Norwich 1945 to 1960

A Journey from Austerity to Prosperity

Pond's flower stall, Norwich Market, 1951

Published by Norwich Heritage Projects, an independent non-profit-making organisation which simply aims to encourage an appreciation of the heritage of a wonderful city.

Norwich 1945 to 1960: A Journey From Austerity to Prosperity
Published by Norwich Heritage Projects
Norwich Heritage Projects
5, Cringleford Chase
Norwich
NR4 7RS
www.norwich-heritage.co.uk

ISBN 978-0-9566272-6-1

Edited, designed and brought to production by Norwich Heritage Projects.
Printed and bound in the UK by
Barnwell Print Ltd, Dunkirk Industrial Estate, Aylsham, Norfolk, NR11 6SU

Front cover: A montage. Background image: the Haymarket *c*.1955. Figures: little girls playing, Stephanie Brooks and friend; girl in Sunday best, Lynn Palmer; teenage couple, Sylvia and Colin Buxton.

Back cover: Montage of the Samson & Hercules Ballroom(page 177)

Image Credits
We are very grateful to our interviewees and all of the following who have kindly allowed us to reproduce images. Where accreditation is not made in the text we have listed the page where the image is located. Subjects have only been specified where more than one person's work appears on the page. In cases where the photographer or artist is unknown the image is accredited to the donor.

Archant Newspapers (*Eastern Evening News* and *Eastern Daily Press*): v, 9 (party), 10 (snow), 14, 16, 20, 21, 22, 23 (Sea Palling), 24 (ER), 25, 29, 33, 35 (Duke), 39, 71, 85, 89, 93, 98, 141, 144 (POW), 148, 150 (queues), 154 (Gorleston), 155, 163, 178, 180, 181, 184 (OF).

Philip Armes: vi, vii, 1,2, 4 (Raven), 6, 18 (Curls), 30, 35 (Queen), 49, 69, 73 (colour), 77 (WS), 108, 109, 110, 118, 119, 120, 121, 122, 125, 127, 128, 129, 137, 139, 145 (SS), 146, 147, 149 (VS), 153, 164, 170, 176, 194.

Compton Verney: Selection of 1950s dresses from the collection of Liz Tregenza displayed in the exhibition Britain in the Fifties: Design and Aspiration, Compton Verney. Photos © Jamie Woodley, 133.

Mike Dixon: 134, 150 (train), 182, 183, 184 (Firs), 185, 186.

Edith Flowerdew: 175.

Simon GP Geoghegan: 142, 143.

Peter Lange: 102, 131.

Charles Nigrelli and the 2nd Air Division Memorial Library Collection: 190.

Norfolk County Council Library and Information Service: cover background image, i, 5, 7, 9 (Norfolks), 10 (Norfolk Show), 11, 15, 18 (Norfolk Show), 19 (Assembly Rooms), 23 (Walcott), 27, 31 (NU), 36, 42, 48, 54 (WP), 59, 74, 75, 77 (MT), 86, 87, 88, 91, 95, 102, 104 (FP), 107, 111, 126, 131, 132, 138 (EP), 139 (CS), 140 (ESH), 149 (CS), 160 (O), 161, 165, 167 (MT), 168, 169, 171 Trafford), 173 (BA), 174, 175, 177 (dancers), 187, 190.

Norfolk Museums & Archaeology Service: 5 (Harmers), 55, 91. Additionally, all images of the Museum of Norwich at the Bridewell and Gressenhall Farm and Workhouse.

Norfolk & Norwich Association for the Blind: 18 (Norfolk Show).

Norfolk Record Office (JLD 2/7/3/1 and ACC 2009/235, 260): 42, 51 (Jarrolds), 52, 82, 87, 114, 115.

George Plunkett (permission from Jonathan Plunkett): 3, 31 (CM), 41, 43, 51 (Dolls Hosp.), 52, 54 (CM), 61, 73 (b&w), 92, 96, 97, 104 (Bonds), 112, 113, 116, 117, 144 (BH), 158, 159, 160 (ABC), 162, 172, 177 (S&H exterior).
John Seymour: 139 (CS)
Tony Skipper: 155
Start-rite: 34.

Contents

Contributors

Many thanks to the following who shared their memories with us.

Andy Anderson: In 1947, when just 19 years old, Andy was serving with the Royal Norfolk Regiment in India, the year of independence. In 1948, after leaving the Norfolks he joined the police force. He left in 1973 to be a social worker, eventually retiring in 1991. He is a renowned local historian, and is a former Chairman and current Vice-President of the Norwich Society.

Philip Armes: Philip spent his life in Norwich. Born in 1923 he witnessed numerous changes which he recorded during the many years he worked as a photographer in the planning department at Norwich City Council.

Rodney Barker: Born during the war, Rodney recalls his family being delighted to be allocated a prefab on Miller's Lane, before moving to the new South Park Avenue Estate. In 1957, at the age of 15, he joined his father at the Jarrolds print works. Both he and his wife Linda enjoy volunteering at the John Jarrold Printing Museum.

Pauline Bell: Born in 1941, Pauline's parents ran several Norwich pubs, including the Red Lion on Bishopgate from 1946 to 1959. After taking a secretarial course at City College Pauline became a PA to the Jarrold family at their print works. She later worked as a PA to Bernard Matthews.

Michael Brett: Michael's family owned Loose's china and glass specialist store on Magdalen Street which was destroyed during WWII and subsequently rebuilt.

Stephanie Brooks: Stephanie was born in Portsmouth in 1951, the following year the family moved back to Norwich. At first they lived with her aunt on King Street, before moving to a brand-new council house on the Heartsease Estate. Stephanie soon found that having a dad who had played for Norwich City (Terry Ryder) made her very popular with the boys.

Avis Brown: Avis was brought up on the Catton Grove Estate. As a teenager she enjoyed wearing the fashions of the day and dancing the night away at the Samson & Hercules. In 1957, when 15 years old, she started her career in the shoe trade which lasted until 2003 when the Start-rite factory closed. In 2015 she returned to the trade, as a tour guide at the Van-Dal (Florida) factory.

Colin Buxton: Colin and his family were bombed out in 1942, when he was just two years old. After the war he lived in a prefab, and as a teenager dressed in the latest fashions.

Sylvia Buxton: Sylvia had a wonderful time growing up on Mariners Lane, where the surrounding bomb sites were her playground. After leaving school in 1956, she worked at the Bally shoe factory until 1967, when she left to start a family.

John Chilvers: Born in 1951, John is a lifelong supporter of NCFC and still vividly remembers the 1959 cup run. After graduating from university, John became a teacher. For the last 16 years of his career he was head at Stalham High before retiring in 2008.

Muriel Chilvers: Muriel was born in 1925. After leaving the Blyth Grammar School she worked for the Norfolk Health Insurance Committee. She left after marrying Leslie.

Albert Cooper: Albert is well known in the City as a musician. In the 1950s he shared a legendary partnership with Black Anna, the landlady of the Jolly Butchers' pub on Ber Street. Fewer people are aware of his time serving in the RAF or of his 'apprenticeship' at the '50 Bob Tailors'.

Roy Cracknell: Roy joined the Norwich Union in 1942 when he was 16 years old. At the age of 18 he was called up to serve in the RAF. Roy spent all his working life at the NU, where he was involved in the installation of the company's early computers.

Pat Gyte: Pat's father worked in the prison service. She spent the 1950s living in prison accommodation on Knox Road.

Stephen Hinde: Stephen was just four years old in 1951 when his father was Lord Mayor. His family owned Bonds and he has many memories of the much-loved department store.

Arthur Holmes: Arthur was born in Norwich in 1921. During WWII he served in the RAF as an aero-engine mechanic. After the war he returned to the City and married Audrey. Arthur spent most of his working life as a cost accountant at Start-rite.

Janice Middleton: Janice was brought up on Marshall Road. She recalls visiting Sandringham on the day of the Coronation, and that school discipline was somewhat different to today.

Barbara Miller: For more than 50 years Barbara has acted as a Blue Badge Guide. Her extensive local knowledge is legendary and resulted in her being a very popular speaker on a range of topics. Born in 1929, as a young lady she enjoyed amateur dramatics and performed at the Maddermarket Theatre under the direction of Nugent Monck.

Martin Miller: In 1944, at the age of 18, Martin was called-up to serve as a 'Bevin Boy' in the Yorkshire coal mines. After returning to Norwich he had a successful management career at the Norvic Shoe Company. He subsequently held the position of Chief Executive at Broadland Housing.

Maurice Morson: Maurice joined the City Police in 1956, when he was 20 years old. He started working the beats as a PC. He was in the force until 1987 when he retired as Detective Chief Superintendent and Head of Norfolk CID. For the next 11 years he worked as Head of Security at UEA. Since retiring he has written a number of books, including *Norwich Murders* and *A Force Remembered*.

Christine Perfect: Christine spent her early life living in a close-knit community on William Street. In 1956, when she was seven years old, she moved with her family to a brand-new council flat on Vauxhall Street.

Lynn Preston: Lynn was born in Norwich in 1948. After leaving the Blyth Grammar School she worked for many years at UEA, during which time she took a break to study for her PhD.

John Rumball: On leaving school in 1952, at the age of 15, John briefly joined the Norwich Union, before embarking in a long career in the print industry. He now works as a volunteer at the John Jarrold Print Museum.

Jude Sayer: In the late 1950s Jude appeared in Crackerjack singing with her heart throb Dickie Valentine. Today, Jude is well known in the City for her work as a Blue Badge Guide and as the Queen of the Norfolk Broads Chapter of the Red Hat Society.

Glenna St Quintin: Born in 1936, Glenna was a teenager in the 1950s. She enjoyed rock 'n' roll and learnt to dance at Eileen Page's school. One of her favourite dance halls was the Lido on Aylsham Road. In 1957 she married John.

John St Quintin: In 1948, straight after leaving school, John started work in the shoe industry, where he worked as a shoe designer until 1981. His family always had cars and as a young man he completed his national service at Horsham St Faith's where he was a MT (Motor Transport) Driver.

Heather Trower: In 1955 Heather started work in the display department at Caley-Mackintosh. Whilst there she posed as Miss Sweetly standing next to Major Quality – the couple that featured on Quality Street advertising and packaging.

Paul Warr: Paul's family moved onto the brand-new Heartsease Estate in 1955, when he was just six years old. As a boy, he enjoyed the freedom of playing with his pals and recalls carefree days. In 2015 he set up a social group called the 'Heartsease Originals' which brings together early residents from the estate.

Peter Watson: Peter's early years were spent living in a Nissen hut on the former Rackheath airbase, he later moved to a new council house on Middleton's Lane, Hellesdon. When he was six, he very much enjoyed taking part in a fancy-dress competition to celebrate the Coronation. After leaving school he worked at Laurence, Scott & Electromotors.

Foreword

In 2015 we published 'The Old Courts and Yards of Norwich' and were amazed at the interest it generated. This left us with the pleasant task of deciding what to do next.

Whilst researching our previous books we came to realise the significance of what happened in Norwich after the war and through the 1950s, and so we decided to tell the story of Norwich from 1945 to 1960.

We soon realised that we faced very different challenges to those presented in our earlier projects. In the past, we have dealt with relatively narrow subjects over a long period, but here we are covering a very wide topic over a short timescale. Knowing the impossibility of covering every aspect in detail, we have aimed to illustrate what was happening by giving the essence of the age. As in our previous books, we have spoken to people who recall the era, combining their memories with newspaper reports, photographs and contemporary records. Additionally, although this is a book primarily about Norwich, the City was also affected by national events, and so we have included these both as background, and to show the impact they had on local people.

In the bibliography we have included sources of information. We must particularly thank Archant for giving us access to their newspaper archive which is full of wonderful stories and pictures, and also to Philip Armes' family for allowing us to reproduce his many superb photos. We would also draw attention to: the marvellous images contained on the George Plunkett and Picture Norfolk websites; the 1950s memorabilia on display at the Museum of Norwich at the Bridewell and the Gressenhall Farm and Workhouse; and the extensive archive held at the Norfolk Record Office.

Finally, as always, we are very grateful to all who shared their memories and stories with us.

Frances and Michael Holmes

Orford Place, 1952

Introduction

On Tuesday 8 May peace was declared in Europe. In Norwich thousands were drawn to the Market Place to celebrate. Amongst their number was Andy Anderson, then 16, he recalls dancing and singing, because 'war was over and there was hope for the future'. Barbara Miller sat with friends on the Castle Mound watching the festivities, she shared Andy's joy and optimism for a world that had been very dark but now seemed bright.

Over the next 15 years Andy and Barbara would be amongst the many who witnessed significant international events, alongside social, technical and cultural changes which still affect us today. This was the era when our longest serving monarch, Queen Elizabeth II, came to the throne. It was also the time when Elvis Presley began his reign as the 'King of Rock and Roll'. These were the years when the teenager came of age and both mass consumerism and the National Health Service were born. As more families benefitted from improved healthcare, the welfare state and a better education system, children from working-class families were increasingly given the opportunity to study at college and university. It was a time of growing affluence, when having a television became the norm, but also one when establishment values were questioned more and more.

Those who lived in Britain during these years were on a journey which saw them travel from the rationing of the post-war years to a time when many 'never had is so good'. It was a roller-coaster trip full of wondrous happenings, people and inventions, but also one of discontent, racism and tragedy.

But what was happening in Norwich? Those who can still recall this eventful period have memories that range from prefabs to Teddy boys, from dancing at the Samson & Hercules to seeing the Canaries' FA Cup run of 1959. They recall a manufacturing city where workers made shoes, chocolates and mustard. It was a time when roads were dominated by bicycles rather than cars and war-damaged buildings were being repaired. Jobs were plentiful, new schools were opened and new-fangled electrical goods were freeing women from the drudgery of housework.

But the story of the City is about more than events, it is also about the individuals who lived through a remarkable time. It is about young men who went to war, children who played on bomb sites and teenagers who witnessed the birth of rock 'n' roll. Ordinary people who saw a city rebuild itself: citizens who were on a journey that took them from austerity to prosperity.

Rampant Horse Street, May 1952

Fish stalls on the Norwich Market, c.1955

1945 to 1960: Austerity to Prosperity

Ber Street, 1949

1945 – 1949: Hard Times

The National Picture

May 1945 was a momentous month. After more than five years of conflict peace was declared in Europe. In August the country celebrated victory in Japan. Britain had won the war, but at a huge cost.

In 2010, when the Conservatives were victorious in the national election, the new Chief Secretary to the Treasury found a note left by his predecessor which famously said: 'I'm afraid there is no money.' Yet the trials faced by the Tories were minor compared to those encountered by the country's first majority Labour Government. In 1945 not only was the country verging on bankruptcy, but the economy was shattered. In a nutshell, the Labour Government needed to generate export income, restart the economy and rebuild homes at a time when the country was on its knees.

Despite these challenges, in the next five years an impressive programme of social reform was instigated, which included the introduction of both the Welfare State and the National Health Service, not to mention extensive improvements in the education system. There were new employment and sickness benefits, free school dinners and milk, whilst 800,000 new houses were built. In any circumstances this was a great achievement.

Meanwhile, on the industrial front a programme of nationalisation – which Prime Minister Clement Attlee preferred to called socialisation – was initiated. This brought a number of industries, including coal, electricity, transport and gas into state ownership and around two million workers into the public sector.

Notwithstanding these achievements, by the end of 1949 the Labour Government was very unpopular. Why? The British public were fed up with endless austerity, epitomised by rationing and increased taxes. There was sound theory behind both. Rationing curtailed demand, reduced imports, encouraged exports and facilitated a fair distribution of goods: it was also a time-consuming and depressing system. Using high taxes to finance social and industrial reform was understood, but death duties of 75% and a 47.5% standard rate of income tax were unacceptable.

By 1950 the British people were tired of queuing, restrictions and abstinence. They'd been on an enforced diet for 10 years, and frankly enough was enough.

Red Lion Street, c.1948

Norwich

May 1945 was a time to celebrate: it was also a time to count the cost of war. Between 1940 and 1943 there had been 45 bombing raids on Norwich which had resulted in 340 deaths. More than 14,000 houses had been damaged, of these 1,200 had been destroyed. Countless commercial buildings had been demolished, including 130 factories and major retail outlets such as Bonds and Curls. Many of the City's young men had been killed or injured in action, others were still held in the notorious Far-East prison camps.

Reconstruction

One of the first tasks for the City Council was to establish a rebuilding programme. In this, they were led by the *City of Norwich Plan*: published in 1945, the document was a blueprint for the development of every aspect of the City for the next 50 years. This far-reaching report covered a range of issues, including transport, industry, homes and markets. It acknowledged that: 'If Norwich is to be re-established as *a fine city* there is much to do, and much to be undone.' This long-term plan influenced decisions, such as the location of industry, housing and schooling. Although in a time of funding constraints many of its proposals came to nothing (in particular the development of an extensive civic centre) many of the concepts, including the development of industrial zones and the building of housing estates outside the City centre, were adopted and remain relevant today.

Like the rest of the country the Council faced the problem of dealing with a huge housing shortage. Building new permanent homes would take too long, prefabricated houses (prefabs) offered a temporary solution. By the end of 1945 such prefabs had already been erected on the Marlpit Estate, and were described in the local press as 'a housewife's dream of convenience and comfort in its kitchen and bathroom equipment'.

CITY OF NORWICH PLAN

Prepared for the Council by
C. H. JAMES, A.R.A., F.R.I.B.A. *and* S. ROWLAND PIERCE, F.R.I.B.A., *Consultants*
and
H. C. ROWLEY, A.M.Inst.C.E., M.I.M.Cy.E., *City Engineer*

With a Foreword by
COUNCILLOR NORMAN R. TILLETT, M.A., LL.B.
Chairman, Town Planning Committee, Norwich City Council

A fine old city, truly, is that, view it from whatever side you will; but it shows best from the east, where the ground, bold and elevated, overlooks the fair and fertile valley in which it stands. Gazing from those heights, the eye beholds a scene which cannot fail to awaken, even in the least sensitive bosom, feelings of pleasure and admiration. At the foot of the heights flows a narrow and deep river, with an antique bridge communicating with a long and narrow suburb, flanked on either side by rich meadows of the brightest green, beyond which spreads the city; the fine old city, perhaps the most curious specimen at present extant of the genuine old English town.

George Borrow, *Lavengro*, 1848

THE CITY OF NORWICH CORPORATION

1945

Prefabs on Ketts Hill, c.1960

Peter Watson's father outside their Nissen hut, Rackheath, c.1948

Around 500 such homes were built in sites around Norwich. Yet despite these efforts the combined effect of under-investment and damage during the war resulted in supply not meeting demand. This was a period when many homeless families crowded in with relatives and friends. The position worsened as servicemen returned from the war. Many, such as Peter Watson's family, sought more inventive solutions: 'We moved into a Nissen hut on the old American base at Rackheath. Just our family lived in the hut, and so it was quite large. It was very basic. It was one big space, and so we created "rooms" by hanging curtains from the ceiling inside. Heat was provided by a pot-bellied fire. We had a bit of a problem with rats, which my mother scared away.'

The Council's commitment to building houses was not in doubt. It immediately began a massive post-war council-house building programme, and as early as 1946 building started on the Tuckswood Estate. In 1948 foundations were laid on the West Earlham and South Park Avenue Estates. On 26 May 1948 the Lord Mayor handed the key of a flat to a Mr and Mrs J. W. Allison. This was a symbolic moment for the City, as it marked the completion of the thousandth permanent home built by the Council since the end of the war. It was also a significant event for the Allisons, whose former home had been destroyed six years earlier in the 1942 Baedeker Raids.

Commercial properties also needed to be rebuilt. It was impossible to construct everything together, and so the authorities prioritised. Pubs were very low down the pecking order, and so many, including the Raven on Guildhall Hill, operated from temporary buildings well into the 1950s. Industrial buildings were slowly restored. One of the first to reopen was Harmers clothing factory. By 1947 the firm had relocated from the City centre to a new building on the Mile Cross Estate. The building was utilitarian in appearance, described in the *Eastern Evening*

The Raven, Guildhall Hill, c.1950

Harmers workers in their new factory, 1948

News as 'a series of Nissen huts joined together'. It may not have been an attractive building, but the owners installed modern machinery which enabled it to be highly efficient. Similarly, when Edwards & Holmes rebuilt their Esdelle Works on Drayton Road, completed in 1948, the directors took the opportunity to update production methods and install the latest machinery, and went so far as to describe their new 75,000 square foot premises as one of the most up-to-date shoe factories in the world.

Edwards & Holmes Esdelle Factory, Drayton Road, 1948

For many people a very visible sign of the hardships faced by the City was represented by the bomb site on Orford Place that had been occupied by Curls department store. For many years it remained an ugly reminder of war. The City was drab. Buildings were interspersed by bomb sites, Andy Anderson recalls: 'St Stephen's was a little bit like someone who'd lost most of their teeth. You'd go up it and there'd be a shop, then a gap, then a shop, and so on. As someone who remembered the City before the bombing I found it depressing and grey, and I couldn't wait for everything to be rebuilt. Even streets you don't think of as being affected had suffered damage, like the City end of City Road. Here, as in so many other streets there were gaps where individual houses had been bombed or burnt out. I thought it was a rather sad old place.'

Rationing and Utility Goods

Before their new store was rebuilt, Curls, along with other City-centre businesses that had been bombed, traded from temporary accommodation. But their main challenge was not so much having premises, it was more the question of having something to sell – because this was the era of rationing and Utility goods. For the consumer, it did not matter if you had money, as there was nothing to spend it on. Barbara Miller recalls people becoming quite ingenious: 'During rationing, many people refurbished old clothes to give them a new lease of life, it really was a period of "make do and mend": I made a skirt in the war out of my father's old grey flannel trousers. I can remember when I was first at the Norwich Union seeing ladies' knitting. At the time (*c.*1948) balls of wool were on ration but darning wool, which was cut into pieces about three foot long, wasn't. So women knitted entire jumpers out of these short lengths, because that was all they could get. Of course, it took for ever to sew the ends in.' Similarly, shops had to adapt to conditions. Stephen Hinde, whose family owned Bonds (now John Lewis), recalls: 'After the war stock was hard to come by, and so we sold quite a lot of second-hand furniture. My father would go to sales and auctions around Norfolk with a cheque book and a Bonds van and buy stock to sell in the shop.'

To address shortages, Utility schemes had been introduced. Covering items such as clothing, furniture and household items, the schemes offered consumers a range of well-designed, practical, durable, mass-produced goods. This meant, for example, that Loose's (the glass and china specialist store on Magdalen Street owned by the Brett family) could only stock limited merchandise, as explained by Michael Brett: 'Immediately after the war when the priority across the country was to export to repay debt, it was difficult to buy stock. You could sell it easily, but you couldn't buy it. We had the austerity period in the 1940s when crockery was white and utilitarian. The return of highly decorative tableware for the home did not come until the 1950s.'

Site of Curls department store, Orford Place, c.1950

Life Goes On

Even the weather conspired to make life difficult, in particular, the winter of 1947 is still considered one of the worst in memory. The *Eastern Evening News* summed up the position: 'Arctic Winter, Floods and Five Months of Drought: The year 1947 will go down in the annals as the year when the weather did its worst to blight hopes of early recovery from the aftermath of war.' The weather disrupted all aspects of the economy. The country relied on coal for fuel, but at the pits coal froze solid and could not be moved. There were power shortages, which meant homes were unheated and streets unlit. Industry ground to a halt: in Norwich factories closed. People could not get food. From the end of January, through February and March, blizzards and freezing temperatures brought two months of hardship to families across East Anglia.

At a time when there was so much doom and gloom, would sport be a source of cheer? In the late 1940s spectators flocked to the City's sporting venues: football fans went to Carrow Road to support the Canaries; the Stars speedway riders attracted similar-sizes crowds at the Firs; whilst supporters literally 'went to the dogs' at the Boundary Park and Norwich City Stadia.

Unfortunately the size of the crowds did not necessarily match results. This was particularly the case at Carrow Road. During the war league games had been cancelled. The FA cup was relaunched in the 1945-6 season whilst the Football League started a year later. Much of the Canaries' bank of pre-war talent had been lost during the conflict, and it would be fair to say that they did not make a particularly good start to the post-war competitions: they had to reapply for re-election to the Third Division South in both the 1947-48 and the 1948-49 seasons. Yet one factor stood out over this period: the depth of the support. The Chairman heaped praise on the Canaries' followers who had 'proved themselves to be fine sportsmen, accepting defeat in the right spirit, and at the same time giving every possible encouragement to the team towards victory.'

Celebrations

Despite the austere conditions there were joyous events. In 1945 crowds gathered in the City to celebrate victory in both Europe and Japan, whilst friends and families rejoiced as servicemen returned from the War. In 1947 the King and Queen attended the Royal Norfolk Show at Keswick. In its end of year summary the *Eastern Evening News* described it as a 'phenomenal success', even going so far as to describe it as the 'outstanding event' of the year' – apparently more important than Princess Elizabeth's wedding to the Duke of Edinburgh. In 1948 the NHS was launched, and for the first time medical treatment was available 'free at the point of need'. By December 1948, 96% of the City's population, were registered with a NHS doctor.

In Conclusion

As the decade came to an end life was beginning to return to normal, but for many it was still hard. Progress was slow, inhibited by shortages, the abysmal weather and lack of funds. The City was drab, children played on bomb sites, young men were sent on national service and rationing continued. Would the 1950s prove to be any better?

In the stands at Carrow Road, 1949

Memorable Events: 1945 – 1949

8 May 1945: VE Day

At 3pm on Tuesday, 8 May 1945, Winston Churchill announced that the war in Europe was at an end. Festivities in Norwich took some time to warm up, but by early evening crowds had gathered on The Walk where a group of British soldiers broke the ice by flinging themselves into an impromptu dance. Very soon the road was a surging mass of servicemen and civilians dancing, chatting, singing and throwing streamers. A local reporter noted: 'A Norwich City police constable...was the recipient of several hearty kisses about 12 o'clock on VE-night from a young woman whose exuberance the PC tried to curb. After she had twined her arms about his neck, she and her companions formed a ring and danced around the PC who after a moment's embarrassment, resigned himself good-naturedly to the onslaught.'

On the following night the celebrations continued. Major City landmarks were floodlit in a blaze of lights, thousands danced and sang on The Walk. Fully illuminated RAF Mosquitoes and American Liberators were caught in searchlights which swept the sky as they flew overhead and dropped scores of coloured flares. After years of blackouts it must have been a wondrous sight. Andy Anderson recalls being caught up in the mood: 'I acted completely out of character! I'd walked into the City with my girlfriend and we found ourselves with an enormous crowd on the Market Place. There was such a throng there, it was like a cup-final. It was riotous, but joyful. People were swinging from lamp posts and I found myself dancing on Gentleman's Walk with people I didn't know. American aircraft circled above, dropping flares. There was, of course, a great sense of relief alongside the celebration. It was a great time. The City I think was careworn; we'd had a rough time with bombs, but now I suppose people were optimistic. War was over and there were hopes for the future.'

Celebratory bells rang out across the City. Norwich's churches and cathedrals held services of thanks and remembrance. Children made full use of bomb sites, reminders of the horrors of war, to build bonfires topped by guys in the image of Hitler. Street parties were laid on. The future Glenna St Quintin lived on Winter Road: 'They put up huge tables and everyone brought along a plate of something or other and we had a very big party there. People were so pleased, we looked for any reason to celebrate. It was amazing where all the goodies came from. I still wonder how people found enough stuff to make buns and sandwiches, because we'd been rationed for years.'

EASTERN DAILY PRESS, WEDNESDAY, MAY 9, 1945

VICTORY SMILES FROM A NORWICH CROWD

VE-DAY CELEBRATIONS IN CITY AND COUNTY

RIVER CRAFT TAKE PART

BIG PARADE FOR NORWICH

VE Day celebrations, 1945

26 July 1945: Churchill Loses the Election

In 1945, when Winston Churchill's Tory Party lost the election, shock waves crossed the world. Just two months earlier huge crowds had gathered outside Buckingham Palace, not only to cheer the Royal family, but also to salute the remarkable war-time leader who was so closely associated with the country's victory. It was almost inconceivable that Churchill could lose. Why did he? Put simply, the vast majority wanted welfare reforms. Labour, with their emphasis on 'Let Us Face the Future', were considered more likely to deliver social reform than the Tories, who based their campaign around Churchill's status of war hero. The *Evening News* commented at the time: 'Our friends in Europe...will wonder what has possessed the British people to vote for a programme of Socialism.'

15 August 1945: VJ Day

In Norwich, the VE Day festivities had been tinged with particular sadness. Our local regiment, The Royal Norfolks, had suffered severe casualties in the Far East. In particular, many local families still had relatives held in notorious POW camps, and so for many VJ Day held much more potency.

By 13 August the civic authorities had announced a programme of events in anticipation of the Japanese surrender. Again the festivities revolved around the City Hall and the Market Place, but extended to the parks and churches and cathedrals. At 9pm the King's Speech was played from City Hall followed by music. On Tombland music blared out from the Samson & Hercules Ballroom. Around 20,000 people converged on the City. In the Market Place there were dancing, fireworks and numerous attempts by the more agile to climb street lamps. An *Eastern Evening News'* journalist took great delight in reporting: 'A solemn-eyed little girl of ten, gazing at what she regarded as all this unusual behaviour, was heard to ask her parent's gravely: "Are all these people nuts?"'

9 October 1945: Former POWs Return to Norwich from the Far East

The *Eastern Evening News* ran a series of reports describing the return to the City of the many local servicemen who had been held as prisoners of war. One of the most poignant occurred on 9 October 1945: 'Last night a crowd of several thousand people gave a tumultuous welcome to the first batch of ex-prisoners of war to arrive in Norwich from the Far East...Every available light at Thorpe Station was switched on and as they passed through the barriers the returned men saw a large notice: "Welcome home to ex-prisoners of war and all members of the armed forces."

'The crowd began to assemble in the early evening, held back by barriers. Then through the loud speakers a girl's voice invited relatives to pass onto number two platform. At about 9.30pm a train approached, and the crowds waved and clapped, only to hear that the train carrying their loved ones had been delayed. Then came the voice of the announcer, but this time it had lost its calmness: "The train now arriving is the London train..." Then her voice was drowned by cheering. Mothers, wives, children and sweethearts ran along the platform and embraced their menfolk.'

Amongst the returning soldiers was Maurice Morson's father: 'He was a regular soldier; I can't remember seeing him until 1945. Before that he'd been stationed in Singapore where he was captured by the Japanese. I'd seen a photograph of him, which had been taken when he was a youngish man with dark hair. When he came home, he had white hair, his nerves were shattered, he was skeletal and he suffered from tropical ulcers. Maybe unsurprisingly, the doctor said to my mother: "You know Mrs Morson that he won't make old bones." However, my father was a very determined man, and in fact outlived the doctor.'

VE party, Cardiff Street, 1945

Royal Norfolk Regiment guard of honour, 1945

January to March 1947: The Big Freeze

Where are my mittens?, 1947

On 23 January 1947, high pressure settled over Scandinavia feeding cold air over most of England. By 28 January the temperature in Norwich at 10pm was -7°C, and snow ploughs were in operation across the county. Meteorologists were predicting a one or two day 'cold snap', in fact Arctic conditions lasted for around eight weeks. During February, the *Eastern Evening News'* weatherman reported that after one of the heaviest falls of snow the thermometer remained below freezing point for a fortnight, or 333 hours. On 23 February it rose above freezing for just 30 minutes. It was a truly miserable month, with only 22.3 hours of sunshine, making it the 'most sunless month' the weatherman had ever witnessed. Avis Brown, who was five at the time, can still picture the snow: 'It was so deep that it came to the top of mother's palings [wooden fence]. Mother shovelled a pathway in front of the house. All our neighbours the whole length of Woodcock Road did the same. If anyone couldn't manage, someone else helped. I still remember walking down the cleared pathway, because on either side there were banks of snow that nearly reached the top of my head.'

25 June 1947: King George VI and Queen Elizabeth Attend the Royal Norfolk Show

The King and Queen, Royal Norfolk Show, Keswick, 1947

In June 1947 the King and Queen visited the City to commemorate the centenary Norfolk Show. They brought a touch of glamour to a city recovering from the drabness of war. Their visit boosted attendance at the show which recorded 27,000 visitors on the afternoon of their visit. The local press commented that despite the austere times, it was an occasion when the City could 'show their majesties that the real spirit of Norwich is unaltered, or perhaps stronger than ever'.

20 November 1947: A Royal Wedding

On a cold November day a beautiful princess and her handsome groom brought much cheer to a nation battered by war and years of rationing. In Norwich, the local press treated readers to columns of detail describing a day designed to lift spirits: but how did local people celebrate?

It was noted in the *Eastern Evening News* that: 'In its outward manifestations of loyal and affectionate interest in the nuptials of the future Queen of England, Norwich is being much less demonstrative than London....We would have liked to have seen a good deal bigger display of bunting, flags and so on to mark the occasion, but we do not think that the lack betokens any indifference on the part of the citizens.'

The article went on to note that although some cinemas were inviting the public into their auditoriums to hear the BBC's radio coverage (without charge) most families would listen to the ceremony at home. The journalist concluded: 'On behalf of readers, the *Eastern Evening News* joins in the heartfelt good wishes of the nation that the wedding of Elizabeth and Philip may be richly blessed.'

17-24 April 1949: Norwich Scout Week

In Norwich, thousands took part in this week of celebration to raise much needed funds for an organisation that offered a ray of hope to boys living in a drab, austere world. With rationing still on, the Boy Scouts Association put on a series of fund-raising stunts at an eclectic range of venues, including bomb sites, ballrooms, youth centres and churches.

Full use was made of the site of Curls department store, which still hadn't been rebuilt since being bombed in 1942. Sea Scouts put on an exhibition at Nelson's Brig, near Pull's Ferry, whilst an auction and carnival dance were held at the Samson & Hercules Ballroom (Tombland), and a grand bazaar was hosted at the Youth Hall on Surrey Street. This was the first week that 'Bob a Job' was introduced nationally, and local Scouts enthusiastically performed small tasks for the public for which they were paid a bob (5p). At the end of the week over a thousand members paraded in front of the City Hall before marching in procession to the Cathedral for the annual St George's Day service.

The organisation had a successful week, and raised sufficient money to build new headquarters for many local troops.

24 April 1949: Sweets Temporarily Derationed

During April 1949 there were celebrations across the country when sweets came off ration.

In their staff magazine, the *Mackintosh Caley Monthly News,* the confectionery manufacturer whose large Norwich factory was destroyed during the war noted: 'What's going to happen is anyone's guess....Some say the shops will be emptied in no time at all, others that the shelves will be bulging with unwanted goods as the nation has forgotten the sweet habit.'

Almost immediately it became very clear who was correct. Four weeks after derationing shops were bare. Producers were only being allocated sufficient materials by the Ministry of Food to manufacture 5 ozs of sweets per person per week, and it soon became obvious that demand was double this amount. One of the big unknown factors had been the spending power of children, which exceeded all expectations.

Sadly, joy soon turned to tears, when after just four months sweets were once again on ration, where they stayed until February 1953.

Scouts and supporters on the site of Curls department store, 1949

Ordinary People Living in Extraordinary Times

WWII may have been over in 1945, but it affected lives for years to come. Despite hardship and disruption, ordinary people went about their lives, adapting to the exceptional circumstances that prevailed.

1946: Arthur Holmes Returns to Civvy Street

Arthur (b.1921) served in the RAF during WWII. In 1946, when he was demobbed, he returned to a very different Norwich to the one he had left. His experiences were shared by many former servicemen:

'During the war I served in the RAF in both North Africa and Italy. As a leading aircraftman I was on the highest rate of pay at my level, some 6s. 6d. per day. I soon realised that I didn't need the money whilst overseas, and so arranged to have it sent to my mother, who I still lived with, to help the family get through the war. When I got home my mother gave me a bank book which showed that I had over £400: she'd saved all my wages for me. That money enabled me to establish myself back into civilian life.

'When I first came home there was very little in the shops: you especially noticed it at Christmas. One of the first shocks I had was when my mother asked what I'd like to eat and I said that I'd love a cheese sandwich – I hadn't had any cheese for a couple of years or more. She gave me the sandwich which I enjoyed very much and after I finished it she said: "Did you know that you've just eaten a week's ration?"

'That gave me a real jolt! People seemed to take rationing for granted. They'd got used to it and just got on with it. I didn't notice much in the way of a black market, but if people heard that something was available in a shop, they flocked there.

'I was very miserable when I came back to Norwich. My sister Betty, her husband Fred and their baby son Gerald, had been bombed out and were living in our house, and so there wasn't much room for me. Then in 1948 I had a stroke of luck. Housing was in short supply but a friend who was an estate agent had managed to find somebody a house to rent and then they'd turned it down. He was rattling the keys in his pocket. So straight away I asked where it was, and when I found out it was a little house in Thorpe I said, "I'll have it". He pointed out that I wasn't married yet, and I replied, "...but I'm getting married very soon". I'd always said that I wouldn't marry until I earned £5 a week, but the opportunity to get a house was too good to miss – luckily, my girlfriend, Audrey agreed! We were married two weeks later and we moved in straight afterwards.'

Audrey and Arthur Holmes on their wedding day, 1948

1947: Andy Anderson Presides Over the End of the British Empire

In 1947 Andy Anderson was involved in a momentous event in Britain's history:

'In 1946, when I was working at the engineering firm Laurence, Scott & Electromotors, I was called up to do my national service and duly joined the Army, which was how, in a very small way, as a member of the Second Battalion of the Royal Norfolk Regiment, I presided over the end of the British Empire.

'Before joining up I hadn't even been to London, and so you can imagine the adventure I had travelling to India. Our journey started when we climbed into a three-tonner at Colchester. We eventually ended up in Liverpool. From there I was at sea for 21 days on the Britannic (a troop ship). Whilst on deck I saw that all the winch gear had large plates on it saying "Laurence, Scott & Electromotors Ltd, Gothic Works, Hardy Road, Norwich". It immediately made me feel homesick.

'We arrived in January 1947. I was only there eight months, but it was a most exciting time; over that short period India and Pakistan were partitioned, and on 15th August 1947 India was given independence. I was in a rifle company for about three days, then on the strength of having been a junior clerk at Laurence & Scotts, I was transferred to the orderly room.

'Soon after arriving we travelled up from a transit camp outside Bombay. We were on the train five days, and as we got up into what we now call Pakistan there was agitation on the stations and we'd hear chants such as, "We want Pakistan, we want Pakistan". Some time later we were sent up to a place called Salt Lake on a camping expedition to gain hard-line experience. The terrain there was so rocky you could hardly get a tent peg in. We'd only been there a few days and all hell let loose, it was the start of the troubles. The Governor of the Punjab asked for military assistance, and so we all packed up and returned to the Victoria Barracks at Rawalpindi (better known as Pindi), which was where we were based. The whole Battalion descended into Pindi in three tonners. I can vividly remember entering the City because what appeared to be its entire male population was out on the streets all waving weapons at us. As you can imagine It was all very, very tense. The night after we got back, buildings around the City were set on fire. There was a lot of violence in the months leading up to Independence, and the Battalion became used to keeping the warring sides apart. A hopeless task, though we did our best. Because I was in the orderly room I avoided most of the fighting. There was a lot of killing, but for a nineteen-year-old youngster like me it was all a bit exciting I suppose.

Andy Anderson, c.1995

'We returned on the HMT Georgic on 17th August 1947, which was the first troopship to leave India after Independence had been declared.'

HMT Georgic, undated

1950 – 1954: Recovery and Growth

The National Picture

This was a period of highs and lows encompassing celebrations and natural disasters, everything from a war to a coronation. The country was on a tumultuous ride which would eventually set it on a road to recovery and growth.

On 26 October 1951 the Tories returned to power, after catching the public's imagination with a promise to create a 'strong and free' Britain. But could they, and their leader Winston Churchill, deliver?

Earlier that year 8.5 million visitors had marvelled at exhibitions showing the best of British art, design and industry at the Festival of Britain. Undoubtedly it had created the desired feeling of optimism, but in many quarters it was insufficient to offset the despondency generated by the start of the Korean War in 1950. A conflict which not only increased the pressure on the country's finance, but also led to a rise in the length of compulsory national service from 18 months to two years.

In the years following the election, the country seemed to lurch from one crisis to the next. In February 1952 King George VI died at Sandringham, and the country mourned a much-loved king. The following December, at least 4000 people lost their lives when London was covered in dense fog (the 'Great Smog') for four days and descended into chaos. The nation was just recovering from this catastrophe when on the night of 31 January to 1 February 1953 gale force northerly winds lashed the British coastline and broke through flood defences from Yorkshire to Kent. In one of the worst storms to hit the country, 307 British people lost their lives, and 24,000 homes were seriously damaged.

Despite all these calamities underlying conditions began to improve. Most importantly, Churchill's Tories did not reverse many of Labour's key reforms. In particular they accepted the concept of the Welfare State and the NHS, which had brought benefits to so many. Living standards were further enhanced when Harold Macmillan, the then Minister of Housing, launched an ambitious construction programme with a target of building 300,000 houses a year: a target he reached in 1953 and repeated every year to 1957. Furthermore, the Tories maintained stability by keeping most of the nationalised industries in government control: only iron and steel and road haulage were returned to private ownership. At the same time the country began to benefit from an improvement in the world economy, which in turn facilitated the easing of austerity measures. As the period progressed, more goods were taken off rationing and taxation was reduced. This all contributed towards an improvement in the country's economic performance: in 1954 the growth in GDP was 4% and unemployment stood at 1.3%.

The spirit of optimism was engendered by national events, none more so than the Coronation of Queen Elizabeth II in 1953, which brought joy to the nation. If this was not enough to raise spirits, the same year saw a British expedition conquer Everest and an armistice signed in Korea.

But the year 1954 was truly momentous: 14 years of rationing finally came to an end. The position was summed up by the social historian, Harry Hopkins: 'Almost at once affluence came hurrying on the heels of penury. Suddenly the shops were piled high with all sorts of goods. Boom was in the air.'

Cobham, Great Yarmouth was badly hit by the floods, 1953

Norwich

Against this backdrop of major national events, between 1950 and 1954 the City gradually recovered from the ravages of war.

Reconstruction

Rebuilding continued to be high on the agenda. The City's house-building programme was particularly impressive. In 1950 Norwich City Council handed over the keys of the 2000th permanent council house built since the war. By the end of 1954 the figure had reached 5000. The same year work started on the Heartsease Estate, described in the press as: 'The last, the biggest and the best'. As more people moved to the new estates on the outskirts of Norwich, the Council recognised the need to build new schools. Between 1950 and 1953 four schools were opened: Middleton's Lane Infants at Hellesdon, Sprowston Infants, Costessey Junior and St William's Junior and Infants at Thorpe. Collectively they cost £230,000 and provided for 1400 children.

In the City centre landmark stores were being rebuilt and modernised, bringing optimism to the City. These included Bonds of Norwich which reopened on All Saints' Green in 1951, in a distinctive new building featured in the *City of Norwich Plan*. Loose's on Magdalen Street reopened the same year. Unfortunately, they had problems buying merchandise for their new store, as explained by Michael Brett: 'When we built the shop after the war we considerably extended the floor space. When we opened in 1951 we had very little stock...The staff had to disperse what we had to make the sales floor look attractive and not too sparse.' Around the City centre there was an element of 'musical chairs' as businesses moved between premises. For example, Barclays St Stephen's branch had been destroyed in 1942. In 1949 the bank constructed a single-storey building as a stopgap on the cleared site, but when Bonds vacated their temporary premises on Red Lion Street the bank took the opportunity to move there. After extensively altering and installing modern equipment, they moved into their new branch in 1953. The local press approved of the renovations: 'On entering, the impression is of lightness and cheerfulness...the bank is fully mechanised for the keyboard is gradually replacing the pen.' The City's factories were also steadily being rebuilt and reopened, including the Caley factory (owned by Mackintosh) on Chapelfield.

New flats, Heigham Grove, 1951

In addition, leisure facilities were being renovated. These included the Assembly Rooms, which was launched as an arts centre and cinema in 1950 and the new, improved Lakenham open-air baths which opened in 1951. The latter was both good and bad news for Norwich's swimmers: good, because it was a popular facility, bad, because the Council announced there was no funding for a 'heated indoor bath for the moment'.

Construction projects helped stimulate the local economy. The cost of the new Caley factory alone was in the region of 'seven figures'. The main contractor on the project was Messrs J Youngs, and it represented the biggest local industrial building scheme in the 105 years' history of the firm.

A further boost was given to the City in June 1951, when Norwich was selected by the organisers of the Festival of Britain to be one of the chief provincial centres to stage its own mini festival. Albert Cooper recalls the Norwich Festival bringing joy and colour to the City: 'All the main buildings were floodlit, the City Hall had all of its big banners. There was a big flotilla near Thorpe Station. I enjoyed it because it was something new.' Similarly, Andy Anderson has fond memories of the event: 'I think the Festival did improve morale. It brought it home that the war was really behind us.'

Tragedy

Against this background of rebuilding and growth, the City shared in the grief and tragedy which saddened the country in this period. The extremes were epitomised on two successive days in 1951: on 18 June Princess Elizabeth opened the Norwich Festival, the following day brought the news that the 1st Battalion of the Royal Norfolk Regiment was to take part in the Korean struggle. Subsequently Norfolk played a central role in two of the major stories of the period. In 1952, the City mourned when King George VI died at Sandringham, then on the night of 31 January to 1 February 1953 the county's coastline was flooded. Across Norfolk and Suffolk around 100 people lost their lives whilst thousands were driven from their homes.

Royal Proclamation to the City on the accession of Queen Elizabeth II, City Hall steps, 1952

Optimism

Then, like the rest of the country, hope and joy returned.

In 1953 the City joined in the national celebrations for the Queen's Coronation. Peter Watson was amongst the many children who attended street parties: 'I clearly remember the Coronation, in particular my mother spending hours making my Robin Hood outfit for a fancy-dress competition held on the Firs Speedway Track, on Cromer Road. She went into great detail and even dyed my boots green. She dressed my sister, Mary, as the Maid of Hearts. The competition took place in the middle of the track. I'd been really looking forward to it – although the shine was taken off it when I found I had to take my sister! It was also raining that day, which didn't help. Once I got there I met up with my mates. John Shaw dressed up as a soldier, someone even dressed up as a postbox! I don't know who won...but it wasn't me. Afterwards we went back home and got changed, and went to a party which was held at 69 and 71 Woodlands Road. The mums all helped prepare the food: there were lots of jellies and sandwiches. We had a really good day.'

Children's party, Woodlands Road, Coronation Day, 1953

Those who bought televisions to watch the great occasion may have been disappointed, as it was later reported in the *Eastern Evening News* that: 'Television reception was practically non-existent. "Nothing but snow," said a viewer at Thorpe, whilst at Eaton a viewer said they had a picture every five minutes but could not hold it.' No wonder so many flocked to the City's cinemas. Phyllis Brighton who worked in the Gaumont (Haymarket) box office recalled the longest queue she'd even seen when the event was screened on Wednesday 3 June 1953: 'It went right round the cinema into Brigg Street and halfway up the Walk.'

Peter Watson as Robin Hood, fancy dress parade, FIrs Speedway Track, Coronation Day, 1953

The following year Barbara Miller was amongst the many in the City who rejoiced when rationing came to an end: 'There was a great sense of liberation when you could go shopping without always wondering if you had enough coupons. After years of shortages you really could buy anything you wanted, the only thing holding you back was having enough money to buy it.'

The period ended with a few landmark events in the City. In 1954, for the first time, the Royal Norfolk Show was held on its new permanent showground at Costessey. In the same year, the local engineering firm Laurence, Scott & Electromotors gained kudos when they made the electric motors for the new Royal Yacht Britannia. Whilst in sport a young man from Sweden, Ove Fundin, arrived to ride with the Norwich Stars at the Firs. Ove went on to clinch five world speedway titles, and needless to say became a hugely popular figure in the City.

Conclusion

By the end of 1954 Nowich was in a strong position. The City's leading sector, the footwear industry, was flourishing and our engineering firms were busy. But, despite all the rebuilding and regeneration, one very visible sign of the austerity years remained: the bomb site in the centre of the City, the former home of Curls department store. Which raised the question: when would this very visible scar be healed?

The Queen Mother, Royal Norfolk Show, Costessey, 1954

Site of Curls department store, 1953

Memorable Events: 1950 – 1954

23 November 1950: The Assembly House Reopens as an Arts Centre

At the outbreak of WWII the wonderful Georgian Assembly House was being used as a warehouse. During the hostilities it was taken over by the War Office for occupation by the Royal Engineers' School of Camouflage. Amongst the officers stationed there was Captain Oliver Messel, an artist and stage designer. Along with colleagues he repainted and renovated some of the reception rooms. In 1944 the rooms even featured in *Country Life*. It must be a unique example of a building benefitting from military occupation. At the time an *Eastern Evening News* journalist hoped the rooms would 'never again be allowed to fall into disuse'. His plea was answered. Later the same year it was bought by Henry Sexton (whose family owned one of the leading shoe firms in the City) and conveyed into a trust.

Assembly Rooms, 1954

In 1950 the Assembly House was opened as an Arts Centre incorporating the Noverre Cinema. At the opening ceremony the Lord Mayor made a wish, which has very definitely been granted: '...[may] this Assembly House, so generously given, so lovely in itself, bring in future much pleasure, much beauty, and much inspiration to the citizens of Norwich.'

3 May to 30 September 1951: The Festival of Britain

In 1951 some 8.5 million visitors flocked to London to visit the Festival of Britain held on 27 acres of cleared bomb sites on the South Bank of the Thames. Here, they marvelled at: the Royal Festival Hall; the 200-foot (61m) Skylon – a vertical feature in steel and aluminium with no visible means of support; and the Dome of Discovery – an aluminium display centre containing a planetarium and other exhibits. Visitors were fascinated by modern designs and entertained at the fun fair and pleasure gardens. The site was designed to inspire, and to promote recovery and hope through the medium of good, contemporary design.

Roy Cracknell was one of the many who travelled from Norwich to London to see the exhibitions: 'We were impressed by the displays which were very modern and so different from what we had been used to during war-time rationing. I think it did a lot of good because people started to realise that things were beginning to look up.' Philip Armes went on a coach trip with colleagues: 'They had a cinema and as you walked in they had a camera on you and your picture was projected on the screen, which was quite something in those days. In fact that was the first time I'd seen live TV.'

Albert Cooper's abiding memory of the Festival is more prosaic: 'It introduced plastic plates: no one had seen plastic plates and cups before. They had them in really bright colours, such as orange and purple. There was a need for everything to be new and refreshed and decorated in what was seen as a modern way, often in gaudy colours. After the war and years of austerity and rationing, I can see why people wanted change, but I'm not so sure it was a good thing.'

18 to 30 June 1951: The Norwich Festival

Norwich was one of the provincial centres selected to play a leading part in the Festival of Britain. From 18 to 30 June a series of events was put on across the City, designed to include attractions that catered for all tastes. In the Festival programme, A. E. Barnes (Chairman) was proud to announce: 'Concerts, recitals, light opera, carnivals, water frolics, plays, exhibitions, processions, lectures, films and dances are intermingled in a constantly varying succession.... The City will be decorated and illuminated throughout the whole fortnight. Gaiety and pageantry will walk hand in hand.'

On the 18 June 1951, Princess Elizabeth came to the City to open the Norwich Festival. An hour before she arrived around 5000 had taken up positions around the Market Place. Their numbers were swollen when local offices and shops closed to allow staff the opportunity to see their future monarch. In the local press it was described as: 'A brilliant scene and a touching demonstration of the loyalty of the City and the county. And the general feeling of the crowd seemed to be: "We have waited and worked for this for a long time. Let us make it an unforgettable day."'

The Princess was met by the Lord Mayor, Eric Hinde, who summed up the sentiment behind the Festival: 'Today...is a tribute to the co-operation of all citizens and traders in Norwich, who have done their best to cover our scars, to lessen our pain, and with decorations of flowers and flags have added grace and beauty to our Historic City.'

Eric Hinde's son, Stephen, was privileged to meet the Princess that day: 'I was only four years old, and so was too young to be part of the official ceremony, but when the formalities were over my father asked the Princess if he could present his young son. I'd been practising my bow in front of the mirror, but the occasion got the better of me, and when the big moment came I was too shy and hung on to my father's trouser leg. But the Princess wasn't going to be outdone by a small boy, and so she got down onto the floor to talk to me. Consequently, my claim to fame was that I am one of the few people Her Majesty has been on her knees to.'

The fortnight was a great success. Amongst the most popular events was the Festival Pageant, when thousands thronged the centre of Norwich to see a procession comprising 25 tableaux, representing 'Norwich Through the Ages'. Whilst the Industrial Exhibition in St Andrew's Hall had 14,500 visitors in a week. In conclusion the local press declared the fortnight a triumph: 'During the Festival as a whole there had been a spirit of gaiety and happiness in the City, a spirit of thankfulness for past glories and a deliverance of our City...[it was a] time to renew our energies for the future.'

Wifflers and Snap the Dragon lead the Lord Mayor's coach, Market Place, 1951

Princess Elizabeth visits the City to open the Norwich Festival, accompanied by Eric Hinde, the Lord Mayor, 1951

6 February 1952: King George VI Dies at Sandringham

On 6 February 1952, when he was just 56 years old, King George VI died peacefully in his sleep at Sandringham. Although the cause of death was a coronary thrombosis he also suffered from lung cancer. He had never expected or wanted to become king, but following the abdication of his elder brother, Edward VIII, in 1936 he reluctantly took on the role of monarch. His steadfastness won both the respect and hearts of the people, especially when he shared the dangers of the Battle of Britain with Londoners.

In the days that followed the *Eastern Daily Press* ran many articles recounting the King's many links with Norfolk and Norwich, pointing out that he both died and was born at Sandringham. The paper looked back on the King's various visits to the City, which included the official opening of the City Hall in 1938, and a wartime visit to Caleys, then being used by Siemens for battery making. On the latter occasion his visit had been kept secret, and factory workers were somewhat bemused to look up one day and see their monarch standing next to them.

On the day of the funeral, 15 February 1952, the Lord Mayor recommended that all Norwich shops were closed from 1.45pm to 3pm. The City Hall and Carrow Works' sirens were synchronised to indicate the beginning and end of the official two-minute silence.

King George VI and Queen Elizabeth open the City Hall, 1938

The floods hit Walcott, 1953

Troops shore up the breach at Sea Palling, 1953

One subject dominated local headlines in early February: the East Coast floods. The *Eastern Daily Press*, summed up the tragedy on 2 February: 'Norfolk Gale Disaster: At least 100 people are reported missing or dead in floods along the Norfolk coast which started with Saturday night's gales and high seas. Many have been rendered homeless. These are the worst floods within living memory in this part of the country. By last night 39 bodies had been recovered along the coast between King's Lynn and Hunstanton.' However, the death rate could have been much higher if it had not been for the 'valiant rescue work' of American air force personnel based at Sculthorpe. Special mention was given of American Airman 3rd Class Reis Leming, who is reported to have saved 25 women and children at Hunstanton's South Beach on a rubber dinghy which he pulled through the flood waters for several hours before collapsing.

2 June 1953: Coronation Day

On 2 June 1953 an estimated 20 million people watched Queen Elizabeth II's coronation on television, a further 3 million lined the streets of London hoping to catch a glimpse of their glamorous new monarch.

Activities were put on across Norwich. The principal event of the official celebrations was a carnival held in Eaton Park where visitors were treated to an eclectic series of events and performances which included: Hell's Angels, the world's greatest trick and stunt motorcyclists; a 'Miss Coronation' competition, featuring 12 of the City's most beautiful girls; a display by members of the Priory Gymnasium; and a performance of ballet and tap by pupils of the Peggy Carr School of Dancing.

Other celebrations included a carnival procession across the City, a Coronation Concert at St Andrew's Hall and a series of dances in Chapelfield Gardens which were 'illuminated with a mass of fairy lights'.

Despite the day itself being somewhat wet and inclement, across both Norwich and Norfolk people rejoiced. Alongside official events there were street parties and many thoroughfares were festively decorated with flags and bunting. Which led to a rather humorous article in the *Norfolk News*: 'A number of people have been amused by the incongruous sets of pennants hoisted to mark the Coronation. A correspondent to a national newspaper noted recently that in his district he noticed that according to the flags displayed outside a house, one resident was making a distress signal, another indicated that he was taking up anchor and a third that he wanted a doctor to come aboard.'

Queen Elizabeth II crowned in Westminster Abbey, 1953

One of the most unusual contributions to the success of the day was made by Albert Cooper: 'I was in the RAF at the time working with B29s, which I can tell you are whacking great planes. For the Queen's Coronation we had three planes from RAF Marham selected to take part in the fly-past over Buckingham Palace. You may know Duraglit, a metal wadding polish normally used to bring a shine to small metallic products. We used a similar product to hand polish the planes so they looked like chromium. It took weeks, but at the end my plane was gleaming. It's a pity it was only seen flying 10,000 feet up in the sky!'

Coronation fancy dress competition, 1953

Ordinary People Living in Extraordinary Times

In the 1950s the impact of WWII still reverberated across the City. Men who had served in the war returned to their families and resumed their lives.

1951: Eric Hinde is Inaugurated as Lord Mayor

In 1951, Eric Hinde, the managing director of Bonds of Norwich, took on the role of Lord Mayor of Norwich. His son Stephen recalls: 'My father had been on the City Council before the war. He was too old to go into a fighting regiment, but was determined to get into the army, and so in 1940 he joined the Royal Army Service Corps. The following year he left for the Far East and my sister Lisa was born nine months to the day after he set off. In 1942 he was captured by the Japanese in Singapore and didn't know Lisa existed until after the end of the war, she was three-and-a-half before she met her father. When she first saw him she ran away! When he came home he was very weak, but by 1947 he was back on the Council. My father had first been put forward to be Lord Mayor in 1949, but the Council decided to "hang on to him" until the Festival of Britain Year.'

In his year as Lord Mayor, Eric undertook numerous official engagements and met many influential people. The highlight was undoubtedly welcoming Princess Elizabeth when she officially launched the Norwich Festival. However, one chance encounter is recalled by Stephen: 'One Sunday evening in 1951, my father was out in his car and saw two small Boy Scouts carrying large kit bags trudging along the side of the road outside the City. He offered them a lift, which they duly accepted. The journey into Norwich was punctuated by the sort of monosyllabic conversation you would expect from young lads. After he dropped them off at home and helped them unload their kit, one of them handed him a threepenny bit saying, "That's for the ride." He was so amused by the incident that he later included it in his speeches. I don't know how he spent his threepence!'

The Hinde Family with the Lord Mayor's Coach, 1951

1951: Martin Miller Marries Barbara

In 1944 Martin Miller was called up. He had hoped to join the Navy, instead he was selected to be a so-called Bevin Boy, and spent the next four years working as a miner down a coal pit in South Kirby, Yorkshire. He was demobbed in 1948, and three years later married Barbara, despite their first date not going quite as planned:

'After I came back from Yorkshire, on Saturday nights I joined up with a group of young people from Norwich who'd quite often go to the Petersfield Country Club at Horning. In those days I smoked a pipe, and one evening I was trying to light it with a match whilst also holding a pint of beer, and a voice said: "Can I hold that for you?" I looked around and saw Barbara.

'Because of the paucity of entertainment in those days, if you wanted to take things further with a young lady you'd invite her to go to the pictures with you during the week. And so, for our first date I arranged to meet Barbara on a Tuesday night outside the Regent Cinema on Prince of Wales Road. I clearly remember the evening because just after we'd been seated eight chaps arrived in the half-dark, as cinemas were in those days, and as soon as I heard them I realised that they were part of the crowd who'd been at the Petersfield the Saturday before. Once they got used to the dim light and they saw me with Barbara, that was it. The remarks they made! In those days there was always a main and support picture. Well the support picture was about a group of girls who went to Blackpool and met these young men and one of the girls said to the other: "I think they're miners." Her friend responded: "We mustn't go with miners; they pollute the sea." Well of course the place absolutely erupted. There was uproar. The noise those eight blokes made laughing was horrendous.'

Martin and Barbara Miller, 1956

1955 – 1960: We'd 'Never Had It So Good'

The National Picture

In 1957 Prime Minister Harold Macmillan made a speech which defined the era: 'You will see a state of prosperity such as we have never had in my lifetime – nor indeed in the history of this country. Let's be frank about it, most of our people have never had it so good.' It is often forgotten that he added a cautionary, and prophetic note, when he asked: 'Is it too good to last?'

By now the economy was experiencing a golden age, epitomised by low unemployment and high growth rates, both driven by a post-war economic boom. These combined to generate improved standards of living. We'd had enough of austerity, we wanted to enjoy ourselves, and for the first time in years we could. Average earnings in the five years to 1960 rose by 37%. At the same time, the prices of many mass-produced electrical goods, including televisions, washing machines and vacuum cleaners were falling in real terms. The ending of hire purchase restriction in 1958 meant that even if you did not have the money to buy an item outright, goods that had been regarded as luxuries became affordable, you could now easily buy them on the 'never-never'. Many availed themselves of this opportunity, and over the next three years total hire purchase and other credit outstanding in the UK doubled.

But was everything as good as it appeared? On the face of it this seems a period of political stability – the Tories had been in power since 1951, and in 1959 they cemented their position when they won the general election with a massive 100-seat majority. But this fact hid underlying tensions. In just five years we had three prime ministers, a failed military expedition to Suez, turned down the opportunity to be a founder member of the European Economic Community, experienced race riots and in 1957 the Campaign for Nuclear Disarmament (CND) was founded.

It is also very clear that in this period of increased wealth there were losers as well as winners. This can be illustrated by two examples: the expansion of television and the growth of car ownership.

In the second half of the 1950s the number of televisions in the UK trebled, and by the end of the decade there were more than 10 million sets in the country. Watching television had a huge impact on the way we spent our leisure time. Yes, it brought people pleasure and enjoyment, but also led to us going out

New cars like the Ford Anglia 105E with its distinctive sloping rear window arrived in 1959, Tombland, c.1960

1950s Display, Museum of Norwich at the Bridewell, 2016

less. One of the biggest losers in this transition was the cinema: over the decade around a third (1500) closed their doors for good.

There was a similar meteoric rise in the number of cars on the roads. By 1960 there were around six million vans and private cars in Britain, a 250% increase since 1950. Vehicles gave freedom, but the country's highways were ill-prepared to deal with these machines. In fact, the country's first stretch of motorway was not opened until 1958, and that was only 8.3 miles long (Preston by-pass). Cities which had not been designed to deal with motor vehicles became jammed with cars. Road-safety procedures did not keep up with the growth of vehicles: in 1958 6000 people were killed in road accidents (compared with 3000 in 2008).

First ITV advert was for Gibbs SR toothpaste

Another downside of the rise in affluence was an increase in lawlessness. Somewhat disturbingly, the second half of the decade saw a 64% increase in indictable offences known to the police (to around 744,000). In particular, crimes against property rose by 72%. Why? Basically, there was more to steal. There were more cars on the road and more goods in houses, whilst a growth in the number of self-service supermarkets was a shoplifter's dream.

Despite such qualifications, millions of people really had 'never had it so good'. These five years were in many ways epitomised by the growth of rock 'n' roll and the youth culture. In this age of prosperity and increased opportunity, for the first time there were teenagers with spare money who demanded goods that would allow them to express their own identity. They no longer dressed, shopped or acted like their parents. Their tastes influenced and dominated the music scene, giving rise to new stars, including Bill Haley, and a man who became known simply as the 'King', Elvis Presley.

By the end of the 1950s, people had plenty of jobs to choose from. Not only did they have money to spend on luxuries, they had goods to buy. Social attitudes were changing. Improved education and health provision had increased young people's expectations. This generation was not going to 'make do and mend'. Modern conveniences were no longer a dream, they were now attainable. The consumer society had arrived.

Norwich

On 6 April 1956, some 14 years after it had been bombed, Curls reopened. Andy Anderson was one of the many who was thrilled, he could finally believe that 'Norwich was coming back to life'. The new store was impressive. The four-storey building plus basement incorporated 97,000 square feet of floor space, where customers could purchase an array of goods, from electricals to fashions, which would have been inconceivable in the austerity years. In 1951, when the newly built Loose's china shop reopened on Magdalen Street, the owners had difficulty stocking the shop. On Curls first day of trading, no such problems existed. Although enough tills had been installed to deal with 40,000 transactions a day, more had to be brought into service to deal with queues of customers. The local press had no doubt about the significance of the occasion: 'The varied examples of rebuilding and extensive renovation which have occurred in Norwich since 1945 now make an impressive total and are an indication of the City's prosperity'.

This feeling of rebirth and growth extended to many aspects of the City. Despite the horrors and destruction of war, the rebuilding that followed led to regeneration: we had new modern houses, new schools, new shops and modern factories.

Curls, drawing by Charles Knight of Curls, c.1956

Norvics St George's factory, 1952

Trade and Industry

The position is exemplified by the state of the local economy. By the end of the decade the City's shoe industry, its leading employer, was operating at full capacity, achieving an output of some eight million pairs of shoes and employing 9000 people. Similarly, the construction sector, with its workforce of 7000, was booming. The City's building enterprises owed their success to a variety of factors: post-war restoration of bomb-damaged properties; the City Council's house-building programme; industrial expansion; and local authority projects, including road improvements.

During WWII 130 Norwich factories had been demolished. As these were rebuilt, they were modernised and redesigned. As a result by the late 1950s the City was home to some of the most

Harmers new factory, Havers Road, 1948

up-to-date industrial units in the country. These included: Caleys huge premises on Chapelfield, described in December 1956 as one of the 'most modern and efficient confectionery enterprises in the world' and Harmers clothing factory, considered in 1959 to be 'one of the leading clothing firms in the country'.

With such reputations it is not surprising that Norwich manufacturers received prestigious orders. Thus in 1955 Start-rite (or James Southall & Co. as it was then) was granted a Royal Warrant for supplying shoes for Prince Charles and Princess Anne. Jean Woods recalls: 'It was a real honour to be selected to work on the shoes for the Royal Family, but making them was a nightmare because they had to be absolutely spot on. Goodness knows how many times a pair went around before it was let out of the factory.' Then, the following year, Thompson & Son (based on Golden Dog Lane) were selected to make shoes for Grace Kelly's pageboys when she married Prince Rainier. Meanwhile, in 1959 Laurence, Scott & Electromotors were delighted to be given a share of a £16 million order from British Rail to build new diesel locomotives.

Laurence, Scott & Electromotors, Hardy Road, c.1960

Cattle Market, City-centre site, c.1959

Cattle Market, after relocation to Harford Bridge, c.1960

Another major feature of the City's post-war industrial growth was the migration of manufacturers out of the City. There were two main reasons for the move: the limited availability of suitable sites within the City and the difficulties of traffic circulation. Such sites were so popular, and the economy so buoyant, that by 1960 the new industrial estate at Harford (Hall Road), was fully occupied. Controversial plans were also well underway to transfer the Cattle Market out of the City to Harford Bridge: the move was completed in 1960.

Expansion also took place in the City centre. The *City of Norwich Plan* had incorporated a proposal to house all Norwich Union (now Aviva) staff in a large modern block of offices facing All Saints' Green. Like many other schemes the idea had been thwarted by post-war austerity measures. However, in 1955 the Norwich Union considered the time was right to make long-term plans, including a significant expansion of its office accommodation. The proposed new buildings were grouped round their existing Head Office, within the perimeter of Surrey Street, Westlegate and All Saints' Green, on what is still known as the Island Site. By 1960 construction had begun on a nine-storey office block designed to accommodate 2000 staff.

New Norwich Union offices arise on the corner of Surrey Street and All Saints' Green, 1961

All this activity translated into high levels of employment, which meant it was also very easy to find work, as explained by Avis Brown: 'I left school in 1957 when I was 15, and went straight to the Caley chocolate factory. After a few months someone said that they were paying more money at Harmers, so a group of us went over there, but I only lasted two weeks because I was put on the hot press, which I really didn't like. I knew about the shoe trade because my mother was in it, and so I left Harmers and walked up the road to Edwards & Holmes on Drayton Road. That's how at the age of 15 I found myself on my third job!'

Entertainment

This was a period that saw a shift in how Norwich residents spent their leisure time. Until the mid-1950s television reception in Norwich was often poor. John St Quintin's family bought their first set in 1953: 'The picture wasn't very good, it looked like snow, and so my dad would twiddle with the buttons. My mum would always be saying, "Leave it!" But we kept losing the picture.' However, this all started to change in 1955 when the BBC began local transmissions from Talconeston (South Norfolk). Then in 1959 the BBC opened television studios in Norwich, and in the same year Anglia TV was launched. The latter was particularly important because it meant that viewers could now access two stations. Over the second half of the decade the number of households with a TV licence in the Norwich postal area increased from around 13,000 to 51,000. Improvement in television reception was the death-knell for many of the City's cinemas and its two professional theatres. Between 1956 and December 1961 seven Norwich cinemas (Regal, Mayfair, Haymarket, Theatre de Luxe, Capitol, Norvic and Ritz) together with the Hippodrome Theatre closed. Although the Theatre Royal remained open as an entertainment venue, in 1956 it had been bought by Essoldo, a national cinema chain, and was no longer a centre for drama. This once illustrious theatre reached a new low in 1959 when it ran a 'Nell-Gwynne Sex-Kitten Contest'.

Music venues held their own, but they did change. Jazz, rock 'n' roll and skiffle all gained in popularity. In 1957 the City's first skiffle contest was held at the Industrial Club (Oak Street) whilst jazz clubs sprang up around the City. Rock 'n' roll reached dizzy heights in 1957 when Bill Haley brought his European Tour to the Carlton (All Saints' Green), followed two years later by the *Oh Boy Roadshow* headlined by a singer described as 'more like Presley than Presley himself' – Cliff Richard – accompanied by the Drifters.

1950s room, Gressenhall Farm and Workhouse, 2016

Eating out also changed. Alongside, the City's traditional venues, cafés which catered for the new brand of teenager arrived, including the Blue Bat on Upper King Street, where Colin Buxton met his mates: 'That's where all the Teddy boys used to hang out. Next door was an amusement arcade. Some bikers came in, but they mostly went to the Boundary Buttery Café. It wasn't rough in the Blue Bat, we used to go there to drink coffee and listen to records on a juke box. It was just a social meeting place.'

Norwich was also at the cutting edge of fast food! As early as 1957 what is believed to be the City's first Wimpy hamburger was sold at Paul's Espresso Coffee Bar. Then in 1959 the Soochow, the first Chinese restaurant, opened in the City. Interestingly both ventures were located on Prince of Wales Road.

Sporting Success

The experiences of one institution sum up the City's fortunes in this period more than any other: Norwich City Football Club (NCFC). Like the rest of the City, they too were on a voyage which saw them travel from the troughs to the peaks. The club was just managing to survive in the Third Division South (between 1948 and 1958 they faced re-election three times) yet fans poured into Carrow Road to cheer the team on. In 1959 supporters had their reward. This was the year Norwich repeatedly took on the giants of the game and won, in an FA Cup run which took them within a hair's breadth of Wembley. The dream came to an end in the semi-final replay, but by then it had uplifted an entire City.

In Conclusion

As the 1950s give way to the 1960s our journey comes to an end: and what a voyage it has been. In 15 years Norwich has been rebuilt and regenerated, housing shortages have been overcome, industry has flourished, television has arrived and, most importantly, optimism has returned.

Terry Bly scores for Norwich against Manchester United, Carrow Road, 1959

Memorable Events: 1955 – 1960

1955: Start-rite Granted Royal Warrant

James Hanly , Start-rite Shoes, c.1955

It was in 1955, when James Hanly was chairman, that local firm Start-rite was first granted a Royal Warrant for supplying shoes for Prince Charles and Princess Anne. In the years that followed the firm fitted hundreds of pairs of children's shoes for members of the Royal Family, including Prince William and Prince Harry. David White, James' nephew and successor recalls: 'Jim loved to tell the story about one of the first times he went with Bill Peake, the firm's fitting consultant, to Buckingham Palace to see Prince Charles. After they'd finished measuring and Prince Charles had decided which shoes he was going to have, the Queen walked in. He was introduced and she was very gracious and there was a bit of small talk. Eventually the Queen said: "We're just going to have tea. Have you had your tea Mr Hanly?" He said no he hadn't whilst thinking: "This is marvellous, here I am selling shoes and I'm going to have tea with the Queen." That was until she said: "Oh dear, we mustn't keep you... Good-bye."'

2 April 1956: Malcolm Flood Dies

Malcolm Flood, speedway star, c.1955

Malcolm Flood was renowned for being one of the greatest cycle speedway riders of his day.

Born in 1931, even as a boy Malcolm was obsessed with speed. He was captain of the Earlham Eagles Cycle Speedway Club as well as both the Norwich and Norfolk teams, winning national titles along the way. Speaking to the *Eastern Evening News* in 1998 Malcolm's brother recalled: 'People loved Malcolm so much. I remember knocks on our front door. When we opened it there was no one there, but presents were left on the step. Sweets, cigarettes...that kind of thing.'

All the time Malcolm wanted to go faster. He soon progressed to motorcycle speedway, and became a rider for the Norwich Stars. He constantly pushed himself and in 1956 he was involved in a horrific crash. He never recovered from his terrible injuries and died later the same year, when he was just 25 years old.

3 July 1957: Queen Elizabeth and the Duke of Edinburgh Visit Norwich

Queen Elizabeth and the Duke of Edinburgh on City Hall steps, 1957

On 3 July 1957 Queen Elizabeth and the Duke of Edinburgh were greeted by thousands when they came to Norwich. This was the Queen's first visit since the Coronation, and the City came out in force to show their support and appreciation for their monarch. The street scenes were described in the *Eastern Evening News*: 'Thousands of children... ranging from head boys and girls from City schools to babes in their mothers' arms, were prominent among the crowds lining Norwich streets to greet the Queen and the Duke. Armed with flags, some almost as big as their bearers, the children were most vocal in their appreciation as the sleek, maroon, Rolls bore the Royal couple through the street's thoroughfares.'

A busy day started with a reception at City Hall. The royal party then went to the Norfolk and Norwich Hospital to open its new operating theatre after which they visited the wards. It was during this tour that an enterprising patient, Simon Warnes, who was recovering from an appendectomy, took the opportunity to have a 1950s-style selfie taken with the Duke of Edinburgh. Simon showed great enterprise when he 'produced a camera from under the bedclothes' before having a flashlight picture taken with his royal guest and telling him: 'Jolly well makes it worthwhile, sir.' The royal party than went to the Costessey showground where they were guests of honour at the Royal Show, which welcomed more than 37,000 attendees on the day of their visit.

A popular Duke of Edinburgh, Norfolk and Norwich Hospital, 1957

The 1959 Norwich City Cup Run

In 1959 the Canaries took on and beat some of the greatest teams in football to reach the FA Cup semi-final. Their legendary performance fired the imagination of the City and won the hearts of a nation.

It was in January 1959 that the impossible happened. The mighty Manchester United, managed by Matt Busby, arrived at Carrow Road to play the third-round tie. The team were chasing the Division One title, and must have expected an easy win. Maurice Morson, was a policeman at the time: 'I'd been allocated point duty, directing the traffic, at Foundry Bridge. Flakes of snow were starting to come down, and people were trickling out of Carrow Road. I shouted across to an early leaver, "How're they getting on?" "Winning three-nil," came back the response. I thought to myself, "He's really taking the mickey." I took real exception to the fact he was taking such a serious subject so lightly. I was quite amazed when I found out that was the result!'

After beating Cardiff at home, Norwich travelled to play Tottenham Hotspurs in the fifth-round tie. They were watched by 20,000 fans who raised the roof in the 64th minute when Terry Allcock put their team in front. It seemed that nothing would stop the Canaries, then in almost the last kick of the match Spurs equalised. More than 38,000 squeezed into Carrow Road to watch the replay. The pressure to get tickets was immense, Maurice recalls: 'It got to the stage that we [City Police] used to parade at Carrow Road, not for the match, but for the ticket queues. They were a real rumbustious affair. Lines of people tailed around over Carrow Bridge, and all the way up King Street.' This time there was no mistake. Terry Bly, City's centre forward, scored the game's only goal and Norwich completed another magnificent giant-killing act. City were in the quarter finals, playing Sheffield United at their Bramall Lane ground.

After two minutes of the match Sheffield scored, a lead they held until, with just 15 minutes left on the clock, Norwich equalised, earning them a replay at Carrow Road. A game of high tension was eventually won by three goals to two by the home side. At the final whistle, delirious fans roared their appreciation and invaded the pitch. The football writer covering the match for the *Daily Express* reported: 'It was the maddest, merriest, nerve-rackingest night I have ever known in my world sporting travels.'

City were now on the brink of playing at Wembley, but first they had to beat Luton Town. The match was played on a neutral ground, White Hart Lane. Norwich drew, and the two teams travelled to Birmingham for the replay. The City held its breath, but their glorious team had come to the end of the road, they failed to score, and lost one-nil. John Chilvers was just seven at the time: 'We were allowed to listen to the replay of the semi-final against Luton in school. But what made it really big for me, was that Sally Nethercott and Michael Ashman, whose fathers played for the Canaries were in school with us. This gave it a real immediacy, and hooked me. You can imagine how despondent we were when they lost.' Meanwhile Andy Anderson had made it to the match: 'It was dreadfully disappointing. We had our chances in the first half and didn't take them and then there was one Luton shot by Billy Bingham, which went in and that was that. When we all left we were a bit down but we had a good run home. The headline the next day summed it up when it said "It's All Over".'

Although there was disappointment, the overall feeling in Norwich was one of pride. As always happened, the players shared the train home from the match with many of their supporters. On this final trip, the train bar was reportedly drunk dry, and it had to make an unscheduled stop at Peterborough to restock. At the same time a pile of *Pink Un* papers, hot off the press, were collected. To show their gratitude for the support they had received the team walked through the train with the papers and led renditions of *On the Ball City*. Thousands of supporters were at Thorpe station to greet the train and the players who had brought so much joy to so many people.

The City's breweries decorated their drays in support of NCFC, 1959

October 1959: Norwich 'Leads The World'

In October 1959 Norwich became the first area of the UK to use post codes. The code, which consisted of 'NOR' followed by a space, two figures and a single final letter were introduced on a trial basis. Albeit in a different format, they have been in use ever since.

The City was selected to run the trial because it already ran automatic sorting equipment which could interpret the codes. By the end of 1959 nine 'Elsies' (electronic letter sorting and indicating equipment) had been installed to cope with the new system. The machines were some 17ft long, 6.5ft high and 3ft wide, leading to a suggestion they should be called 'Elongated Elsies'.

The introduction of post codes caused both confusion and anger, resulting in some rather interesting articles in the local press. A letter from J. A. S. read: 'I would like to express disapproval at the system of postal codes now imposed upon the Norwich area. The majority of my firm's clients are from the rural areas and quoting their full postal address is certainly not their strongest point. Now to expect them to remember a code number and use it, is rather wishful thinking.' Meanwhile Lucy Lawrence made her feelings very clear, even before the trial started: 'Sir – May I endorse [recent] views regarding the Postmaster General's new postal code. To me it appears an unintelligent move....Instead of having to pay heavily for electronic equipment give the public a cheaper telegraph service.'

27 October 1959: The Launch of Anglia Television

At 4.15pm on 27 October 1959, much to the delight and excitement of viewers, both in Norwich and across the region, Anglia TV was launched.

The opening transmission featured an iconic model of a knight on horseback which represented the channel until 1988. The figure, which was more than 100 years old, had originated in the Netherlands, and was discovered in the window of a London jeweller's shop. After certain modifications, including the addition of a pennon on the lance bearing the word 'Anglia', the magnificent silver trophy became one of the most widely recognised symbols in British broadcasting.

The new organisation was based in Norwich in the former Agricultural Hall [Agricultural Hall Plain], renamed Anglia House, where they had installed offices and three studios. It brought glamour to Norwich as summarised by Anglia TV Director Aubrey Buxton: '...[It] will attract personalities, stars and notabilities from all walks of life into the heart of the area. The glamorous pop-singer or the distinguished archaeologist may soon be heard declaring with undisguised relish: "I'm off to Norwich!"'

On launch day, the *Eastern Daily Press* ran a supplement which introduced the new channel to its readers. A diverse range of articles included everything from advice on how to get a good picture to an introduction to Susan Hampshire who would be singing in the channel's *Mid-Day Show*.

From the start the new channel acknowledged they had to perform a fine balancing act, not only between high and low culture, but also between national and local programmes: 'Many viewers will complain if peak viewing hours are devoted too much to "highbrow" features – and a number will complain at a diet of cowboys and murder. Well-known features such as *Wagon Train, Emergency Ward 10, Sunday Night at the London Palladium* and *Song Parade* will be taken from the national network, but much of the quota originated in the Norwich studios will be strongly local in appeal.' This approach was clearly illustrated in the opening day's programme.

Opening Day's Programme

4.15	*Introducing Anglia*: Official opening of Anglia's Norwich studios by Sir Ivonic Kirkpatrick, chairman of the ITA (Anglia).
4.45	*Small Time*: Children's programme (Associated Rediffusion).
5.00	*Lucky Dip*: Children's magazine (A-R).
5.55	News (ITN).
6.08	Local News (Anglia).
6.15	*This Wonderful World*: Magazine documentary (Scottish).
6.45	*Birth of a Regiment*: Documentary on the amalgamation of the Norfolk and Suffolk Regiments filmed in Germany (Anglia).
7.00	*Song Parade*: Musical with the Grenadiers - TV's most popular song and dance team (Granada).
7.30	*Emergency Ward 10*: Serial on life in Oxbridge hospital (ATV).
8.00	*Concentration:* Panel game.
8.30	*Knight Errant '59*: Playboy detective series (Granada).
9.25	News (ITN).
9.35	Play of the Week: *The Violent Years,* starring Laurence Harvey and Hildergarde Neff (Anglia).
11.05	News (ITN).
11.07	*Introducing Anglia*: Film of Anglia opening (Anglia).
11.37	Epilogue (Anglia).

Throughout the 1950s young men were called up to do their national service. For some it was two years of hardship, for others a stepping stone to a successful career.

1956: Maurice Morson Completes his National Service and joins the City Police

Maurice Morson, c.1955

Between 1954 and 1956 Maurice served with the Royal Norfolks. Once he'd completed his ten-weeks' basic training Maurice expressed his ambition to eventually join the civilian police force. In response, he was given the opportunity to train as a provost (army term for regimental police). By the time he left the forces he was a corporal, and a senior provost.

'As I got near the end of the two years the army allowed me to come back to Norwich for an interview with the City Police based at Bethel Street. After sitting the recruitment exam, which wasn't very strenuous, I was invited to come back and see the Chief Constable, who offered me a job as a constable for two years on probation. And so I went back to the army, went to W. H. Smiths and invested in a book, "Moriarty's Police Law", which I used to sit in the guard room, studying, in anticipation of my new career. I left the Norfolks on a Friday, and the following Sunday I went to the police training centre in Oxfordshire.

'When I joined the police force it was a regimented existence, because those were the days when police constables were on the beat. Looking after property was a prominent part of our duties. And so you tried door handles by night and directed traffic by day. This routine was punctuated by one or two incidents. You hoped that at the end of your two years' probation that you would be accepted.

'I still have my beat book, which told you exactly where you had to be at any one time. It was very regimented. You worked to a strict timetable. As you walked the streets, every hour and 20 minutes you made a call from a flashing pillar phone. You didn't have a radio, and so this was how we communicated.

'Working on nights tended to be boring. The last bus would have left by about 11 o'clock and, as people didn't have cars, at that point the City would die – and I do mean die. At one or two o'clock in the morning you had the City to yourself. You could actually stand at Stump Cross, in Magdalen Street, and hear the inspector's car starting up in Bethel Street. It was like that until the early hours of the morning when bakers and railway men were coming in to start their shifts. You could walk around the City and hear the clanking of the engines and wagons down at Thorpe Station.

'There was a lot of semblance between the army and the police force. You've got to remember that in those days all the force was ex-military, because if you weren't fit enough for military service you weren't fit enough for the police force. I worked with people who'd served in Korea. And so, there was a common bond.

'The public showed the force respect. You don't see it today. If there was a fight in a pub, you could open the door and walk in and it would stop. Just because the uniform was there.'

This was the start of a long and successful career for Maurice. He eventually retired from the force in 1987, by which time he was a Detective Chief Superintendent and Head of Norfolk CID.

The National Health Service

The Queen visiting the Norfolk and Norwich Hospital, 1957

The Birth of the National Health Service

The National Picture

Aneurin (Nye) Bevan, c.1950

It seems incredible that at a time when both government finances and the economy were in such a fragile condition two bastions of the current age were born: the National Health Service (NHS) and the country's modern welfare state.

Before the war healthcare in Britain encompassed a mix of private, charitable and municipal schemes which varied significantly in terms of structure, effectiveness, hygiene and access. Services included:

Voluntary Hospitals: These operated as independent charities financed from a mixture of sources, including investments, fund-raising events, gifts, payments for services and a mishmash of insurance schemes.

Municipal Hospitals: Run by local councils, many of these institutions had grown out of workhouses. Some were relatively modern places, where beds were generally kept for the poor, others were squalid and poorly run.

General Practitioners: These doctors ran private practices. Although they depended on private fees to generate an income, most also took in poor patients via health insurance schemes. Many also worked as surgeons in municipal hospitals.

In 1911 the National Insurance Act had established a state health insurance scheme which gave lower paid workers free access to a doctor (but not a hospital). However, it did not cover dependents or the unemployed. Those who could not afford the premium relied on a variety of health insurance schemes, many run by Friendly Societies. Services for the poorest were limited to voluntary/charitable schemes or very basic public provision. As a result, visits to the doctor would only be made in an emergency. Dentistry and optical services were only available to those who could pay for them.

Then in 1942 William Beveridge, the lIberal economist, produced a report identifying five 'Giant Evils' in society: squalor, ignorance, want, idleness and disease. He went on to propose a series of reforms to the system of social welfare which would address these 'giants'.

When they were elected in 1945 the Labour Government, led by Clement Attlee, had a clear mandate to implement Beveridge's plans. Almost immediately they put them in motion with the introduction of a new system of social security. During their term in office they introduced extensive legislation, including the National Insurance Act 1946. Under the act people in work paid a flat rate of national insurance. In return, they (and the wives of male contributors) were eligible for a range of benefits, including flat-rate pensions and sickness benefit. Various other pieces of legislation provided for a range of groups and situations, including the elderly, children and the disabled.

Central to Beveridge's vision was the creation of the National Health Service. Aneurin Bevan was appointed by Clement Attlee as the Minister for Health, and so the responsibility fell to him to institute a new and comprehensive National Health Service 'free at the point of need'. During the war Britain's hospitals had been brought into a single national emergency medical service. Bevan decided that a similar system should continue after 1945. He proposed that all hospitals, both the voluntary ones and those run by local councils, be operated under a single nationalised system. There would be regional boards but these would come under the control of the Ministry of Health in London. Bevan's National Health Service Bill was published in March 1946 and enacted two months later. There followed a period of protracted dispute during which time opposition from the Conservatives, members of his own party and the British Medical Association (BMA) threatened to derail the scheme. Members of the BMA particularly objected to: being 'nationalised'; being paid a flat salary rather than paid on the basis of how many people they treated; and losing the option to treat private patients. In February 1948 the BMA and government were still in deadlock. In April Bevan conceded to the BMA's major objections, later saying that to broker the deal he had 'stuffed their mouths with gold'.

On 5 July 1948 hospitals, doctors, nurses, pharmacists, opticians and dentists were brought together under one umbrella organisation: the NHS was born.

The Health Service in Norwich

Norfolk and Norwich Hospital, 1955

At the outbreak of WWII, for most people in Norwich access to healthcare relied on membership of quasi-insurance schemes. The main suppliers of cover in the City included:

- A Norwich-based hospital contribution scheme, under which regular weekly payments to the Norfolk and Norwich Hospital exempted contributors and their dependants from hospital charges. In the 1930s, around 80% of hospital in-patients were members of the scheme.
- The Norwich Friendly Society, whose members had access to the doctors at the Medical Institute on Lady's Lane.

Memories

Barbara Miller recalls: *'There were always people who stood around on Norwich Market, never visibly working. After the launch of the NHS they suddenly all had new glasses and new teeth: it was a transformation really. I think the free access to dentists and opticians had more of an effect than free medical treatment, largely because the Norfolk and Norwich Hospital had been greatly loved and well served before the NHS.'*

Christine Perfect recalls: *'My father was a civil servant. He'd been badly injured during WWII when he had been a motorcycle dispatch rider. On returning to Norwich he started work at the Artificial Limb Centre in Norfolk House on Exchange Street. Although he didn't have an artificial limb, one of his legs had been badly injured, and so he had great trouble walking. I remember visiting him in his office, and him opening a drawer that was full of artificial eyes. As a child I didn't know whether to be frightened or to laugh.'*

In the News

On 5 July 1948 a jubilant journalist reported on the birth of the NHS in the local press: 'The great venture of a nationwide joint health and insurance scheme which comes into force today will undoubtedly consolidate Britain's eminent position among nations which lead in the field of social services. It is a bold project to be introduced at a period when this country is still beset by grave perils. If the Government can make it work efficiently as a whole and sympathetically in relation to the individual, they will have accomplished something very big indeed.'

Hospitals

Before WWII the major providers of hospital care in the City were:

- The Norfolk and Norwich Hospital (St Stephen's Road): A voluntary general hospital with 448 beds and an out-patients' department.
- The Jenny Lind Hospital for Children (Unthank Road): A voluntary children's general hospital with 80 beds and an out-patients' department.
- The Woodlands Hospital (Bowthorpe Road): A public-assistance institution under the control of the City Council. Before war damage it had 823 beds of which some 530 were for the infirm and mentally incapacitated.
- The Isolation Hospital (Bowthorpe Road): An infectious diseases hospital adjoining the Woodlands Hospital that was also under the control of the City Council. It was designed for 94 beds, although it housed more.
- The Norwich City Mental Hospital (Drayton High Road, Hellesdon): This 750-bed hospital for the mentally ill was again under the control of the City Council.

As the hostilities ended, doctors at the region's leading hospital, the Norfolk and Norwich (N&N), were questioning the possible format of a NHS. The main point at issue was the Government's proposal for placing hospital control in the hands of an area committee representing local government authorities. By 1946 they were backing a model put forward by the British Hospital Association (a body representing all voluntary hospitals), for an independent hospital service which could work within the NHS. The proposal involved the government paying to use the services offered by the voluntary hospitals, which would continue to operate as independent, self-funding bodies. It was believed that such an arrangement: 'Would maintain...a balance between the organisation required for a National Health Service and the dangers in any national hospital plan – loss of the personal and human touch, loss of local interest, and making the patient fit the scheme instead of the scheme being made to fit the patient.'

As we all know, the proposal was rejected. Under the new NHS all hospitals were brought together in a single system run by one of 14 regional boards overseen by local management committees.

In June 1948, a month before the launch of the NHS, the board of the voluntary run N&N presented their 176th, and final, annual report with a 'deep sense of regret'. They concluded: 'In bidding farewell to the old order, the Board and all who have supported the hospital can boast that they are handing over to the State a first-class institution with the hope that the future will show that though changed in form it will remain the same in spirit and purpose.'

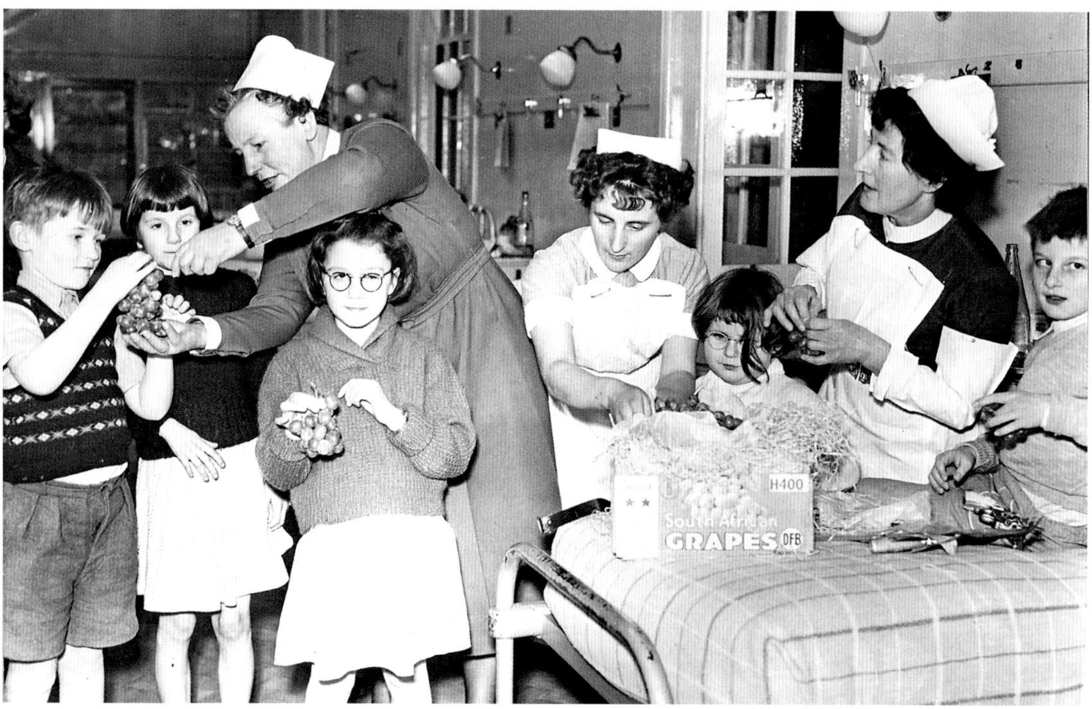

Children and nurses at the Jenny Lind Hospital, c.1955

GP Surgeries

GP surgeries did not experience the same revolutionary changes. Along with dentists, opticians and pharmacists they remained self-employed but acted under a contract for services from the NHS. Thus began the GP's role of gatekeeper to the rest of the NHS, referring patients where appropriate to hospitals or for specialist treatment alongside prescribing medicines and drugs.

The launch of the NHS marked the end of a Norwich institution: the Medical Institute. Until then, the Institute's five doctors and support staff had provided treatment for both state-insured patients and members of the Norwich Friendly Society.

Roy Cracknell's family was one of the many who relied on the Medical Institute: 'It was a big old house, which housed four or five doctors' surgeries. It was a wonderful place. When you went in you'd be faced by a row of boxes containing numbered tickets. You'd tear off the ticket for the doctor you wanted to see, and then you picked up your packet of papers from the receptionist. Next, you'd go and sit on one of the benches in the waiting area. Because there were so many doctors there, we'd all be looking around saying: "Do I follow you?" The walls were festooned with big old photographs of the elders of the Friendly Society, all in their suits. The surgeries were down the end behind a screen. Once you'd seen your doctor you went to another part of the building where they had a dispensary – which also had pictures of the elders all around it. You left your papers at a little wicket with a glass screen, then in due course you were handed your bottle of medicine.' With the launch of the NHS and the provision of free treatment the Medical Institute became superfluous and on 4 July 1948 it was dissolved, leaving its patients (some 13,000) to register with the new service.

By December 1948, 96% of the City's population, including 55,000 women and children who'd never registered before, had signed up with a NHS doctor. Pent-up demand for treatments put a huge strain on Norwich's new NHS. In its first six months 260,000 prescriptions were issued, 14,000 sight tests undertaken and 9850 pairs of spectacles supplied.

In the News

In March 1948 a letter appeared in the 'Eastern Evening News' which summed up public feeling regarding the Medical Institute: *'I am sure there are many members like myself who join with me in praise for its great service and would like to offer their thanks and gratitude for all the goodness and devotion given to us by the doctors, never forgetting Doctor Flack, especially through the years of the war.'*

The Medical Institute, Lady Lane, 1938

Would this happen today?

Christine Perfect:

'We had a lovely doctors' surgery on Willow Lane. I remember seeing a Doctor Napier – every time we visited he was smoking.

'You didn't make an appointment. When you arrived you'd be given a blank prescription by the receptionist. You then waited in a very long room, with chairs along one side. Every time someone went in the rest of us moved up a chair. You didn't have your name called, instead you'd hear the doctor holler, "next". No one pushed in: it was all very civilised.'

Stephanie Brooks:

'At our surgery on the Heartsease Estate you never made an appointment. Everyone raced to get there, and you got to see the doctor based on what time you arrived. We all worked out the order ourselves: strangely enough, I think it worked better than the appointment system we've got today.'

The 1950s

In the years that followed major investment took place in the City's hospitals, including improvements to the Woodlands (later the West Norwich) Hospital and the Norwich City Mental (later the Hellesdon) Hospital. At the N&N, improvements included the opening of a new operating theatre in 1957 and a new nurses' school in 1959. Meanwhile GPs' surgeries and health centres were incorporated as a matter of course into the many housing estates built around the City.

It is interesting to note that many of the shortcomings in the health service that were identified in the 1950s are similar to those that hit the headlines today. Thus, in 1956 the local press ran the story: 'Shortage of Nurses Still a Problem'. In 1957 we learnt: 'The N&N radio-therapy department is so short of radiographers that superficial X-ray therapy is stopped.' Demand always seems to outstrip supply.

Yet, despite the many criticisms levelled at the NHS, it is impossible to imagine Britain without it. The ideal espoused by Bevan is as relevant today as it was in 1948: 'Good healthcare should be available to all, regardless of wealth.'

Nurses served Christmas dinner by surgeons, 1954

In the News

In February 1955 *a local journalist reported that a growth in the number of TVs in Norwich had led to an interesting innovation: 'A television set has been added to the eye-testing equipment at Messrs D. R. Grey the Norwich opticians...[they] installed the set so that people can see for themselves whether they need spectacles for looking at televisions.'*

In August 1959 *the 'Eastern Evening News' ran an article on the new Nurses' Training School attached to the N&N. Costing £19,000, the self-contained building housed a variety of rooms, including a classroom, a model ward and sluice room. Here, the students learnt 'practical work such as bed-making, moving and tending the patient and the correct handling of that feature of hospital routine that looms so incredibly large and all-important in the life of every patient – the bed pan'. The school had been a long-time coming: its predecessor had been destroyed in the war.*

Did You Know?

In 1954 the Norwich Executive Council of the NHS were given the responsibility of inspecting GPs' surgeries. Before the review started, the Norwich Local Medical Committee sent a letter to doctors saying although it was impossible to lay down rigid standards, inspectors expected:

- *Consulting rooms to have running water or at least a wash basin with water, soap and a towel*
- *A separate examination room or screened-off couch*
- *A waiting room large enough to seat all in reasonable comfort (unless there was an unusual amount of illness)*
- *Well warmed and cleaned premises*
- *Domestic rather than institutional furniture*
- *Patients to have access to a lavatory and washbasin.*

Avis Brown (right) and friends at Hemsby, 1957

Children

If you took a child of today back in time to the immediate post-war era, they would have a shock. What would they make of a world where food was rationed, where there were no mobile phones or social media, and televisions were few and far between?

Weren't children bored? Wasn't it awful? Wouldn't everyone be happier growing up today? For many the answer to all of these questions would be a resounding no. Of course, it would have been lovely to eat what you wanted, and live in a warm house, but would you substitute that for having so much independence; and why do you need 'Facebook friends' when you could go out and play with a real-live friend? The position is neatly summed up by John Chilvers: 'For me, being a child in the 1950s was vintage. I couldn't have wanted any more. We didn't have the material goods that most children have today, but we had freedom.'

Responsibility and Independence

From a very young age most youngsters were allowed out with no supervision: older children would be told to look after their younger friends and siblings, and that would be it. Kids, like Rodney Barker, would be waved off in the morning and be expected home by nightfall: 'We'd be given a jam sandwich and what we used to call baby orange juice, which was a tiny flat bottle of thick concentrated juice that was supposed to be good for you. We'd go out first thing and come back late afternoon, when our tummies were telling us that we were hungry.'

Young children would also be allowed out on buses and into the City in a way that would never be contemplated today. Since being a small boy John Chilvers has been a great NCFC fan: 'I had very careful, loving parents, but they didn't think twice about letting me go into Norwich by myself. In January 1959, when we went to see the Manchester United cup game, I was just seven. Mum packed up mine and dad's dinner, I got on the bus and took it down to his office on Prince of Wales Road, where we sat and ate it before going to the match.' When he was even younger, just six years old, John was regularly sent by himself to walk from Hotblack Road (off Dereham Road) to Ripley Close (off Colman Road) – a distance of over a mile – to visit his grandparents: 'It was the same with my friends: we had so much freedom. It really shows how parenting has changed. We had a degree of movement and independence, that if allowed today would be regarded as child abuse. It really was a different world.'

Also, from a young age children were given a lot more responsibility. Typical of this generation is Avis Brown, who lived on Woodcock Road: 'When I got to junior school, I'd be first home. When I got in I'd set the fire, lay the table, put the kettle on, and then from 6pm I used to watch at the gate looking for the people walking up the hill from the bus: I knew that mum would be amongst them. Then I'd run back indoors, boil the kettle again and make a pot of tea. We all used to have to help, in them days. That's why you grew up quick.' Similarly, from an early age Peter Watson had chores: 'When I was around eight years old one of my jobs was to go and get the fish and chips for Friday night's tea. I used to get onto the bus outside the house, which took me on a journey down Middleton's Lane and along Reepham Road to Thompson's fish and chip shop at Mile Cross. When I got there, I'd hand over the money from a purse and a bit of paper which had our order on it together with a request for them to take me back across the road. Then I'd catch the bus back home.'

John Chilvers (centre) with family, Clacton, 1947

Playtime

Playtime meant going out with friends, running around, using simple props and above all having an imagination. In the words of Stephanie Brooks: 'We didn't have many toys, and so we made up our own games.'

Lynn Preston recalls that she mostly played street games, including *Release-O, Port and Starboard, Chocolate, Pigeon Toes* and *Two-balls*. Avis Brown was typical of many girls of her generation: 'We used to play hopscotch. We'd draw the squares with chalk on the path, and then when mother came home I used to have to get a bucket of soapy water and wash it all out. There'd be loads of us from school all playing skipping with a long rope which went right the way across Woodcock Road. There were hardly any cars, the only thing we needed to worry about was when the bus came: it was great.' Meanwhile boys entertained themselves with cigarette cards and maybe Dinky toys, they'd play football, chase and catch.

Children developed games based on where they lived. Sylvia Buxton's home was in the City centre: 'By the end of the war we had loads of bomb sites around us. As kids, we thought ourselves very lucky, because they made brilliant playgrounds: we'd build houses and little dens on them.'

Maurice Morson lived on Hilary Avenue, off Plumstead Road: 'I spent a lot of time playing with my mates on Mousehold, and on what we called the "four miles square", which lay between Heartsease Lane, Salhouse Road, Woodside Road and Plumstead Road East. Later it became home to the Heartsease Estate, but the houses weren't there then, and it was just a huge open space. We used to go over there quite a lot. We'd often just run around or play at hide and seek; there was always something to do. I even remember playing on a tip at the bottom of Plumstead Road and making a cycle speedway track at what was the end of Lloyd Road, which was a cul-de-sac at the time. We also used to try and get into the sand martins' nests in the cliff face at the back of Hilary Avenue, where it bordered Valley Drive. We used to dangle over the top and try and put our arms down. We never got the sand martins, but it was something to do. There were quick sands there, and our parents always cautioned us not to go down an area known as "the pit". We always promised not to...but we always did.'

When the Heartsease Estate was built, children living here, and on the other estates, thought themselves especially lucky, as explained by Paul Warr, whose family was amongst the first to move onto the Heartsease: 'It was a brand-new house, which was surrounded by fields. It was fantastic because the rest of the development was being built, and so as a child I had a huge "gymnasium" on my doorstep. Luckily

Stephanie Brooks (right), in the 'farmer's den', c.1957

Paul Warr (centre front) dressed for a party, c.1958

for me it was before there were any worries about health and safety. This meant that me and my mates, including my neighbour John, had a wonderful time. We climbed everywhere, played hide and seek within the structures, built dens with the window frames and even had great fun starting up cement mixers. There was nothing in the mixers, but as lads we'd seen the men running them during their working days, and we just wanted to see if we could set them going as well. We sometimes used to take the putty out of newly glazed windows. Not only did we have fights using the putty as ammo, but we also used the fresh stuff as a plasticine substitute: we'd make models out of it. Unfortunately, I wasn't very artistic, and my limit was making little men in houses. Our relationship with the builders was somewhat mixed. Some would give us rides around the estate on the lorries and dumper trucks while others gave us our first insight into their colourful language! I vividly remember getting a good hiding from my father for trying these new words out at home!'

The Marlpit Lane area was also very popular, it was here that Colin Buxton used to '...play on the marshes, near the river. We used to swim at Hellesdon Mill all the time. On the meadow near the mill, we had a big bicycle track that we all raced around.'

Then, of course there were the parks. Rodney Barker lived on the South Park Avenue Estate: 'I must have gone over every inch of Eaton Park, every inch of it. As young boys we went over there whenever we could. In those days there was a fellow called Reggie Ward who was the park keeper. He was a tallish man who always wore a uniform: a dark navy blue or black jacket and trousers and a flat peaked cap. As a boy I was always fascinated by the fact that you could see a bit of a bump, which was the outline of his head, under the material of his cap. The gates used to be locked up at night times. There are lots of football pitches at Eaton Park, but we were never allowed to walk over them. If Reggie saw you walking across those pitches, he'd really yell out at you. Well of course, as youngsters we were frightened of him and ran away. I suppose we respected him. There was another field that we called the circus field or the third field, which is where they now do pitch and putt. We'd go there with binoculars to do some bird spotting, I recall even seeing skylarks.'

Saturday

Every Saturday, across the country children flocked to the cinema. In Norwich it was no different, but there were also other attractions, not least of which was the Cattle Market.

The cinemas put on special shows and clubs on Saturdays for children who'd all have their favourites. Peter Watson used to go to the Odeon on Botolph Street where, like other venues, they showed a lot of cowboy films: 'It was brilliant. I loved it, because after the film they'd call up all the birthday girls and boys onto the stage to get a lollipop. I couldn't wait until it was my turn. Thinking back, it was strange, but none of us ever dreamt of telling a lie.' Meanwhile, Maurice Morson enjoyed going to the Regent Cinema on Prince of Wales Road with his mates: 'It was a riotous affair; there was a continuous barrage of noise in the auditorium. They used to screen cartoons, and a variety of westerns featuring stars like Gene Autrey and Roy Rogers. All the kids would pile in whooping and shouting and pile out...still whooping and shouting. The audience was made up mostly of children – in fact I can't remember an adult

Castle Book Stall, Agricultural Hall Plain, c.1955

in there.' The Capitol Cinema on Aylsham Road was Janice Middleton's favourite: 'They ran a programme for kids called the Sixpenny Rush: because it cost sixpence to get in. They always showed a cowboy and Indian film, and then a horror film. I went with my friend from next-door and we used to sit on one seat, and then when they showed the horror film we'd put our coats over us.'

After leaving the Regent, Michael Holmes and his mates often went to the Castle Book Stall: 'The left-hand side of the stall was a brilliant place to buy a great selection of comics, such as *Superman*. Even better, after you'd read them you could take them back, and buy your next one half-price.'

The Cattle Market and its surrounds provided just as good entertainment, especially if, like Sylvia Buxton, you could get involved in the action: 'As kids, we used to go up to Old Joe's on Ber Street and get four penn'orth of chips. We'd then sit on the pig pens on the Cattle Market for half the day. My brother, used to go bullock whopping; the farmers would give him a shilling or two and he used to get a stick and drive the cattle along Ber Street and down to the Pineapple pub in Trowse. We used to run behind them sometimes. I didn't mind going behind, but I didn't like walking in front – they were very big, and I would have been only eight years old.' Similarly, Maurice Morson and friends used to find sticks and then 'help' the drovers direct the cattle down Plumstead Road: 'Once at the market we could go and see other animals, including rabbits and chickens, then just across the road at the top of the hill, where Archant is now, was a pet shop: Wicks was the name. I particularly remember the mice, because I used to keep them as pets. On Saturdays the whole area was like a treasure island.'

Other Saturday attractions may have included a trip to Thorpe Station to see the steam trains or, like Michael Holmes and pals, you might have swung around to the Castle Museum: 'Not only was it free to enter, but it was like an Aladdin's cave. We were fascinated by the mummy and its tomb, and spent hours looking at the stuffed lions, tigers and polar bear. We'd never been to the zoo, and so it was our only chance to see wild animals close up. We obviously gave the art galleries a miss, but the castle keep was a great place to play.'

Then in 1955 when Curls, now Debenhams, reopened, their new escalators (the first in East Anglia) brought a whole new dimension to Saturdays. From the outset children had a whale of a time. Some did circular tours, up by escalator and down by lift or stairways, whilst the more adventurous went up on the escalator: 'forwards, backwards, standing and sitting' and particularly enjoyed running down what was an 'up' escalator. All-in-all a brilliant way to round off a very enjoyable day.

The Cattle Market, c.1955

Would this happen today?

Maurice Morson and his pals were among the many children who learnt how to use their initiative from a young age: *'Hilary Avenue backed onto the prison at Britannia Barracks. The prisoners used to earn money for doing little jobs, but all they could buy was chocolate, when they really wanted cigarettes. We soon realised the potential of the situation, and so we used to pick up the dog ends of cigarettes from the gutters and trade them through the fence for chocolate from the prisoners.'*

In 1959 Paul Warr was delighted when the City Council left an unorthodox piece of equipment on the Heartsease Estate playground: *'Through the 1950s building continued on the Estate, and so one day when we saw a steamroller being driven through we just thought they were doing roadworks. But it carried on to the park, turned around close to the toilets, and stopped. Well, it was another toy for us boys to play on. You can imagine. We'd climb up there and pretend to drive it. Boys being boys, we soon realised that if we climbed on the roof then ran fast on the fly wheel whilst someone in the cab quickly put it into gear, it would move forward. Once we'd perfected our technique we got it moving three foot at a time: then we'd move it back. Eventually common sense took over, and the Council disconnected the drive chain.'*

Boys on the Heartsease loved playing football with the former NCFC player Terry Ryder (played 1946 to 1951) who lived on the estate with his family. His daughter Stephanie takes up the story: *'I was very conscious that my dad had played for Norwich City: it made me a very popular girl. We used to have lots of boys visiting our house, they'd come to play football with dad. On Manby Road we lived in a row of terrace houses, but between every couple of houses there was a little passage way. Well, all of these boys would trot through the passage, and then they'd come in my back garden. It was then a short trip down the garden, over the fence and into the field which housed the old aerodrome, where they'd play football. It wasn't a proper pitch, the goal post was nothing more than a space between two jackets, but my dad just loved playing, it was his life, and so I think he enjoyed the games as much as the lads. My mum was concerned that I was being left out – but not for long. At the time I wanted to be teacher, and so dad soon found a way to involve me. I used to sit at my very own little wooden desk and as the boys walked in one-by-one I'd tick them off my register: just like I'd seen the teachers do in school. After the last boy arrived, my dad would instruct two of the lads to pick up my desk and chair and carry them over to the field. I'd then sit back down with my pen and paper and was in charge of keeping the score. That said, I was a very good footballer, I could (and probably still can) head the ball fantastically, my dad saw to that.'*

Paul Warr (centre front), c.1959

Stephanie with her Dad, Terry Ryder, c.1960

Toys

Toy Cave, Jarrolds, 1950

As we progressed through the 1950s and families became more prosperous, parents could treat their children to new toys. These tended to follow gender stereotypes, and so girls would typically be given dolls or skipping ropes, whilst boys favoured cowboy guns, Dinky cars or building sets, such as Bayko or Meccano. Like today, each year there were different crazes. In 1958 hula-hoops were the must-have toy (there were even competitions on Saturdays at cinema clubs); in the same year Lego bricks appeared in their familiar form. Then in 1959 an iconic doll made her first appearance: Barbie.

Major stores selling toys in Norwich included Langleys, Hovells and Jarrolds. In December 1958 Jarrolds advertised that it had the largest toy fair in East Anglia and invited children to visit Father Christmas in the Land of Nursery Rhymes. That year they were promoting a variety of toys, including pedal cars, Hornby train sets and Meccano for boys, whilst girls were being tempted with dolls and related items, such as prams and houses.

See all these Tri-ang Toys & thousands more at

Jarrolds

TOY FAIR

THE LARGEST IN EAST ANGLIA

TEDDY BEARS from 10/2

HUNDREDS of DOLLS AT ALL PRICES

DOLLS' PUSH CHAIRS from 15/11

A large Selection of BABY TOYS

HORNBY TRAIN SETS from 28/6

Herald (Unbreakable) TOY SOLDIERS from 1/- each

COWBOY SWOPPETS from 1/3 each Mounted 2/11

MECCANO Full Range in Stock

DOLLS' HOUSES from 49/6

TRI-CYCLES from 27/6

PEDAL CARS from

DESK and CHAIR SETS from 38/6

ROCKERS from 31/-

TIPPER LORRY 19/6

DOLLS' PRAMS from 32/6

WHISTLE PUFF-PUFF 49/6

FATHER CHRISTMAS in the LAND OF NURSERY RHYMES

Your children will be thrilled by FATHER CHRISTMAS and the life-size working models of favourite NURSERY RHYMES.

Admission: Children (with mystery present) 1/-; Adults 6d.

CHOOSE FROM OUR LARGE SELECTION OF CHRISTMAS CRACKERS

FROM OUR SPORTS DEPARTMENT

FOOTBALLS from 15/6
ROLLER SKATES from 21/-
HOCKEY STICKS from 17/6
TABLE TENNIS SETS from 12/6

Joe Davis BILLIARD TABLES from 4 ft. £6/12/-
A Large Selection of BOWS and ARROWS
DARTS and DARTBOARDS

★ See a DEMONSTRATION of the Exciting Game SUPER (MAGNETIC) SOCCER. Sets from 34/11.

Gift Vouchers available in all Depts.

JARROLDS

LONDON STREET, NORWICH Tel. 21481

Jarrolds advert, 1958

Memories

Janice Middleton recalls a City institution: *'For us, going into the City really meant going to Magdalen Street. It was a lovely street in the 1950s. As a girl I particularly remember taking my broken dolls to be mended at the Dolls' Hospital. When you went in you entered a dark little room, which had lots of repaired dolls and teddies on shelves, waiting for their owners to pick them up.'*

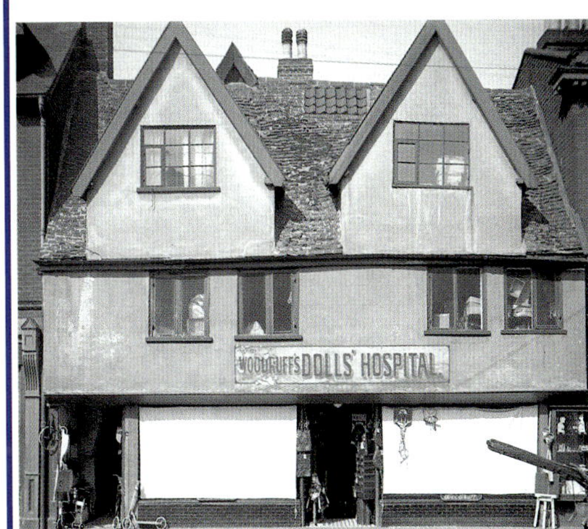

The Dolls' Hospital, 1935

Toyland, Jarrolds, 1950

Toy Department, Jarrolds, c.1959

Toy Department, Jarrolds, c.1959

Children's book fair, Jarrolds, c.1959

Television and Radio

Home entertainment was very different to today.

Most households had access to a wireless, although like Lynn Preston you may have had a 'radio relay', a system whereby set stations were piped to the house and accessed via a control switch screwed to the window sill. Shows, such as *Children's Hour*, featuring *Larry the Lamb* and a host of other characters were very popular with young children. Whilst serials, such as *Dick Barton – Special Agent*, appealed to an older audience. This popular radio thriller which was transmitted between 1946 and 1951, had over 20 million listeners at its peak. Another great favourite with children was *Journey Into Space*: it kept children (and their parents) entertained between 1953 and 1958, and was the last UK radio programme to attract bigger audiences than television.

In 1945 few households had a television, but by the end of the 1950s there were 10 million sets in use across the country. Sales had been boosted by the Coronation in 1953 and by the launch of ITV, which came to Norwich in 1959 with the birth of Anglia Television. If, like John Chilvers, your family did not have a set, it was not necessarily a problem: 'In 1956, very few people in our neighbourhood around Hotblack Road had a television. By 1959, most of my mates did have one, although we didn't. It didn't bother me, if there was something on I particularly wanted to watch I just used to make sure I got an invite to a friend's house. At the time I was particularly fond of westerns. I knew a girl who lived six doors away, Jenny Bell, whose family did have television. Luckily her mum was really nice as well. I must admit that I infiltrated myself into their household, mainly because of their TV.'

One of the most popular children's TV programmes of the era was *The Lone Ranger* which ran from 1949 to 1957. Even today, when people of a certain age hear the *William Tell Overture* (the programme's theme tune) they are taken back to the days of their youth, and can imagine the Lone Ranger jumping onto his horse with the cry 'Hi-Ho, Silver! Away!' Younger children were entertained by *For the Children* (renamed *Watch With Mother in 1950*). Many of the characters featured in the programme are still recognised today. Favourites included: the marionette Andy Pandy with his sidekicks Looby Loo and Teddy; Bill and Ben, the Flowerpot Men, accompanied by Little Weed; and Muffin the Mule. Other programmes, launched in the 1950s, which stood the test of time, include *Crackerjack*, which ran from 1955 until 1984 and *Blue Peter*, which was launched in 1958 with presenters Christopher Trace and Leila Williams.

Memories

'Crackerjack' was first shown on 14 September 1955, when it was presented by Eamonn Andrews. *Until 1963 the programmes were broadcast in front of a live audience, mostly of children, at the King's Theatre on Hammersmith Road [London]. The show was quite frantic, it had everything including corny jokes, appearances by pop stars and a singalong finale. It featured the game 'Double or Drop', where kids' arms were piled high with prizes which they took home if they answered questions correctly or with cabbages if they got them wrong. Crackerjack pencils were much treasured. In the late 1950s Jude Sayer, well known in Norwich for her work as a Blue Badge Guide, appeared on the show: 'At the time I lived in Cliftonville [Margate] where our next-door neighbour was Bert Hayes, who was the musical director for Butlins and was also renowned for his work on the "Lenny the Lion Show" and "Crackerjack". Bert had a daughter, Janet, who was about the same age as me and we became friends. This meant I was invited along to help with the rehearsals for "Crackerjack", and I even took part in the test-run for "Double or Drop". They also needed groups of children to sing along with performers. Being a born show-off I was in my absolute element. In 1958 I performed with Michael Holliday who sang his hit "The Story of My Life". But the absolute highlight came in 1959 when I sang with Dickie Valentine, who was a big star at the time and my absolute heart throb. I remember Bert Hayes introducing me and telling Dickie he was my hero. At that point, for the one and only time ever, I was absolutely speechless. All I could do was stare at him with my mouth open, but I still remember it as being one of the best moments of my young life.'*

Jude Sayer, 1953

Wensum Park playground, c.1955

The Cattle Market, c.1960

Paul Warr and Dad, c.1953

Lynn Preston, c.1955

Miller family, Sheringham beach, 1955

Young Cracknells, Gorleston beach, 1959

Teenagers

Would this happen today?

As a child growing up in the 1950s, Lynn Preston (born 1948) recalls rules created by adults who were afraid of the new youth culture:

1. *Teddy boys and girls were dangerous and should be avoided at all costs.*
2. *Jeans were allowed but only to play in. They could not be worn to visit relatives, on a Sunday or to go 'up' the City.*
3. *On Sundays you still wore your 'Sunday best' and were not allowed to go to the pictures.*
4. *There was a strict dress code covering all aspects of clothing and make-up. There was a constant litany of restrictions and everything had to be run past mother for approval which was only reluctantly given. I think she gave up, finally, in about 1964.*
5. *There was a great fear of anything that didn't originate in Norfolk – despite both my parents spending six years in the armed forces during WWII.*

In the 1950s a new social group emerged: the teenager. The word 'teenager' was not new, but the 1950s was the first decade that people thought of the teenage years as a separate stage of life between childhood and adulthood. Until then children had been regarded as young grown-ups from the age of 12, becoming full adults by the time they were 21.

This group of young people was now spending more time in education than earlier generations, and when they left school they had access to jobs with good wages. As they became more affluent, they demanded goods that would differentiate them from the adult world and enable them to express their own identity. Manufacturers were happy to meet this demand and developed products specifically for them. For example, after discovering that on average teenage girls bought five pairs of shoes a year, twice as many as the average woman, Norvic (the Norwich-based shoe manufacturer) decided they could not afford to ignore them. In their 1959 annual report the directors announced they had set up a Teenage Council, which was described as: 'A group of seven alert young women with just the right mixture of intelligence, wit and fashion-sense.' To add 'authority', and no doubt a bit of star quality to the Council, it was headed by Judy Grinham who had won a gold medal in the 100m backstroke at the 1956 Olympic Games.

Norvic's Teenage Council, Judy Grinham is second left, 1959

Bill Haley, 1957

Teens wanted their own fashions. Jeans were particularly popular with some youngsters, a reaction against the more formal clothes worn by their parents. In contrast, others enjoyed being Teddy boys, and dressed up to the nines in long, bright jackets, 'drainpipe trousers' and 'slim-jim' ties.

Styles were often linked with popular music or films. For example, skiffle fans were influenced by the American folk scene, and so boys sported lumberjack shirts and turned up jeans, whilst the girls favoured flared dirndle skirts or tight mid-calf-length pedal pushers, worn with flat shoes.

Several American films had a huge impact on the British youth movement. One of the earliest was the *The Wild One* (1953) starring Marlon Brando, which featured a leather-and-denim-clad motorcycle gang: a look emulated by many teenagers. Two years later the similarly attired James Dean appeared in both *East of Eden* and *Rebel Without a Cause,* and in so doing became an icon of teenage rebellion.

However, for many teenagers of the 1950s, one film and performer came to epitomise the era, as explained by Glenna St Quintin: 'We went to see Bill Haley in *Rock Around the Clock* at the cinema. Everyone was shouting and hollering. It was such a different thing. You could feel yourself getting excited and worked up. We were all so quiet before, and there wasn't too much going on, and then suddenly rock 'n' roll arrived. We all learnt to jive, which was great. It did have a real impact. The excitement came from the newness, and with the music. Everyone else was doing the same thing, and you didn't think that anyone was looking at you especially, and so you felt as though you could let rip and let go and just thoroughly enjoy it.' You can imagine the excitement in March 1957 when the man himself came to Norwich and performed on stage at the Carlton Cinema [All Saints' Green]. Despite the evening being lively, with reports that the crowd reached 'fever pitch', fears of an uprising were not met.

All-in-all it would seem that the City's teenagers embraced the new rock 'n' roll phenomena with an acceptable level of enthusiasm, as reported in the *Eastern Evening News*: 'There has been no rowdyism occasioned by it, said a spokesman for the management of the Samson & Hercules Ballroom. Occasionally jive enthusiasts give vent to their abundant energies in corners of the dance floor invariably without inconvenience to other dancers.'

Avis Brown (second right) and friends, Butlins, Clacton, c.1959

Education

One of the pivotal changes of the post-war era was the emergence of an improved and state-funded education system. This particularly had an impact on children from poorer families, enabling greater numbers to extend their studies at college and university.

Christine Perfect, left, with family and friends, William Street, c.1954

The National Picture

In 1938 around 80% of children left school when they were just 14 years of age: most had only ever attended an all-age elementary school. Like other social reforms introduced by Attlee's Government, the war acted as a catalyst for improvement. In the case of education, the evacuation of millions of working-class children from big cities to the countryside forced people from all backgrounds to mix and brought to light the abysmal state of the system. After the war people wanted to believe that Britain would be a better place that offered opportunities for all.

The legislation that formed the basis of post-war education policy was passed in 1944. It was the brainchild of a Conservative, R. A. Butler (sometimes described as the 'best prime minister we never had'). It developed from a White Paper he published in 1943 entitled *Educational Reconstruction*. Butler had a simple mission: 'To secure for children a happier childhood and better start in life' and to open the way to a 'more closely knit society'. The Attlee Government ensured the provisions of Butler's education act were fully implemented. As a result, for the first time free secondary education became a right. One of the act's main thrusts was the introduction of a three-tier secondary school system made up of:

- Grammar Schools: designed for children with academic ability. Entrance was based on children passing a test (11+) in their final year at primary school.
- Technical Schools: for pupils who were as intellectually able as grammar school entrants, but whose aptitudes were better suited to technical subjects than to subjects of an academic nature.
- Secondary Modern: for the rest.

Other key policy changes included:

- An increase in the school leaving age to 15 (implemented in 1947).
- The introduction of university scholarships, which aimed to ensure that no one who qualified for a university education should be deprived of their place for financial reasons.
- An extensive school-building programme.

One of the major achievements of the Act was the abolition of fees in grammar schools. In the interwar years about 60% of places in grammar schools were taken up by middle-class fee payers, whether they were suitable for an academic education of not. It was hoped that free places for more intelligent children of poorer means would give them better life opportunities. Although many did benefit there was a major deficiency with the selection process: the 11+ exam. The most successful, around 25% of pupils, were allocated to grammar schools; for many this was a gateway to better qualifications and jobs. Those who 'failed' were sent to secondary modern schools, where they had less opportunity. The exam ignored both the fact that children develop at different ages, and that some went to poor primary schools and were ill-prepared for the exam.

During its term of office, the Attlee Government increased spending on education from £6.5 billion to £10 billion. The funds were used for a variety of measures, including the construction of 928 new primary schools, the expansion of free school meals, an increase in state scholarships to university and raised expenditure on technical education. Although the act was not perfect, it resulted in a significant improvement in the country's education system.

Orchestra, Colman Road School, c.1958

Education in Norwich

In Norwich, the Labour-led Council clearly recognised the importance of education, as evidenced in the *City of Norwich Plan*: 'If we are thinking in terms of affording full opportunity for children and building up local communities, then new housing, allotments and other aspects of planning should not have priority over other educational facilities.'

In the years that followed, the City Council's Education Committee faced many challenges, not least of which was competing demands for public money in a time of economic constraint (sounds familiar!). Other issues included coping with an abnormally high birth-rate in the two or three years after the end of the war (which produced the so-called 'bulge' babies or baby boomers), and providing school places for families living on the new housing estates.

Although not perfect, there is no doubt that educational provision at the end of the period was significantly better than at the beginning. This is clearly illustrated by the fact that by 1961 21 new schools had been built in Norwich: nine infants, seven junior and five secondary. These included many schools built to serve the new and expanding council estates, including primaries at West Earlham, North Park Avenue and Heartsease, and secondary schools at Lakenham and West Earlham. Despite all the challenges of the post-war years, by 1960 some 70% of Norwich children were attending a school which had not been built before the war, or had been completely modified since: an admirable achievement.

Memories

After the war, children from poorer backgrounds had opportunities which had not been available to their parents. Michael Holmes lived on Woodcock Road, on the Catton Grove Estate: *'As kids, we were all a bit rough around the edges but we did have our Catton Grove School.*

'There is no doubt that the teachers had a challenge, but they were well up to the job. Many had spent time in the forces during the war and had been fast-tracked to a teaching qualification. This meant they understood discipline, which was strict but far from harsh, and also they could tell stories of the exotic places they had visited during their time in the Services. I vividly remember one teacher talking about plucking oranges from trees and how they tasted so good. When he got to Paris he saw cakes the like of which we could not even imagine: soft crusts filled with creamy custard and exotic fruits covered with jelly.

'But it was the likes of Mr Brown, Mr Roe and Mr Thurston who helped some of us pass the 11+, which eventually led to us going to university – a step well within the capability of our parents, but an option that was never open to them.'

The City of Norwich School, 1939

Secondary Education in Norwich

In the years after WWII, in line with national policy, Norwich's secondary schools underwent significant changes. By 1960, around 25% of the City's secondary-school pupils in state education went to selective schools, including the City of Norwich School (C.N.S.) for boys, the Blyth Grammar School for girls and the co-educational Hewett School, with its emphasis on technical training. The remainder attended secondary modern schools.

Grammar and Secondary Modern Schools

Mr Jex (Chairman of Norwich's Education Committee) was very much in favour of the post-1944 grammar schools. He did not see the 11+ as a deterrent, instead he believed that 'for the first time young people from modest homes [had the opportunity] of proceeding to a university and then reaching administrative positions...equal to and standing side-by-side with those of boys from public schools.'

However, although in favour of the grammar-school system, investment was not made in selective schools to the detriment of secondary moderns. Indeed, one of the major thrusts of post-war provision in Norwich was the criteria set by the Education Committee that schools for secondary-modern children should have the same standard of facilities as those provided for grammar-school pupils. In fact as new secondary moderns were built facilities were often better than the older grammars. For example, the Blyth Grammar School, which was opened in 1929, was built to accommodate 490 girls, but by 1958 it had 750 pupils. Despite investment in various extensions an inspection report completed in 1958 noted: 'The premises remain very considerably below what is required for a five-form entry grammar school, not only in teaching space but in cloakroom and lavatory provision.' In contrast, in 1951 proposals were in place to build a brand-new secondary-modern girls' school at Lakenham, complete with 40 classrooms, gymnasium and halls. Pupils at some new secondary moderns also profited from another key policy which had been an integral part of the *City of Norwich Plan*: the amalgamation of school and community facilities. For example, the Earlham and Bluebell Secondary Modern Schools at West Earlham benefitted from a 62-acre site adjoining Earlham Park, which incorporated over 40 acres of playing fields.

Although they lacked facilities, there is no doubt that the teaching at grammar schools was generally excellent. In 1959 the C.N.S. ranked as one of the leading maintained grammar schools in the country, as measured by awards of scholarships and exhibitions at Oxford and Cambridge. In this one year 34 of its boys qualified for university places. Similarly, in 1957 three pupils from the Blyth Grammar School won open awards to attend women's colleges at Oxford and Cambridge, an achievement that ranked it as the top maintained girl's school in England. However, although not so exam driven, there is also much evidence of high-quality teaching at the secondary moderns: in particular, the Alderman Jex School for Boys had an excellent reputation. Here, lads who showed academic promise were given the opportunity to study for the General Certificate of Education, whilst all pupils took part in school excursions, open days and dramatic performances. The school was much admired by inspectors who reviewed it in 1959: 'Much has already been achieved in this school, and there is much promise for the future. It is a community with abundant vitality, aware of its problems and intent upon their solution.'

Technical Schools

As the Norwich City College and Art School (previously the Technical College) already offered technical training for youngsters over 13, the City should have had no difficulty introducing a technical secondary school meeting the criteria laid out in the 1944 Act.

The College must have seemed ideal for the role. It had originally been set up by the Mechanics' Institute to train employees in new industrial processes. By the 1940s it provided training for many of the City's workforce (on both a part-time and full-time basis) in a variety of trades, including engineering, printing, boot and shoe manufacturing, commerce and domestic science. As early as 1919 a Junior Technical College had been created as a full-time day school offering courses in craftsmanship for boys. A Junior Art Department followed in 1935 and a Junior Commercial School in 1937. The college was based on St George's, but by the 1930s it had outgrown its original buildings and land was purchased on Ipswich Road for expansion. By autumn 1939, plans had been agreed and the steel framework of a new building was completed. This was put on hold during the war, but

Would this happen today?

Rodney Barker, recalls that despite all the improvements, facilities at some schools were not quite up to scratch: *'The other day I was speaking to my grandchildren who asked if we had showers at school. I said, not only didn't we have showers, but at Avenue Road School, we had an outside toilet in what looked like a stable. The urinal was outside in the open air: it ran along the side of the building.'*

City College, 1991

a workshop and some classrooms were completed in the expectation that they could be used for industrial training purposes.

To meet the requirements of the 1944 Education Act, the three 'junior' divisions (technical, art and commercial) were collectively designated as a junior college. Which was good, but it did not meet two important criteria i.e. pupils should have started at the age of 11 after passing the 11+. Instead, even in 1949, pupils who were selected from secondary moderns could only enter the college from the age of 13. This resulted in an inspection report noting: 'It appeared... that a good many of the boys were not of the mental calibre which is generally associated with the idea of secondary technical education.' The inspectors also criticised inadequate facilities, including small and badly ventilated classrooms, and commented that coursework and teaching was both unco-ordinated and lacked direction. It was very clear, that whilst an excellent institution of higher education, the College was not the appropriate home for the City's Technical School. The City Council addressed the issue head on and in 1957 opened the Hewett Secondary Technical School on Hall Road.

Memories

One of the biggest criticisms of grammar schools has always been the 11+ examination. Albert Cooper recalls the stigma of failing the test: *'I failed my 11+, which was a big thing in those days. If you passed you might end up working for a solicitor or for the Norwich Union, in general doing a more professional job. If you failed you might work in the shoe trade, Laurence, Scott & Electromotors or the Co-op bakery: the more artisan jobs. At the age of 11 your future was almost mapped out, and so if you were a late developer or hadn't been prepared for the exam, you were already viewed as a failure.'*

Rodney Barker, took the 11+ at the Colman Road Junior School. He was terrified the day he took it and can still remember what it was like: *'When we were practising for it the teacher wrote out ten words on the board, and you had to look at them for five minutes and then they'd turn the board around and you'd all have to write out what you could remember. You were then asked, "Who got ten?" Of course, the same two kids always stood up, then those who got nine stood up. They then came down to me who had three or four. I'd always be right at the bottom, which was very demoralising. And so, when it came to tests and stuff, I was never very confident, and no-one was surprised when I failed the exam and went to the Avenue Road School, between Recreation Road and College Road.'*

Although for many children going to a grammar school was the stepping stone to university and better paid jobs, failing it was by no means the end of the world. *Despite their experiences, both Rodney and Albert have gone on to have successful and happy lives, as has Janice Middleton: 'After I failed the 11+ exam I went on to the Angel Road Secondary Modern, if I'd have passed I'd have gone to the grammar school. I never felt that I had missed out. I passed the same number of O levels as friends who went to the grammar school, and then I went on to train to be a teacher.'*

Primary Schools in Norwich

The combined effects of war-time bombing and the migration of families to the new housing estates resulted in a revamp of junior and infant school provision in the post-war years. As new premises were built, efforts were made to house junior and infant schools on the same site, to form primary schools.

Throughout the 1950s primary schools were particularly hit with transient increases in numbers as the 'baby boomers', children born in the years immediately after the war, passed through their ranks. Additionally, schools located near to the new council estates had to cope with huge increases in pupils pending the opening of the associated school. In response schools resorted to using every spare space, from corridors to halls, as temporary classrooms. In 1951 there were reports of classes as big as 45 children, but by 1960 classes of around 30 were the norm.

As more people moved to the outskirts of Norwich and into its suburbs, the Council concentrated on building new schools in 'the fringe area'. Between 1950 and 1953 four new schools were opened: Middleton's Lane Infants at Hellesdon; Sprowston Infants; Costessey Junior; St William's Junior and Infants at Thorpe. Collectively they cost £230,000 and provided for 1400 children.

The new school buildings were significantly better than their predecessors. In all cases schools were allocated adequate playing facilities. Typical, was St William's School, which was built in 1953. Here, classrooms were paired and each pair had its own cloakroom and lavatories. Additionally, the juniors and infants each had their own assembly hall. Particular thought had been given to aesthetics, and the school had been planned to 'give maximum sunshine to the various rooms'. Changing rooms and showers were provided for the junior children.

In contrast, the Colman Road Infant School had been built in 1906. In 1953 it comprised a hall, six classrooms, two cloakrooms with wash basins and a staffroom. In 1946 it served 130 children from an established estate plus older terraced houses. Seven years later, following the construction of houses on two new estates (North Park and South Park Avenue) the school had 369 pupils. A new school had been approved on North Park Avenue, but until its completion, there was no choice but to soldier on. To create more teaching space, two classes were run in the hall, which was also used for school dinners. The pupils had to manage with only eight toilets, located in a detached block on the other side of the playground. However, despite the conditions, the staff, which consisted of a head mistress together with eight full-time and one part-time teacher, received a glowing school report when it was inspected in 1953. They were praised for their varied and well-balanced approach to their fundamental work in reading, writing and numbers, which produced as a minimum 'satisfactory results'. The inspectors going so far as to say that children's speech was good whilst older children wrote with ease and fluency. Nature study was well taught, despite limited space 'music and movement, singing games, percussion band work and singing' all received attention.

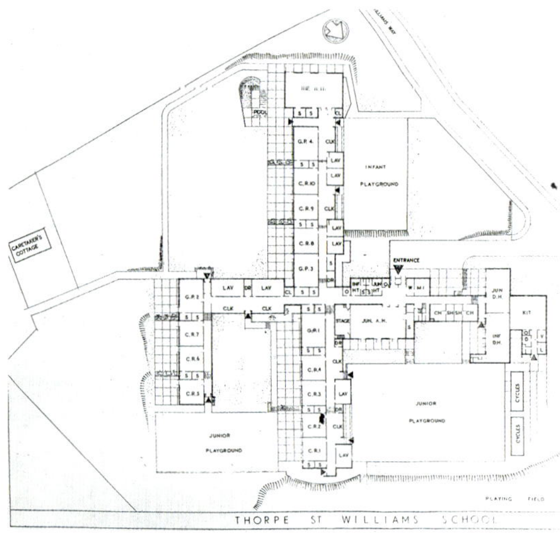

The new St William's Primary School plans, 1953

Did You Know?

In the years following the war there was concern that children were undernourished and needed extra care. *Avis Brown is among many whose earliest memory of going to school was having an afternoon nap: 'After dinner the teacher would help us get little canvas fold-up beds out of a cupboard, we'd put them up, and lie down and have a sleep.'*

Others recall, not always fondly, school milk. The 1944 Education Act decreed that all schoolchildren under 18 were given a third of a pint a day. Additionally, younger children were given a dose of cod liver oil and a little bottle of orange juice. It was not until 1968 that free milk was withdrawn from secondary schools. Then in 1971 Margaret Thatcher (as Secretary of State for Education) abolished it for children over seven, earning her the nickname 'Thatcher, the milk snatcher'.

Memories

Like today, playtime was a very important part of the school day. Paul Warr and Stephanie Brooks were amongst the first pupils at the brand-new Heartsease Junior School (opened in 1956). They recall the many games they enjoyed playing:

Paul Warr: *'At school us boys found lots of ways to entertain ourselves. We often played with cigarette cards or charged around playing chase and catch in teams. We also used to have fun with Dinky cars, because there was a slope on the Heartsease Junior school playground, and they used to really zip along. In the autumn term we had hours of fun with conkers.'*

Stephanie Brooks: *'I loved going to the Heartsease infant and junior schools: they were happy days. We were all friends together. In the playground we played things like hop-scotch, skipping and five stones. When we were younger we'd play singing and dancing games, like 'The Farmer's in His Den'. It was great when it was icy because we used to make big slides on the playground and whizz across them, until the caretaker came along with a bit of salt and spoilt our fun.'*

Like today, in the 1950s school dinners divided opinion:

Sylvia Buxton was not a fan: *'I lived near school, and so went home at lunchtime, but all my friends had school dinners and I begged my mum to allow me to stay. Eventually, she let me stay one week, but I hated it. The food was revolting, and so I hid it in my pockets, and then threw it out. '*

Stephanie Brooks thoroughly enjoyed her school dinners at the Heartsease School: *'Mondays was stew with mashed potatoes – the stew had big lumps of gristle in it and Fridays was always fish pie. In between we had a variety of meals. I can remember having beef olives, which today would be served at a dinner party, and egg and bacon pie. I used to really like the puddings, especially anything that came with custard, including syrup pudding and pineapple. We also had rice pudding or semolina with a lump of jam in the middle, and every now and then had jelly.'*

Would this happen today?

One of the big changes in school life is the approach to discipline: in the post-war years corporal punishment was the norm. Teachers could be cruel, with many firmly believing in the adage: 'Spare the rod and spoil the child.' Although it was accepted at the time, today it would not be allowed.

Avis Brown attended Catton Grove School until she was 11: *'I remember a teacher in the last year at school, a Mr Brown, he was strict. He once threw the rubber with a wooden handle, which was used to clean chalk off the board, at me, because I wouldn't stop talking...some things don't change. He used to slap the backs of the kids' hands with a ruler if we weren't paying attention. If the boys were naughty they used to be sent to the headmaster for the slipper.'*

Sylvia Buxton has a very clear recollection of how the headmistress at the infant school on Horns Lane instilled discipline: *'When I was five years old [1945], I started at the infant school. I particularly remember the headmistress: she was very strict, and a real character. In morning assembly, she'd pull a hanky out a pocket in her knicker leg – she wore big bloomers – and say to us all, 'hankies out'. And so, everybody would get their hanky out, and we all had to blow and wipe our noses. If there was any trouble she used to take the boys' trousers down in front of all the pupils and smack their behinds, and once she washed a girl's mouth out with soap because she swore: you wouldn't get away that now.'*

Janice Middleton went to the Norman Primary School: *'It was a good school, though if you upset the headmaster he used to throw the blackboard rubber across the room at you, and so you had to duck to avoid it. We didn't get caned, but if we misbehaved we were hit across our legs with a book.'*

These were also the days before a national curriculum, which meant that teachers had more flexibility in how they taught individual subjects. *Michael Holmes, is one of the many boys who attended the City of Norwich School, when the third year (13/14 year olds) dropped English, geography and history to do local studies in their place: 'This involved a weekly visit to somewhere local such as the gas works, a farm, a museum but most often to a factory. I really enjoyed the year. It gave me a real understanding of my home city, and inspired me to learn more.'*

National Service

Basic training in the RAF, c.1950

Compulsory national service was introduced in the UK in 1939 and any hopes that it would come to an end with the cessation of WWII were soon quashed.

It remained mandatory for every youth to register with the Ministry of Labour on his 18th birthday. Assuming they passed their medical, the new recruits then undertook a three-to-four-month introduction to service life. After training the men were posted: where you went was a matter of luck, with around one in 12 seeing action. Conscripts were initially obliged to serve in the armed service for 18 months and remain in the reserves for a further four years. However, after the outbreak of the war in Korea in 1950 the length of service was increased to two years. National service was gradually phased out from 1957. The last call-ups were made at the end of 1960.

Although some men enjoyed their national service and used it as a springboard for their future careers, for the majority it disrupted all aspects of their lives, including relationships, careers and education. During WWII the need to defend one's country was understood, but as the 1950s progressed national service became synonymous with square bashing, lack of privacy, mindless training and unnecessary violence and bullying.

A total of 2.3 million men were called up in this post-war period. The army took around 70% and the RAF most of the rest: very few entered the navy. Somewhat ironically, most of those called up were deemed able to fight for their country, but not able to vote: the voting age was only reduced to 18 in 1970.

Roy Cracknell, Martin Miller, Maurice Morson and Albert Cooper were all called up at the age of 18. Their stories and experiences are typical of the many young men who put their lives on hold to serve their country.

Roy Cracknell (left), RAF Raynham, 1947

Joining Up

Although conscripts could express a preference for the service they wanted to join, they soon found they had little control over their fate.

Roy Cracknell was 13 when WWII broke out: 'The Air Training Corps (ATC) [a British youth organisation sponsored by the Ministry of Defence and the RAF] was a big thing in Norwich in those days. I was one of many boys who knew they'd probably be called to do national service at 18. Being interested in aeroplanes, we all wanted to go in the air force, and so we joined the ATC. There were four squadrons in Norwich: 230, 231, 232 and 233. I joined the 232 squadron which met at the Alderman Jex School. When the ATC got out on parade on a Sunday it was something to see. I don't think that we worried about joining up, we just accepted it would happen. My ambition was to be aircrew, and when I was approaching 18 I went to a selection board. All went well until they shone a light down the end of a tunnel and asked me its colour. "Red," I said. "No it isn't," they replied, "It's green." So that was the end of that.' Although Roy's colour blindness dashed his ambition to be a pilot, at the age of 18 he was still recruited to the RAF where he served as a 'Range and Detecting Finding' (RDF) mechanic, working on radar systems. After completing a six-month basic radio training course at Dagenham followed by two months' radar training at Cosford, Roy served at a Sunderland Flying Boat station in Sierra Leone for the remainder of the war.

Martin Miller, also had a clear idea which service he wanted to join, but unlike Roy was recruited to a totally different type of war work: 'In 1944, as my 18th birthday approached, I knew that I would be called up. I'd always enjoyed sailing and boats, and so I volunteered for the Navy, passed my medical, was duly accepted and was all ready to go. Once I was 18 I expected that my next brown envelope would tell me which ship I would join. I was quite excited when I received it, and quite looking forward to being in the Navy. But, lo and behold, the brown envelope didn't hold the expected news, instead it contained Mr Bevin's requirement that I would go down the mines. I had quite a shock and I was terribly disappointed, but I didn't have any choice. If I'd refused to go, I'd have been sent to jail.' And so for the next four years Martin worked down the pits as a so-called Bevin Boy.

Similarly, after WWII, recruits had little choice where they were sent. Albert Cooper was 18 in 1951: 'I was all set to do my compulsory national service in the air force. I went to Martineau Hall, in Colegate, to do my medical and proficiency tests, and all that sort of thing. I passed everything and then just had to wait for my papers to come through. Then a couple of months later I got a letter from the Ministry of Defence. This said that owing to international problems all of my intake was being directed to join the Norfolk Regiment. It was because of the Korean War which was at its height. I just couldn't see myself killing anybody, and I didn't want to join the army. Instead I signed on to become a "regular" in the RAF, which meant I had to do service for three years but could choose which service I joined. I hated doing it, because I didn't want to leave home and three years seemed like a lifetime. I was sent to RAF Cardington, in Bedfordshire, to get my uniform and all that sort of stuff, and then went to RAF Bridgnorth in Shropshire to do my square bashing.'

Maurice Morson is three years younger than Albert, and so was called up for national service after the Korean conflict. Any dreams he had of choosing where he served were similarly dashed: 'I'd been in the ATC, the 231 Squadron, based at Catton, and so I'd hoped that I had a chance to join the RAF. I'd also been in the Sea Scouts, and so I thought that I might qualify for the Navy. However, as soon as they saw me they said: "Your father is a professional soldier in the Royal Artillery, you are entitled to claim his regiment." "Not likely," I replied. I didn't want to join the Royal Artillery, and, to be honest, wasn't keen on joining the army, but I didn't have much choice. They asked what I would like to do, and so I asked if I could join the commandos, tank corps or parachute regiment. They just looked me up and down and said: "Righto: the Royal Norfolks".'

Did You know?

The need to conscript men to mine coal became clear in 1943. The coal industry had lost many of its young men to the forces (before it became a reserved occupation), and we only had weeks of coal stock left. Ernest Bevin (Minister for Labour) was given the task of increasing coal production, which he did by drafting one in ten of all conscripts aged 18 to 24 to work underground in the British mines. All conscripts had call-up numbers. Every month Bevin picked a number from 0 to 9 and if that was the last digit of your call-up number you were selected to go down the mines.

Training and Discipline

Maurice Morson completes his basic training in the Royal Norfolks, 1954

All new recruits undertook a three-to-four-month introduction to service life. Typically they lived in barracks, sharing a dormitory with 20 fellow recruits. They'd be woken by 6am, and after breakfast they'd endure a day of parade-ground drills, weapon training and field craft.

Some of the biggest criticisms of national service after WWII were the mindless and pointless rules and training regimes, epitomised by square bashing – a military drill performed repeatedly on a barrack square. New recruits were often the subject of verbal abuse, violence and bullying.

On his first day in the Royal Norfolk's Maurice went to their training depot, the Britannia Barracks, where he was greeted by the Regimental Sergeant Major, Winky Fitt: 'I think that the thing people disliked most about national service was the discipline: the fact that the army was very pedantic. You'd been a free spirit up until then. I never did see people whitewashing coal, but that was the sort of thing they got the men doing. For the first ten weeks we did non-stop training, square bashing and obstacle courses. I have vivid memories of spending a night in a water-filled trench at the Stanford Battle Area, an army training site some seven miles north of Thetford, with a Bren light machine gun. It had so much mud on it, it would never have fired anyway. Soldiers kept coming up and throwing thunder flashes and shouting you're dead, to which I responded, with heartfelt relief, "Thank the Lord for that." It was an adventure in a way. To be honest, I didn't mind it, but I can understand why some didn't like it. We used to sit there at nights around one of those central stove fires polishing our boots, "bulling boots" they used to call it. Woe betide you if you didn't get a good enough shine. You had a little cloth and you put spit on it and a little bit of polish, and you'd be there all night just bulling your boots. You'd have inspections when all your kit had to be laid out precisely. I got four days in jankers, a form of punishment which meant I had to undertake lots of extra duties and lose privileges, just because I had dust on top of my locker. It was all about discipline. There were one or two who cracked, who didn't make it, also a couple who pulled fast ones, imagined injuries and that. But I don't regret it.'

As a member of the regular air force, Albert had similar experiences at RAF Bridgnorth in Shropshire, where he was under the orders of a particularly unpleasant officer: 'The corporal would come up behind you and say: "You're a horrible little man. What are you?" "I'm a horrible little man, corporal", you'd reply. I got jankers for seven days just for having a dirty hat badge. As a result I had to report every morning with my full kit on: large pack, small pack, water bottle, bayonet, strap, puttees, the lot. The officer would come around, look you up and down, and say, "Off you go." You then took everything off and got on with your square bashing. Then, as part of your penalty, you'd do fatigues in the evening. Doing fatigues normally meant you'd be sent into the spud room or the tin room. Both were pretty bad. In the spud room you had a machine like a cement mixer and a heap of around three tons of unpeeled potatoes. You had a spade, which you used to shovel the spuds into the mixer, which peeled them. When they came out we had to take all the eyes out. Then they'd be washed and then sent to the cookhouse. In the tin room you had to wash all the huge tins that the cooks used to bake in. They were greasy and horrible. You'd have to scrub them until they were spotless. Being quite small, and not a typical soldier – I hadn't even shaved before I joined up – I was bullied in the air force. But it didn't really bother me, I just got on with it. I know it's an old adage, but it did make a man of me. No doubt about it.'

Serving in the Forces

After successfully completing their training new recruits were then sent to serve their country, often learning new skills in alien environments.

As a Bevin Boy, Martin worked in extreme conditions. He had little choice but to buckle down: 'I was sent to South Kirby in West Yorkshire, which was a very old pit, where we still used picks and shovels. In the seam I was in there were 100 pit ponies hauling the coal, they only saw daylight once a year when they came up out the mine for the annual pit holiday. Even their stables were underground. I soon discovered that the pit ponies were canny: they had a sense of danger. There were no reins, they acted on commands. When the ponies knew they had a new "driver" you'd tell them in best Yorkshire to turn right and they'd turn left, and vice versa! One day, I was going along with a load to the coal face and the pony, who I can still remember was called Drummer, stopped absolutely dead. Nothing I could do,would make Drummer go on. Then suddenly a piece of the roof fell in: Drummer was injured but I was unharmed. If we'd have kept going we'd both have been killed. I worked with the ponies for six months before I moved on to the coal face which was 3200 feet below the surface. As you walked from the shaft to the coal face it would get warmer and warmer and warmer. And so we used to go down in winter muffled up and leave our various bits of clothing en-route on nails which jutted out of the pit props, we'd then retrieve it all on the way back. When I got to the coal face I had the biggest shock of my life because the men were working naked, except for a belt where they hung their lamp and their socks and boots, and that was all. I worked on the coal face for around three and a half years.'

Once he'd qualified as an aircraft engineer, Albert began to enjoy his work as a mechanic. But looking back he can hardly believe the responsibility he had: 'I was eventually stationed at Marham where I repaired aircraft and signed their airworthy certificates. At the time I was totally confident, but now I wonder how I did it. I used to strip pieces of aluminium from the body of an aircraft, then I'd make a new piece, rivet it in and then I signed it off as being airworthy. I used to marshal the planes along the runways, and not any old planes, they were B29s which were huge. I'd stand in front of them and bring them into my 'pan', which was where they parked. You'd have a marshalling wand, a short stick with a circular disc on the end, and run backwards whilst an enormous plane towered over you, following your directions. You had to hope that the pilot knew what he was doing. When it was in position, you crossed your wands, and let out a huge sigh of relief. Mind you, I loved it.'

Similarly, once he'd finished his basic training, Maurice enjoyed his time in the army, and put his time to good use, preparing for his post-service career: 'Once I'd completed my ten-weeks training I went in front of the Personnel Selection Officer (PSO) who asked what I wanted to do after completing national service. I said that I wanted to join the police force. I'll give the army its due they sent me to Colchester Training Depot Provost [Provost is the army term for regimental police]. I was sent on a regimental police training course, after that I was posted to Salisbury Plain, to the school of infantry. Very rapidly they decided I should be a lance corporal, and even more rapidly a corporal, which meant that I was the senior provost. So I had my own room, I could go to the canteen and have meals when I liked, I could walk down to the local village. I had a lot of freedom. I was quite content, but I never thought about staying on longer.'

Life After National Service

After completing their national service the men returned to Civvy Street.

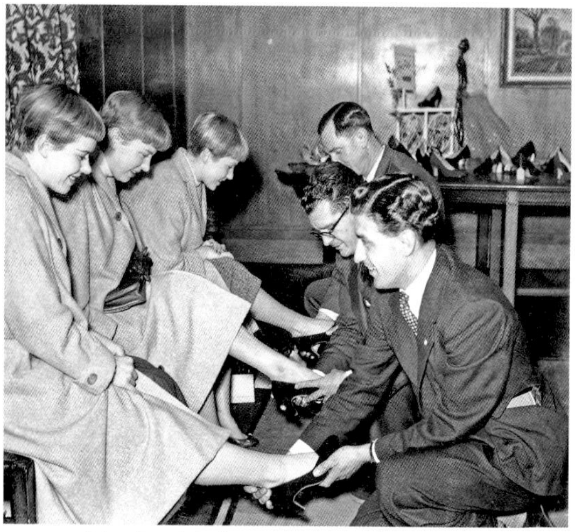

Martin with the Kaye Sisters (vocal group), 1958

Roy and Jean, 1948

Martin Miller worked in the mines until 1948: 'I always remember arriving home after I was demobbed because the first thing my mother inadvertently asked me to do was to fill the coal scuttle!' After returning to Norwich he had a successful management career at the Norvic Shoe Company. He subsequently held the position of Chief Executive at Broadland Housing.

Roy Cracknell was released from the RAF in 1948 and resumed a very successful career in IT at the Norwich Union, where he worked until retirement. In the year he was demobbed he married his sweetheart, Jean, who he'd met at a works' dance just before joining up – he still remembers asking if he could write to her whilst he was away.

Maurice as a young policeman, c.1957

Albert performing, c.1959

Maurice Morson went on to join Norwich City Police. He left the army in 1956 and two days later started at the police training centre in Oxfordshire. He was in the force until 1987 when he retired as Detective Chief Superintendent and Head of Norfolk CID.

Albert Cooper returned to his job at the Fifty Shilling Tailors in 1954. In the same year he first performed at the Jolly Butchers with the legendary Black Anna. In a musical career spanning five decades he has established himself as a popular local celebrity.

Housing and Homes

Marlpit Prefab Estate, c.1960

Housing

The National Scene

The shortage of housing was one of the country's most pressing immediate post-war issues.

Across the country enemy action had destroyed some 450,000 dwellings, an additional 3,000,000 had been damaged: simultaneously the population had grown by around 1,000,000. During the war, when labour and materials were in short supply, new building projects had been a luxury, repairing war-damaged houses was the priority. Therefore it is unsurprising that in 1945 housebuilding moved to the top of the government's agenda. The clear objective was to increase the country's housing stock, and so slum clearance, which had dominated interwar housing policy, was suspended.

As a direct result of legislation introduced by the Labour Government, local authorities (as opposed to private builders) dominated housing construction in the immediate post-war era; in fact 80% of all new permanent dwellings constructed between 1945 and 1950 were built by local councils. Like the years immediately after WWI, when Lloyd-George exhorted the nation to build 'homes fit for heroes', in the aftermath of WWII the government expressed its intention to build superior houses. Thus, despite severe shortages and economic turmoil, in both periods local authorities erected exceptionally high-quality properties.

The recommendation to improve standards had been outlined before the cessation of hostilities in the Dudley Report of 1944, *Design of Dwellings*. Its recommendations included the need for:

- Better heating and constant hot water
- A kitchen-diner rather than a parlour, which was now considered to be old fashioned
- An improved scullery, now called a utility room, for laundry.

However, with labour and traditional building materials in scarce supply, how would the government meet the pressing demand for housing? The answer: build prefabricated bungalows. These prefabs, constructed mainly in steel, aluminium, cement and asbestos, were issued to local authorities who were responsible for providing the sites. Although only designed for a few years' use, some were still being lived in 60 years later.

Between 1945 and 1949, under the *Temporary Housing Programme*, more than 156,000 prefabs went up. They were a lot more than mere huts, as exemplified by the prototype 'Portal' bungalow. Made in 1944, it came complete with cooker, sink, fridge, fitted cupboards, bath and boiler. Although at £550 it would have been cheaper to build a traditional brick terrace house, at a time of scarce resources, it used significantly less materials. Typically, the prefabs were built in converted aircraft factories. Once completed they could be transported by lorry to a cleared site, where they were simply unloaded and screwed together on a concrete plinth. There were 13 designs, each with slightly different features. Although some residents complained about living in a rabbit hutch or a tin box, often they were better than the houses they replaced, and objections were raised when the time came to demolish them.

When they came to power in 1951 the newly elected Conservative Government attempted to limit public expenditure and at the same time expand the building programme. As a result, new council houses were of a lower standard and higher density than their predecessors. Additionally, largely due to smaller family units, councils were increasingly building one-bedroom dwellings: from 1945 to 1950, just 5% of homes built by local authorities had one bedroom, by 1960 the figure had reached 25%.

Around 1954 policy underwent a further change. After sustained activity it was assessed that the housing crisis was over, and so the Conservative Government relaunched a slum-clearance programme. Simultaneously they removed the licensing system that had constrained private building since the outbreak of WWII. This triggered a reorientation in post-war housing policy. From now on private builders were given a more dominant role in housing provision whilst local authorities focussed on slum clearance and associated rehousing.

These factors contributed to a complete change in the British housing market which had previously been dominated by privately rented properties. Between 1945 and 1961, the percentage of all households living in public rented accommodation more than doubled to 27%, whilst the proportion living in private rented accommodation halved to 31%. Over the same period an increase in the supply of private housing, higher wages and easier accessibility to a mortgage facilitated an increase in owner occupation, from 26% to 43% of households. For thousands of families owning their own house had become more than a dream: it was now an attainable goal.

Housing in Norwich

In Norwich, at the outbreak of the war there were around 36,000 houses. Between 1940 and 1943 there were 45 bombing raids on the City which had resulted in damage to more than 14,000 houses, of which 1200 were destroyed.

In the interwar years, the Labour-led Norwich City Council had overseen an extensive and effective slum-clearance programme involving approximately 10,000 people and 3000 properties. Although the worst buildings had been demolished, the war had interrupted the work. That there was still much to do was highlighted in the *City of Norwich Plan,* which estimated that around 25,000 of the City's houses had been built before WWI. The authors reckoned that 80% of these would need to be rebuilt over the next 50 years.

Like the rest of the country, in 1945 the Council's immediate challenge was to provide housing for the many blitzed families who had been living in temporary accommodation and to provide a home for returning servicemen and their families. Building permanent homes would take too long; prefabs offered a temporary solution to this conundrum. Simultaneously, the City Council swung into action with its long term plans. Between 1945 and 1955 it oversaw the building of over 6500 new homes. Post-war council estates included Tuckswood, West Earlham and the Heartsease.

The housing stock was further boosted from the mid-1950s when the private sector entered the market. At first, private building mainly took place in the south-west sector across the outer ring-road at Eaton. However, by the end of the 1950s homes for purchase were being built by commercial builders outside the City, but in areas contiguous to it, including Thorpe St Andrew and Hellesdson.

The Council's house-building programme was so successful that in 1954 they believed there would 'shortly be no real shortage of houses in Norwich'. Then in 1957, the local press ran the headline: 'Too many houses'. By then it was estimated that Norwich's population of 120,000 lived in 42,000 dwellings. Although the statistic hides underlying problems (in particular some 30% of dwellings within the City boundary lacked one of the four basic amenities: a cold water tap, a hot water tap, a fixed bath or a water closet) it was a significant achievement.

Lord Mayor Eric Hinde and the Bishop of Norwich open new flats in Old Palace Road, 1951

Memories

During WWII many families made room in their houses for bombed-out relatives. As servicemen and women returned there was often insufficient space, which resulted in some people seeking out alternative accommodation.

Peter Watson explains what happened to his family: *'My grandparents lived down Mountfield Avenue, off Reepham Road. During the war their daughters had been sent out to Gorleston to stay with friends, as it was considered safer than Norwich. After the war they all came back. By then mum and dad were married and I was on the way. My grandparents were very short of space and so mum went to live with her sister, which I believe was in a prefab off Angel Road, and dad moved back in with his parents during the week and stayed with mum at the weekend. Dad worked at Laurence and Scotts, and he always told me that every day in his lunch break he used to cycle up to the council offices to see if there were any houses available. Eventually they got annoyed with him and gave him a Nissen hut on the old American Base at Rackheath. Just our family lived in the hut, and so it was quite large. It was very basic. It was one big space, and so we created "rooms" by hanging curtains from the ceiling inside. Heat was provided by a pot-bellied fire. We had a bit of a problem with rats, which my mother scared away.*

'For me, growing up there was fantastic. I was only a little tot, and I loved running around the open spaces. Although some areas were fenced off because they had potentially dangerous underground installations, the runways were still there, and we ran up and down them pretending to be aeroplanes.

'When I started work one of the guys asked where I'd lived, when I told him about the Nissen hut, he assumed we'd been squatting there. But my parents were there officially. They paid rent to the Council, I think that it was around 14 shillings a week.

'We moved to a semi-detached council house on Woodlands Road in Hellesdon when I was about six [1952]; it was a big step up from the Nissen hut.'

Similarly, Janice Middleton's family couldn't afford to be choosy: *'My mum and dad were bombed out three times during the war. Eventually, together with my brother, they moved in with a friend's family on Bolingbroke Road. Then, just after the end of the war, mum saw people being turned out of a council house on Marshall Road on the Mile Cross Estate, and so she went to the council and successfully applied for it. When they moved in, it was in a terrible state. My mum and dad had to scrub it from top to bottom with disinfectant, mum always said they got through ten bottles, but with so many people without a home they were just pleased to get a roof over their heads.'*

Peter Watson's father outside their Nissen hut, Rackheath, c.1948

Norwich Prefabs

Under the provisions of the Housing (Temporary Accomodation) Act, 1944, Norwich was granted 1000 temporary houses, around 500 of which were eventually built. The two main sites for the buildings were at Marlpit Lane (where 229 were erected) and Millers Lane (location of 83 prefabs). Others were built at Tuckswood, Lakenham and on bomb-damaged sites around Norwich.

In December 1945 the *Eastern Evening News* columnist known as the Whiffler provided a contemporary opinion on one of the first prefabs erected in Norwich when he attended a viewing on the Marlpit Estate: 'For such an unprepossessing exterior...inside is a housewife's dream of convenience and comfort in its kitchen and bathroom equipment...there seems nothing lacking except the compact gas refrigerator not yet delivered. The modern streamlined gas stove with its absence of bars, the steam-heated towel rails over the enclosed bath, the ingeniously ventilated pantry, and the built-in wardrobe and ample cupboard space were severally admired.' Colin Buxton's family was one of the first families to move to the new estate...but it wasn't perfect: 'We thought the prefab was marvellous. We had all the mod cons: a refrigerator, a bathroom, everything. The problem with living in a prefab was that they used to rattle like anything when the wind blew, it was like being in a shed. They had insulation inside, but you always heard the patter of rain.' Rod Barker's family were equally impressed with their prefab on Miller's Lane. The family now had facilities which were significantly better than they were used to: 'To me it was just a new house, but for my mother it was wonderful. We had a toilet inside and even a little fridge in the kitchen, things we'd never had before. We had two bedrooms, a bathroom, a lounge and a kitchen complete with stove. At the front of the stove were two doors with little square windows. I think they were made from reinforced perspex.'

Napier Street prefabs, 1960

It was originally intended that the prefabs would have a lifespan of ten years, but some were occupied for well over 25 years. In 1957 they were still very popular, as discovered by a local reporter: 'Most of the tenants with whom I chatted said that they liked living in the prefabs and particularly liked the low rent of 11*s*. 2*d*. a week. Together with rates and electricity assessment they pay about 18*s*. a week, much below the cost of a post-war council house.'

50s Memories

Prefabs on Ketts Hill, c.1960

In 1974 Mary Ellen Hall celebrated her 88th birthday in her late 1940s prefab at 17 Little Armes Street. It was one of 11 prefabs still standing in scattered sites across the City, including three which had been occupied by the original tenants for 28 years. Mary Ellen loved living in her prefab so much that she refused offers to move: 'I shouldn't want to be surrounded by all those brick walls,' she said. 'It's nice and open here.'

Similarly Kenneth Miller and his wife first moved to their brand new prefab on Magpie Road in the late 1940s. When they moved out in 1976 he commented: 'We made a nice home and we have been very comfortable here. My wife says she is going to miss the kitchen. The one we shall have now won't be so big and we shall have to buy equipment for it. This one was fully equipped when we first arrived.' Their prefab was one of the last in Norwich to be demolished.

Would this happen today?

The prefabs built on the Marlpit Estate and Millers Lane were all made out of asbestos. Those built on other sites were made out of aluminium, not because the material was considered safer, but because it was more durable.

Council Housing

The main thrust of the Council's housing investment was the erection of large new estates on what would now be called 'greenfield' sites.

Tuckswood and the West Earlham Estates were the first to be laid out after the war. Subsequent developments included South Park Avenue and North Park Avenue, followed by the biggest estate of all, Heartsease (built 1954 to 1964). As happened nationally, in the 1950s the standard of council houses declined. This is clearly evident on the 360-house extension built on the South Park Avenue Estate. From the outside the properties did not look much different from their higher-spec predecessors, but inside there were no fireplaces in the bedrooms, no picture rails, no second WC and no fitted cupboards in the kitchen. As had happened after WWI, a period of higher standards had been followed by one of stringent economy. Although the interior of these later houses was very plain, a 'woman reporter' writing in the *Eastern Evening News* in 1952 about properties on the South and North Park Avenue Estates did not see this as a problem: 'None of the houses have the pretensions of being anything other than simple and habitable homes, but their very simplicity affords an opportunity for tenants to make of them what they will...certainly the long sitting-room in the new type houses offers endless possibilities to the artistry of the housewife.'

Other factors also came into play. In particular, by the mid-1950s it was evident that there was a shortage of building land. Estates built immediately after WWII had been laid out at low densities (e.g. Tuckswood at 8 to 9 houses an acre), but the Heartsease was built at a density of 15 per acre. As a result, the City Architect, David Percival, designed an estate with terraces, flats, maisonettes and in-fill developments. His intention was not only to make best use of the space available, but also to create a close-knit community.

On the 25 November 1954 the *Eastern Evening News* ran a headline describing the new Heartsease Estate as 'the last, biggest and best...'. The estate had four natural boundaries: Heartsease Lane, Salhouse Road, Woodside East and Plumstead Road. A variety of house and flat designs were adopted, particularly notable were the two-bedroomed houses: 'They are economical and do not waste space. They have a delightful large living room and a nice sized kitchen, two fair sized bedrooms and a bathroom upstairs.' Although the houses were smaller than many post-war houses, any initiative to improve appearance was carefully assessed. Thus, although the City Architect was given permission to use a variety of different porches and front doors, it was stressed that these would not cost more, with the expense of wider doors and sidelights being offset against savings in brickwork.

Sandy Lane, Tuckswood, 1954

Memories

Rodney Barker's family moved to their new council house in 1951: *'When I was about nine we moved from our prefab on Millers Lane up to Sotherton Road, on the new South Park Avenue Estate. Our road was one of the first ones to be built up. There were hundreds of new houses there, and so I had a wonderful childhood, because for years I had a huge, huge builders yard as my playground! Health and safety didn't come into it. Once the builders had left for the day us kids used to run up and down their ladders and onto the roofs. You'd see us walking along the rafters, and we even used to take all of the putty out of the newly fixed windows and roll it into huge putty balls. We can't have been very popular with the glaziers! The sites weren't fenced off. They used to have night watchmen, but they couldn't look after the entire area.*

'The house was brilliant. I think that the lounge was about 20-foot long, and it had a little tiny fire place, no one really had central heating then. When it was cold we'd light a little fire, and we'd all sit huddled around it, in fact we almost sat on it! I remember my legs been mottled with the heat, but my back was freezing.'

Stephanie Brooks recalls the contrast between her homes on King Street and the new Heartsease Estate: *'Mum and I lived with my aunt at 222 King Street for around three years. With two families living in one house there wasn't a lot of room. It was an old house: three storeys. The toilet was at the bottom of the garden. My bath night took place at the end of wash day. We were very small and so the copper that my aunt had boiled the towels in doubled up as the bath. Once the towels had been taken out and the water had cooled, my two cousins and I were put one by one into the soapy water. I can tell you that Omo is no substitute for Lux!*

'Then in 1955, we moved to the Heartsease Estate, to a brand-new house. My mother thought it was wonderful: the house was her palace. We used to have brass handles and catches on the windows, and every single Friday night she used to Brasso them until they shone. Even though she worked five days a week mum was so house proud that if a weed dared to grow in the pavement in front of our house, she'd be out there pulling them up. She even used to put disinfectant down the drains in the road.'

New homes on the Heartsease Estate, 1954

Slum Clearance

Until the immediate post-war housing shortage had been addressed, slum clearance was low down the City's agenda. However, by 1953 it had built 4000 new properties and so turned its attention back to the City's poor-quality housing.

The Council, which estimated that Norwich had some 1600 slum dwellings, began to look at the possibility of rehousing families from decaying houses in the centre of the City to the new estates (particularly Heartsease). Once cleared of residents, the sub-standard properties could be demolished and new council-owned properties built in their place. Examples of such programmes started and/or completed in the late 1950s included schemes in and around West Pottergate, Vauxhall Street and King Street.

The latter was the biggest area tackled by the Council. It incorporated some 56 acres of land lying between King Street and Ber Street extending from Cattle Market Street southwards towards Carrow Road, which was reported to contain around 670 'unsanitary properties'. After the worst buildings had been cleared the Council instigated a huge redevelopment scheme, which included the building of Rouen Road (1962) and a reconfiguration of the area between the east side of Ber Street and King Street. Low-rise council flats were built, together with Normandie Tower (completed in 1966), one of two high-rise flats erected in the City centre: the other was located on Vauxhall Road.

Bartholomew Street, c.1960

Thorn Lane looking down from Ber Street towards King Street, c.1960

Memories

Amongst the properties cleared as part of the King Street Redevelopment area was Sylvia Buxton's home: *'37 Mariners Lane was next door to the Mariners Tavern (39). Saturday night was horrendous, because they had a piano in the pub, and the walls weren't very thick! All we could hear all night was the piano pedals banging away, and the plonking of the piano – which wasn't always very tuneful. Mum sort of got used to the noise, but she got very upset by the awful smell in our kitchen, which stood on the other side of the wall to the men's toilets. The stink from their urinals was terrible. Mum often complained, but it was just one of those things that you had to put up with.*

'It was a rented house. We'd moved in with my granny who lived three doors down when my father was in the army, but the lady renting number 37 died, and so the landlord let us have it. Because of wartime housing shortages we were pleased to get it. We had no running hot water, an outside toilet and coal fires. There was no such thing as toilet paper, we made do with squares of old newspaper which were threaded together with a piece of string. My granny didn't have any electric lights, they were all gas. She had a copper built out of bricks with a cast iron insert, and she used to light a fire under that on Mondays, which was wash day, and boil all the water up. As we lived so near my mother used to take all our washing up to her, and they used to spend all day doing the laundry. They'd boil everything, take it out, put it in a big bath, scrub it, then mangle it. They were doing that through the 1950s.

'The first time I had a proper bath, rather than a tin bath in front of the fire, was after I met my future husband, Colin. Colin lived in a council house on Sycamore Crescent and his mum used to let me use theirs: and that was only once a week! That would've been when I was around 17 (1958). We would have loved to have moved from Mariners Lane, but there wasn't anywhere to move to. Mum finally moved around 1961 when the area was redeveloped.'

In 1956, when Christine Perfect was seven years old, she moved with her family from a sub-standard house on William Street to one of the new flats in the Vauxhall Street development: *'My earliest memories are of my family home in William Street, off Grapes Hill. It was a fabulous street, full of terrace houses. They were two-up-two-down with outside toilets that were shared with about three other houses. We were conscious of being hard-up, but I think because we didn't have much we really appreciated everything that we did have. Looking back, you weren't looked down on if you were poor because so many people were in the same boat.*

'Six houses shared the yard at the back of our house. We had a toilet at each end of the yard, which we all used. We all knew each other, and were always going in and out of each others houses. It seemed that everyone helped each other.

'The new council flat in the Vauxhall Street Development Area was wonderful. It was brand new, clean and bright, and when we moved there we thought we'd gone to heaven. It had two bedrooms, a kitchen and even a bathroom – something we'd never had – and even an inside toilet.'

The Mariners Tavern on Mariners Lane, undated

Georgian terrace, William Street, undated

Homes

It is hard to imagine how drab and run-down houses would have looked in 1950. For years only a very few, including newly-weds and those who had been bombed out, had been able to buy furniture and crockery, and these items would have been made to 'austerity' designs (the Furniture Utility Scheme was not wound up until 1952).

However, after years of abstinence and self-denial, the 1950s marked the decade when Britons embraced modern technology and designs. As war-time austerity came to an end and the economy improved, there was hope that Britain would be a better place for all. By the end of the decade families expected to own household goods which before the war had been regarded as luxury items only available to the most privileged. Why? Between 1955 and 1960 average weekly earnings rose by 34% whilst in real terms the cost of many consumer items fell and the availability of HP grew. Higher living standards and improved technologies made household goods, including fridges, vacuum cleaners and televisions, available to most people for the first time.

Very simply, by the end of 1959, the average consumer had more money to spend on goods and more goods to choose from.

Did You know?

'Which?', the consumer magazine was first published in 1957, to advise people what they could buy in an ever-expanding market.

Electrical Appliances

After WWII new houses were wired for electricity as standard whilst older houses were updated to include an electricity supply. By 1951 almost 90% of houses were connected to the National Grid, and as the decade progressed the range of electrical appliances for the home grew.

For many households one of the most welcome additions was the electric washing machine, particularly the twin tub: a machine with two agitating drums, one for heating the water and soaping the clothes, and one for spinning them. Although a far cry from the machines we take for granted today, they were a huge boon. Fridges were slowly becoming available. They were often rented from local authorities or bought on hire purchase from local electricity boards. In 1948 just 2% of households in Britain owned one, but by 1960 around one in three households had them. Less fortunate households continued to rely on a separate larder, as explained by Janice Middleton: 'Before we had the fridge, we only had a pantry in the kitchen on the end of the house, with a little window covered by mesh, to let air in. Mum kept a bucket with cold water there, and she used that to keep the milk cool.'

For centuries an open fire had been the main (often the only) way of warming a room. Although in the 1930s new houses had at least two fireplaces, many of those built in the 1950s only had one fireplace located in the living room, the other parts of the house were heated by electric fires, paraffin burners or gas heaters. Some smaller properties did not have fireplaces, instead they may have had electric

Murphy radio with Kodak Brownie 127 camera

Hotpoint electric toaster with Falks 'Globe Trotter' travel iron

heaters fitted as standard or 'warm air heating'. The latter produced heat from a single boiler located in a cupboard, with ducts piped out which fed warm air into the rooms around it. However, the low hum of its fan, the dry atmosphere it created and its spasmodic performance limited its appeal. Even by 1960 only around 5% of homes had central heating. For years the fireplace had been more than a source of heat, it had also been the focal point of the main living area. But in the 1950s there was a new kid on the block: the television.

The television came of age in the 1950s. In 1953 demand for these tiny convex screens set in a large wooden box was stimulated by the desire to watch the Coronation. By the end of the decade there were 10 million sets in Britain. TVs could be either bought or rented. Arthur Holmes recalls: 'There was only one other person in our street [Falcon Road East] who had a television in the early 1950s. He used to invite us there every Wednesday night; we used to look forward to going. We especially enjoyed a programme on music and after a bit I started to think that I'd like a television of my own. I remember getting my first television in the mid-1950s. I bought it from Wilmotts in Prince of Wales Road: it was a tall box, with a small screen set in it at the top. It cost £70, which was quite a lot of money then, and so I had to save for it. You wouldn't buy anything on credit, you'd only buy what you could afford. I recall it going wrong on Christmas Day, the valve had gone – valves used to go wrong all the time. There was only one channel, BBC. We had to wait until 1959 for the launch of Anglia TV, which meant we had a second channel.'

The vacuum cleaner had been around since the turn of the 20th century, but it was rather superfluous to households that didn't have carpets. Before the war fitted carpets had been considered a luxury. More commonly people had painted or polished floors, or they may have had lino, covered in part by a rug. Avis Brown's home on Woodcock Road was typical of many: 'In the 1950s we used to make rag mats. We'd cut up old clothing into bits and use a sort of crochet hook to pull them through a half sack and knot them at the back. We'd all help mother make a new mat for the fireplace or for alongside the bed. We didn't have carpets, at first mum just polished the floorboards, later we had lino, but that used to tear.'

In the 1950s the invention of synthetic, machine made carpets made them affordable, whilst vacuum cleaners meant they were easier to look after. By the 1960s around two-thirds of homes had carpets.

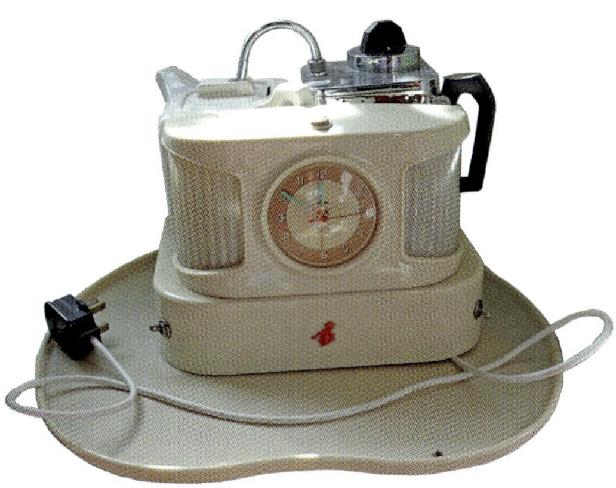

Goblin teasmade

All these electrical appliances from the 1950s are on display at the Gressenhall Farm and Workhouse, 2016

Furniture and Décor

Because of the shortage of materials during the war it was virtually impossible to buy new furniture, all that was available to many households were second-hand pieces. In 1943, to alleviate the problem, the government introduced Utility furniture whereby 150 companies manufactured items to official designs. The furniture was specifically intended for families who had been bombed out, or for newly-weds setting up home. The Utility scheme was not wound up until 1952, and had even been extended in 1948 when restrictions on design were lifted and manufacturers allowed to innovate – though they still had to meet strict guidelines. Despite criticism of the scheme, including the poor quality of some items and lack of traditional pieces, Utility furniture brought a new modern style into the home for the first time.

Initially such contemporary designs, which were further promoted at the Festival of Britain (1951) and in glossy magazines, tended to be more popular with the middle classes in London, but harder to find elsewhere. Generally, people wanted furniture which fitted with their existing traditional pieces. However, as the decade closed there was much more blending of the old with the new.

1950s' kitchen cabinet, Gressenhall, 2016

There was a particular divergence between fantasy and reality when it came to kitchens. Magazine adverts showed luxurious fitted cabinets presided over by beautiful housewives in improbably elegant dresses, but for most households such fittings were little more than a pipedream. Most kitchens were smaller and less luxurious, such as the one that Christine Perfect's family had in their council flat on Vauxhall Street: 'Mum didn't have much kitchen equipment: we had a gas fridge (unfortunately the pilot light kept blowing out, which was a bit of a nuisance), a gas cooker and an Ascot water heater. We didn't have fitted cupboards like you have now. Our main piece of kitchen furniture was a sort of dresser, with a front panel that pulled down to form a table top, where mum prepared food.'

However, there was one aspect of contemporary style which was easy to adopt: a bright new palette. New production techniques in the manufacture of materials, wallpaper and paint meant that householders could easily and cheaply put years of austerity behind them simply by adding colour to their homes.

New decorating materials also contributed to the emerging Do it Yourself (DIY) movement. Before the war, those who had the money to improve their homes more often than not employed a professional craftsman. The less affluent either received little encouragement or were restricted by tenancy agreements. In the decades that followed a number of factors converged to inspire millions to make improvements to their homes. These included:

- A shortage of skilled tradesmen
- The 'make do and mend' mentality engendered by the war
- Cheaper mass-produced decorating materials coupled with a more affluent population
- A plethora of home-interior magazines which encouraged the public to buy modern furniture, wallpapers and fabrics
- National exhibitions promoting new products and modern design, including 'Britain Can Make It' in 1946 and the Festival of Britain in 1951.

When Curls department store reopened in 1956, management were very aware of this trend. In the booklet produced at its launch they advised: 'In line with today's popular "Do-It-Yourself" movement, every department which sell tools of any kind is under the charge of an expert assistant who can not only advise customers what to buy but how to use it. This service applies to paints and wallpapers...and curtain fabrics.'

50s Memories

In 1954, Loose's shop on Magdalen Street sold a range of 'furnishings and equipment for kitchen and pantry' which give an insight into what we were buying in Norwich. In the following descriptions they refer to items which could enhance a 'picture' kitchen, as opposed to the utilitarian kitchen of previous years. Items included:

'**Formica Top Tables:** In colours to match cabinets and kitchen chairs, with brightly upholstered seats in modern, washable fabrics to complete your "picture" kitchen.'

'**Aluminium:** Teapots, kettles, stewpans, egg-poachers and frying pans (polished to a mirror finish) for electric and gas cookers or Aga stoves, to brighten your "picture" kitchen.'

'**Wallpapers and Paints:** Crown [wallpaper] and Sherwood's paint are a combination essential to a modern "picture kitchen", and it is not expensive to decorate with these long-wearing materials.'

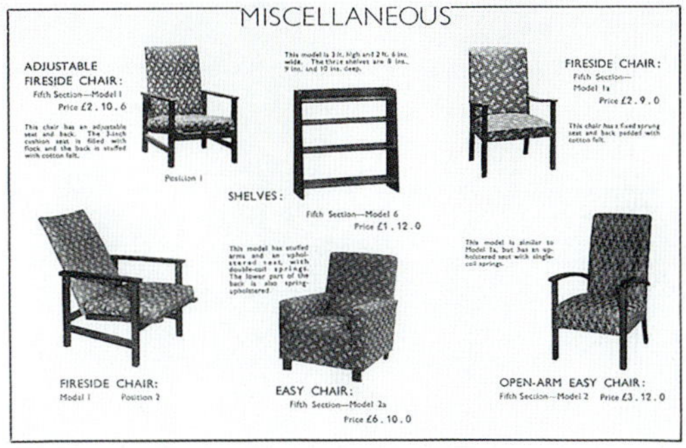

MISCELLANEOUS

ADJUSTABLE FIRESIDE CHAIR: Fifth Section—Model I Price £2 . 10 . 6

This chair has an adjustable seat and back. The 3-inch cushion seat is filled with flock and the back is stuffed with cotton felt.

Position I

This model is 3 ft. high and 2 ft. 6 ins. wide. The three shelves are 8 ins., 9 ins. and 10 ins. deep.

SHELVES: Fifth Section—Model 6 Price £1 . 12 . 0

FIRESIDE CHAIR: Fifth Section—Model 1a Price £2 . 9 . 0

This chair has a fixed sprung seat and back padded with cotton felt.

This model has stuffed arms and an upholstered seat, with double-coil springs. The lower part of the back is also spring-upholstered.

This model is similar to Model 1a, but has an upholstered seat with single-coil springs.

FIRESIDE CHAIR: Model I Position 2

EASY CHAIR: Fifth Section—Model 2a Price £6 . 10 . 0

OPEN-ARM EASY CHAIR: Fifth Section—Model 2 Price £3 . 12 . 0

Barbara Miller recalls the challenges she and her husband Martin had furnishing a new home when they married in 1951: 'Various people used to laugh and say that we should call our house "Cornhall", because we bought so much second-hand furniture. Not only because we couldn't afford new, but also because we didn't particularly like Utility furniture [pictured above]. At the time I was working at City College, where I met Billy Meek the cabinetmaker. Although he shouldn't have done, Billy made us a sofa and chair that we still have in our living room today. We now have covers on them, but underneath you can still see the original material, which was shoe lining that Martin got from the Norvic factory where he worked.'

1950s living room, the Museum of Norwich at the Bridewell, 2016

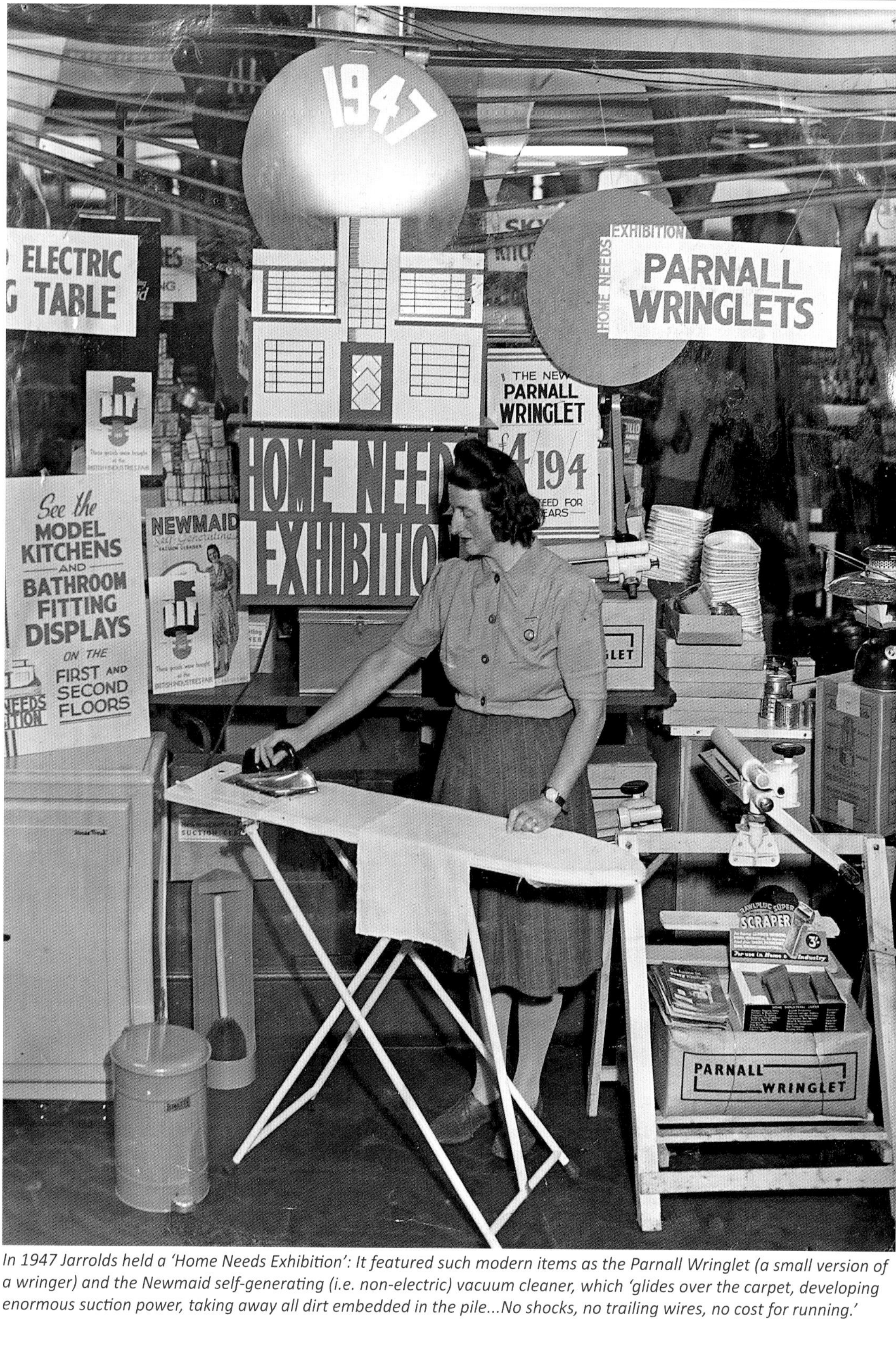

In 1947 Jarrolds held a 'Home Needs Exhibition': It featured such modern items as the Parnall Wringlet (a small version of a wringer) and the Newmaid self-generating (i.e. non-electric) vacuum cleaner, which 'glides over the carpet, developing enormous suction power, taking away all dirt embedded in the pile...No shocks, no trailing wires, no cost for running.'

Memories

Roy Cracknell recalls fitting out his home on Thunder Lane:

'For the first three years of married life we rented a flat but were then in a position to buy our own house, and eventually bought a plot of land on Thunder Lane for about £160. We moved in on 1 January 1953, 64 years later I'm still there.

'In those days you didn't have a fully fitted kitchen. You'd have a kitchen cabinet, a cooker and a table; we didn't have a fridge. We'd had one when we lived in the rented flat. We'd been really pleased when our landlords, the Norwich Union, said they were going to install one, it was only small and we had to pay extra to have it, but it was a great boon.

'I think we bought a fridge soon after moving to Thunder Lane. In those days you had to either have the cash or apply for HP, which meant you had to fill in an enormous form. Most people only embarked on one thing at a time. And so, for example, we didn't get a washing machine until we'd paid off the fridge. The big day was when we finally got central heating, but that wasn't until 1963.

'We just had a little radio when we got married, and were really excited in 1956 when we bought our 14-inch, black and white television set.'

Barbara and Martin Miller recall their first home together:

'Just as we got married [1951] Hoover had brought out the first twin tub washing machine. It had a mangle on top with rubber rollers and when you finished the wash you turned the mangle over into the washing machine. It also had a spinner which made it so much easier to dry your washing. We had a cupboard on the landing and Martin fitted it all up with slatted shelves and we had a heater in the bottom, and so we had an airing cupboard. But that is something my mother, for instance, never had.

'In the kitchen we had a dresser which had an enamel counter that you let down, I'd use it to make pastry on. We had a gas oven and a pressure cooker.

'We didn't have a television, it was too expensive. My mother and father had one, and so I used to push our daughter Charlotte up to see them after lunch, and she could see "Andy Pandy" and the "Woodentops" and all things like that on "Watch With Mother". It was only in 1958 when we went to London that we bought a television.'

Muriel Chilvers bought her first home in 1950:

'I married my husband, Leslie, in 1950. He was a Building Society manager. He started there before the war, and when he was in the forces they saved up what would have been half his wages, which amounted to five shillings a week. When he came back in 1946 this was given to him as a lump sum, and it eventually went towards the deposit on our first home on Hotblack Road: a small terraced house. Because he worked for a building society, we also got a mortgage at a very good rate. We lived there until 1959, when we moved to a much larger house on Bluebell Road.

'At Hotblack Road I used to have a copper and mangle in the kitchen. We mostly had a lino floor and a few rag rugs, and so it didn't occur to me to have a vacuum cleaner. I eventually got a washing machine, a twin tub, when we went to Bluebell Road. When we moved we had more carpets downstairs, although they weren't fitted, and so I also got a vacuum cleaner. We didn't buy a television until 1961.'

Avis Brown recalls her home on Woodcock Road in the 1950s:

'Because we only had a fire in the living room, we used to sit there. If mother couldn't afford to have a chimney sweep the fire would still be lit, but every five minutes or so you'd have a cloud of black smoke billow into the living room. When it got really bad mother used to waft the smoke out of the living room with a towel.'

Mangle, Gressenhall, 2016

Memories

Do you remember Barry Bucknell?

Barry was television's first 'Do it Yourself' expert, encouraging viewers throughout the 1950s and 1960s to beautify their homes. Barry's techniques to 'modernise' older properties typically involved using cheap materials, particularly plywood, to cover up architectural details such as period doors and fireplaces, which at the time were considered unfashionable. In some circles this technique earned him the nickname 'Bodger' Bucknell.

There is an argument today that Barry saved many valuable Victorian treasures by encouraging them to be covered awaiting the day when the hardboard was removed to reveal the hidden gems.

In the late 1950s Barry launched the long-running BBC series 'Barry Bucknell's Do It Yourself' which at its peak attracted audiences of seven million. The programmes were presented live and occasionally resulted in mishaps, which gave rise to the catchphrase: 'This is how not to do it.'

Did You know?

Both the Gressenhall Farm and Workhouse (Dereham) and the Museum of Norwich at the Bridewell (Bridewell Alley, Norwich) contain displays from the 1950s.

The combined kitchen and living room at Gressenhall includes a wonderful array of memorabilia which will be very familiar to people of a certain age. Here you will find everything from a twin-tub washing machine to a Sky Baby portable radio: all evocative of the era. At the Museum of Norwich you are invited to sit in the retro 1950s living room and play board games, or just look at their fascinating collection of everyday items.

1950s kitchen display, Gressenhall Farm and Workhouse, 2016

A Manufacturing City

Closing (machine) room, Sexton, Son & Everards shoe factory, 1959

Manufacturing

The National Picture

By 1950, after a decade of austerity, most of the developed world was experiencing a 'Golden Age': a period of high growth and low unemployment. Led by America, improvements in the world economy were largely attributed to the thawing of international trade barriers and a gradual move towards greater economic freedom. The shift was epitomised by the General Agreement on Tariffs and Trade (GATT), which was initiated in 1947, and the founding of the European Economic Community in 1957.

Britain shared in this affluence. In fact one of the most positive aspects of the country's immediate post-war economy was the maintenance of high employment and a rising level of output. Both were achieved despite a number of detrimental factors, including years of under investment, run-down capital equipment and shortages of both raw materials and fuel. Advancement was placed firmly at the door of science and technology which, of necessity, had moved on apace during the war years. Between 1948 and 1960 industrial output in Britain rose on average by 3.8% p.a. compared to 3.1% in the interwar years.

Progress was uneven. Immediately after WWII sectors linked with the war effort, including metals, engineering, chemicals and related industries registered the highest growths in output. Firms and industries which produced consumer goods (e.g. clothing) showed relatively modest increases, largely because they tended to supply the domestic market where demand was curtailed by rationing. As we moved through the 1950s, industries that combined rapid technological progress with the potential to displace older industries and create new markets, such as car making, grew the most.

This 'Golden Age' has to be viewed with a note of caution. Yes, in the 1950s the British economy flourished, but we were already under performing relative to other countries. For example, between 1950 and 1973 the average annual growth of GDP in Britain was 3%. Over the same period in West Germany it was 5.9% and in Japan a massive 9.4%. Similarly, although between 1950 and 1963 our volume of exports rose by some 25% our export growth was trailing behind other developed countries. The result was a dramatic decline in Britain's share of the world's manufactured exports: between 1950 and 1960 it fell from 25% to 16.5% of the total.

There were a number of reasons for this relative decline, one of the most important was the fall in price competitiveness experienced by British manufacturers. This, in turn, was caused by a number of factors, including a lower level of capital investment and a greater reluctance to innovate than our competitors. Very clearly, as evidenced by growing output, we did invest and innovate, but relative to other countries we began to under-perform. These few facts already allow us to answer Harold Macmillan's question: we may have 'never had it so good' but was 'it too good to last?' The answer, as we now know, was 'yes'.

A view from St James Hill, 1951

Norwich

Through the 1950s light industry flourished in Norwich. 30,000 people, around 35% of the City's workforce, were employed in manufacturing and construction. Firms such as Harmers, Bullards, Laurence, Scott and Electromotors, Start-rite, Caleys and Colmans, were synonymous with the City, and central to its prosperity.

The importance of the sector to Norwich's success was clearly illustrated when Curls department store reopened in 1956, and asked the question: 'Who will be the customers of the new Curls?'

The answer was unequivocal: 'They are the men and women at work in the important industries of Norwich – 10,000 of them in the shoe industry alone. Others are employed in the large Norwich Union offices nearby, in the two big engineering firms of Laurence & Scott and Boulton & Paul, in mustard and flour mills, chocolate and Christmas cracker factories, and printing works and breweries.'

St Mary's Foundry, Barnards Ltd, 1949

The War Years

During the hostilities much of the City's industrial capacity had been diverted to military production. In particular, the City's engineering firms played a major part in the war effort. For example, Laurence, Scott & Electromotors had been on a war footing before 1939 and at the outbreak of WWII were already manufacturing a range of military equipment, including searchlights for air defences and submarine motors. Boulton & Paul made wooden buildings for army camps and 40-ton trailers for tank transporters. Mann Egerton manufactured more than 4000 military vehicles, whilst Barnards made artillery shells and aircraft parts. Other sectors also contributed. Harmers, the clothing firm, made more than two million garments for the Armed Forces and Civil Defence Services whilst the Norwich shoe factories produced thousands of pairs of boots and shoes for the women's services. Of course, civilians also needed footwear, but with raw materials in limited supply the Norwich firms were ordered to manufacture Utility footwear, designed to be practical and made with the minimum of materials, rather than their normal fashion shoes.

Caleys chocolate factory destroyed, c.1942

As the conflict came to an end local industries were counting the cost. During the war 130 Norwich factories had been demolished, numerous others suffered bomb damage. Buildings that had been occupied by some of Norwich's most illustrious firms had been wrecked, including Caleys chocolate factory on Chapelfield Road, Harmers clothing factory on St Andrew's Street, Edwards & Holmes shoe factory on Drayton Road and Morgans Brewery on King Street.

Did You know?

Because of war-time restrictions, during the 1940s no snaps were produced for use in Christmas crackers. However, one company, Reliance, began manufacturing them specifically for military training purposes. A local firm, Tom Smith (cracker manufacturers), was then given the job of folding and tying bundles of snaps together using regulation string and knots. These bundles were used to simulate the sound of machine-gun fire during army training exercises.

50s Memories

Barbara Miller recalls: 'Everyone in the City knew when Caleys was bombed because of the very strong smell of roasting chocolate that wafted everywhere.'

Did You know?

At the outbreak of WWII Caleys had three factory buildings on their Chapelfield site. However, they couldn't get supplies, and so during the war they reduced production. Meanwhile, under the 1939 Trading with the Enemy Act, the Government had taken over the German-owned Siemens factory in London. Siemens were manufacturing batteries for the forces, which were particularly needed in the wirelesses used for communication by British troops. There was concern that the London-based Siemens factory would be a prime target for bombing, and so they were pulled out of the capital and relocated to one of Caleys' buildings. In 1942 when Caleys was bombed this seemed like a bad decision. However, although both of the factories making sweets were hit and went up in flames, the one in the middle occupied by Siemens survived. Siemens remained there throughout the war.

Post-War Regeneration

As the war came to an end attention turned to reconstruction. With more than a third of the workforce employed in manufacturing, the City Council were understandably concerned that firms needing to rebuild premises might choose to redevelop elsewhere. A survey assuaged their fears: of 26 firms approached 20 intimated they intended to stay in Norwich, whilst most of the others indicated they would stay subject to 'reasonably attractive conditions [being] afforded to them'.

Rebuilding gave firms the opportunity to review their premises. Very definite trends emerge during this period of reconstruction:

Location: Historically, Norwich industry had been based in the City centre near to its workforce and transport networks. The Norvic Shoe Company, for example, dominated St George's and the streets around reverberated with the pounding of their heavy machinery. After the war, as transport improved and new council estates were built on the outskirts, industrial sites were progressively established outside the centre. This trend was encouraged by Norwich City Council and had been included in their 1945 Plan. Proposals included the development of a large new industrial area between Hall Road and the main line railway at Harford, part of which was allocated for the Cattle Market, which eventually moved here in 1960. Small industrial zones were also designated, with the intention of 'providing employment close at hand for some of the residents in the larger housing estates near the present City boundary'. Although many firms rebuilt new factories on their existing sites, others, including Harmers, took the opportunity to move their operation out of the City.

Staff Welfare: In response to changes in public attitude and in anticipation of new workplace legislation, more staff facilities were introduced in factories. These included new canteens and purpose-built welfare departments.

Modernisation: New premises were redesigned and updated, allowing firms to introduce the latest production methods. This made them more efficient and increased their productivity.

Marketing and Distribution: During rationing consumers couldn't afford to be too fussy. However, as the decade progressed manufacturers realised customers, especially housewives, were becoming more choosy. For example, as supermarkets began to open the public started to declare a preference for pre-packaged goods. Discovering the views and needs of consumers became an essential part of business planning. Also, as competition increased advertising grew in importance and the more innovative firms took advantage of a new medium: the television.

Boulton & Paul, official opening of new offices, 1951

Norwich: Sectors and Firms

A look at a selection of the City's manufacturers illustrates how they faced the challenges of post-war Britain.

The Shoe Trade

In 1959 9000 people were engaged in the Norwich shoe industry making it the City's largest employer. The vast majority worked in approximately 20 factories based around the City centre. The industry had a national reputation for the production of high-quality footwear for ladies and children.

The shoe trade had been badly hit during the war. In fact it is estimated that as a combined result of enemy action and requisitioning the industry lost 316,000 square feet of productive floor space, an overall reduction of 40%. Shoe factories, such as Edwards & Holmes Esdelle Works on Drayton Road, were totally annihilated, as explained by Peter Holmes, who recalls his father, Geoffrey, viewing the devastation: 'He found that there was nothing left of the huge, red-brick, three-storey building, but rubble, twisted girders and molten machinery. When he saw it his hair, literally stood on end. Everything was destroyed, including, stock, fixtures, lasts and patterns.'

The fact that so many companies survived, owes much to the support they gave each other. Manufacturers even gave up space in their factories to competitors whose premises had been bombed until they could rebuild. It was even commented on in the *Eastern Evening News*: 'One splendid feature to offset against the whole sorry mess of war damage has been the co-operation between companies, and the way the luckier firms have helped those less fortunate.'

As they rebuilt, directors took the opportunity to modernise their factories. The directors at Edwards & Holmes going so far as describing their new 75,000-square-foot factory, which was built on the site of the bombed premises, as being one of the most up-to-date shoe factories in the world.

Over the decade, the shoe manufacturers were adept at introducing new marketing methods to meet the challenges of a post-war era. One of the most inventive was the Norvic Shoe Company, which by 1956 was advertising on television. This was quite a novelty at the time as the Independent Television Authority (later ITV), with its capacity to show commercials, had only been launched in the previous year. Meanwhile, in 1955 Start-rite received a major marketing coup having been granted a Royal Warrant for supplying shoes to Prince Charles and Princess Anne. Subsequently, Edwards & Holmes promoted themselves by making footwear for a number of major London shows, including *South Pacific* and *My Fair Lady*. The latter opened in 1958, and starred Julie Andrews.

Over this period the Florida Group also developed new marketing strategies when it began manufacturing its trademark wider-fitting shoes, as explained by former chairman Simon Goodman: 'We started making narrow-fitting footwear named "Norfolk Narrows". The joke is that Billy Waller, a designer, made a small mistake and instead of the lasts coming in as narrow fitting they were made as wide fitting. So rather than making "Norfolk Narrows" we made "Norfolk Broads".' Until then women with wider feet had to buy shoes designed for older women irrespective of their age. Florida introduced the 'Italian look', which was considered to be fashionable, into wider-fitting footwear, which was sold under the Van-Dal brand name (introduced in 1946): a brand still made in the 21st century.

Similar to other sectors, technological advances led to improved productivity, which translated into a reduction of the workforce (it had stood at 10,000 in 1949) rather than a significant increase in output. Despite this, times were good. Although through the 1950s the trades' fortunes fluctuated, overall it flourished, with firms producing between seven and eight-and-a-half million pairs of shoes per annum.

Did You Know?

The shoe manufacturer W. H. H. Clarke was reputed to have been the unluckiest firm in Norwich during WWII, the 'Eastern Evening News' going so far as to dub it 'probably the worst-bombed firm in Norwich'. *The company's problems started in April 1942 when their Northumberland Street factory was completely destroyed in the Baedeker Raids. Undeterred they took up space with box manufacturers Mansfields (Norwich) Ltd on St Saviours. Sadly, a few months later Mansfields was also burnt out. At this time Clarkes relocated to the Sexton, Son & Everards shoe factory on St Mary's Plain, that is until the August Bank Holiday (1942) when the same fate befell them. It says something for William Clarke's fortitude that he never gave up and instead moved across to Dibden Street, where the firm was taken in by fellow shoe-producer Chittock & Sons Ltd. Here they remained until the end of the war. One can't help but think that Chittocks, was very generous to invite a company as jinxed as Clarkes into their premises.*

Harmers new Havers Road factory, 1948

At the end of the 1950s around 1000 Norwich workers manufactured clothing. About 150 made men's outer garments for the Cox Clothing Co. Another two or three small firms made a variety of garments, but by far the major clothing manufacturer in the City was Harmers. During the war its St Andrew's Street factory was hit by a number of incendiary bombs, and in 1943 it was completely destroyed.

After the war the firm relocated to Mile Cross. By 1947 they were operating from a newly constructed, purpose-built factory, which had an output of around 10,000 garments a week. By 1959 production had doubled and it was one of the leading clothing firms in the country, employing around 800 people at the main site, plus an extra 70 staff at a factory in Watton.

Increased output was attributed to improved productivity which could be partially ascribed to the efficiencies of the new building. The factory would not have won any architectural awards, being described in the local press as: 'A series of large Nissen huts joined together.' However, what it lacked in aesthetics was more than offset by the practicality of its layout which engendered the introduction of modern production methods. As the directors explained: 'This factory is as far removed as possible from the crowded, ill-designed buildings which were representative of industry all over the country in past generations.'

A few men were employed on cutting, engineering and maintenance tasks, but the vast majority of the workforce were women and young girls operating huge banks of sewing machines. This put Harmers in competition with the City's shoe firms, all of whom required skilled machinists. One way to attract employees was to offer good working condition and staff perks – which the firm was now able to do. Despite the utilitarian appearance of the factory from the outside, the interior had 'a pleasant atmosphere which predominates throughout'. The firm was also keen to promote its Staff Welfare Department and even went so far as to open an on-site hairdressing salon. Here, they anounced, 'girl employees' (but not the men) could visit Mrs Rackham, 'a hairstylist with 14-years' experience who will tackle anything from the simplest trim to the most intricate styling and tinting'.

In the News

In November 1947, a reporter from the 'Eastern Evening News' visited Harmers new factory, prompting him to run an article entitled, 'Good out of the Blitz?'. It read: 'Terrible as the raids were in toll of life and despoliation of property, one good result of the Luftwaffe 'blitz' on Norwich is that it has caused a great deal of factory rebuilding, in which the latest ideas and methods of production have been incorporated far more successfully than they could have been in old buildings...here, on a site in an area by the river scheduled for industrial building they have a splendid...large, light and cheerful factory.'

The Food and Drink Manufacturers

In 1959 this sector employed 5700 people, 6.8% of the City's workforce. Major companies included John Mackintosh & Sons Ltd (better known locally as Caleys) and Reckitt & Colman Ltd (known as Colmans).

Former Caleys factory, 1996

In 1933 the chocolate factory originally set up by Caleys had been bought by the Halifax-based John Mackintosh & Sons Ltd. In 1942 the business suffered a devastating blow when the factory was bombed and destroyed. The *City of Norwich Plan* advocated the redevelopment of the cleared site for professional and commercial offices and suggested that the company, which before the war had employed over 2000 people in Norwich, relocate to an industrial zone. However, this presented a problem. Under the rules of the War Damage Act it was decreed that the full price of the factory would only be paid to the owners if they rebuilt on its former site. If it were relocated compensation would only be based on the 1939 value plus 30%, which would leave Mackintosh's out of pocket. As the business had no long-standing links with Norwich, the City Council were concerned that if they remained intransigent the firm would leave. After efforts to secure a modified ruling failed, the Council backed down, and in 1946 rebuilding started on the old site.

The factory was rebuilt in stages, which enabled production to recommence before it was finished. In 1956, when H.R.H. the Duchess of Kent opened the completed Norwich factory and offices, the business had 2100 employees. Understandably, the new factory was built to high specifications. As explained in the *Eastern Evening News* in 1956: 'Everything In the factory is streamlined. The liquid raw materials flow through overhead pipelines to the various chocolate-producing processes. There is not a belt drive to be seen. Nearly 900 electric motors give power to the hundreds of machines. Temperatures and humidity, vital to the sustained success of this industry, are controlled by the newest scientific apparatus.' By 1958 the factory was being described as 'the most modern confectionery plant in the world'.

However, in the new post-austerity era, the directors were very aware that success depended on more than manufacturing a good product. If they wanted to attract and retain customers they needed to be inventive, as regards both their products and marketing. The firm rose to the challenge, and after the end of sweet rationing (2 February 1953) they became more innovative. A succession of new lines were made in Norwich, including Week-End, Munchies and Caramac. They also started to advertise on television. According to the *MC Monthly News* (in-house magazine), in 1959, when the firm launched Caramac, their marketing campaign included: 'a 15-second commercial which will be transmitted frequently on independent television...In the modern idiom, this film features two teenagers eating Caramac to a very catchy jingle based on the old nursery-rhyme tune Knick-nack Paddy-wack.' No wonder it was so popular!

Like Caleys, the other major employer in the sector, Colmans, was no longer independent. In 1938 this long-established Norwich firm had merged with Reckitts of Hull to form Reckitt & Colman. Historically the firm had been quick to realise the importance of product recognition, and even in the 19th century had sold their merchandise in distinctive tins and packets. But as the 1950s progressed the company became even more sophisticated in its approach to sales. By 1958 it had started its own market research department and food research laboratories, and even had a 'tasting room' where a panel tested new products. This forward thinking resulted in an average of one new line a year being introduced at their Carrow Works. One of the most innovative, first marketed in 1956, was the Jif lemon, which is still sold in a plastic container 'shaped and squeezed like a lemon'. During the 1950s the firm also introduced many ground-breaking production processes including electronic control and automation in the flour mill. In addition, a new soft drinks factory was opened which produced more than 100 bottles a minute. In 1958 the local press drew particular attention to the firm's new-found ability to produce 'powdered lemonade...in laminated foil envelopes at a retail price of a penny a packet'. Sounds delicious! Like other companies, technical advances resulted in improved productivity. This translated into an increase in output, but also to a fall in employees: from 2200 in 1900 to 1200 in 1958.

50s Memories

Avis Brown has happy memories of her first job:

'When I was still at school I went around Caleys factory and saw all of the big mixers. They were like cement mixers, but they had liquid chocolate going around inside. I loved chocolate, and so when I left school in 1957, I started work there.

'At first I worked on the Week-End line. They were boxes of sweets. You got chocolates in the box, but also candies, like orange and lemon jellies. I used to sit there and the production belt ran above my knees. On the belt was a box which needed filling. We had a shelf underneath which held whatever you were packing. You used to have a little packet of brown paper cups, like the ones you use for cupcakes. You had to peel one off onto your finger, pick up whichever sweetie you were responsible for, put the sweetie in the case and put both in the box. Each person did one sort. The box would move down the belt and when it reached the end it was weighed, and if it was under they'd put an extra sweet in.

'Just before Easter they'd want some help in the Easter-egg room, and so I used to go in there. The eggs used to come down on the production belt; by then they'd already got a bag of Quality Street, or something like that, inside them. We'd have a large sheet of fine, silvery or coloured paper, and when the eggs got to us we'd pull the sides of the paper up around the eggs and, using a cloth, smooth it around the egg. We'd put the egg back on the line and when It got to the end someone put it in a box.

'I can't remember how much I earned, but I know what I did with my money. At first mother let me keep it, and I used to spend it on the pictures or going out with the girls down the City. I just used to waste it: I was really naughty. But then once I got into it, mother said that she wanted some board money, which I gave her. I used to be paid on Friday – and was broke on Monday.'

Rolo line at Caleys factory, c.1959

The Engineering and Electrical Trades

Laurence, Scott & Electromotors Ltd, Hardy Road site with new heavy machine bay centre left, c.1960

In 1959 more than 10% of Norwich's workforce, some 8500 people, were employed by the engineering trades. It was quite remarkable that despite being located far away from the major centres of British engineering, the Midlands and the North, we had firms that enjoyed remarkable success in this field.

Within this sector, Laurence, Scott and Electromotors Ltd (LSE) had a workforce of 3000, making it the City's largest single employer. During WWII the company had been at the forefront of technological change. In particular, technicians, engineers and craftsmen at the Norwich firm experimented with new scientific advancements which were then incorporated with electrical gear vital to the supremacy of the Royal Navy. The contribution made by LSE is exemplified by the fact that there was hardly a ship in the British or Allied navies which did not use machinery made in Norwich. Post-war this placed them in an ideal position to exploit new markets. Amongst their achievements was the development of control gear for electrically-powered units on board ships, which they managed to halve in size. Their reputation was such that in 1951 two-thirds of all motor vessels constructed in Great Britain contained some LSE apparatus. Therefore it is not surprising that the firm was involved in building the Royal Yacht Britannia. In all they made 122 motors of varying sizes for the new vessel (launched in 1954) plus two electric winches.

During WWII innovative production methods had brought great changes to industry and its needs in relation to electric power. LSE was well placed to meet the new demands, but to do so had to embark on its own ambitious programme of re-equipment and expansion. This included a new heavy-machine bay, brought on stream in 1959. By then, around 25% of the company's labour force were engaged in producing a range of high-quality specialised equipment for government departments. Another 25% made ships' winches and corresponding control gear, whilst the remainder made electrical rotating machines and associated control gear and systems.

Memories

In 1944, at the age of 16, Andy Anderson started work at LSE: *'It was an exciting place to a young lad. They made electric motors of all sizes, including motors for submarines, which were colossal things. I used to take correspondence around the various departments. As a boy I loved the test bed, where they had enormous motors roaring away. It was mostly men working there, although ladies did some of the more intricate wiring jobs. It was a happy place, people were friendly.'*

Part of Boulton & Pauls Riverside Works, 1953

The City's second largest engineering firm, measured by the number of employees, was Boulton & Paul. They operated at the 14.5-acre Riverside Works (named after its location). Like LSE the firm had made a huge contribution to the war effort, including the manufacture of more than 100,000 Morrison air raid shelters.

After suffering bomb damage during the war, their capacity had been seriously reduced, and in 1946 the firm's priority was to restore its plant and machinery.

Initially, attempts to revive the firm's fortunes were thwarted by post-war shortages. Although, demand was high for their renowned greenhouses and sectional bungalows, Mr Jean Tresfon (Director) explained they were unable to meet orders because: 'There is only a certain amount of seasoned timber available, and we are quite properly restricted in the use of it for the most needed articles.'

However, all was not gloom and doom.

At the end of the 1950s the firm was flourishing. By then, 35% of their workforce (totalling 1300) was involved in the fabrication and erection of structural steel, an essential component of many modern buildings. As experts in this field the firm won both national and international contracts, including work for the Metro-Goldwyn-Meyer studios at Elstree and for several big motor factories in the Midlands. The remainder of employees were mainly involved in standard joinery (in particular the manufacture of doors and windows) or fencing contracts, including the manufacture of wire netting. Interestingly their biggest competitor in the field of wire netting was another local firm, Barnards Ltd, whose Mousehold-based premises was believed to be the most modern netting factory in Europe.

Although after the war both these firms lost their independence – in 1948, a controlling interest in Boulton & Paul was bought by Anglo Transvaal Industries, whilst in 1955 Barnards was purchased by Sheffield-based Tinsley Wire Industries – they continued to be regarded as local Norwich firms.

Memories

***In 1955, when he was 15 years old, Colin Buxton worked at Boulton & Pauls Riverside Works**: 'The place where I worked was covered in smoke all day long, and I hated being shut up. In the eight months I was there I did the same job all the time. I was given a template and I'd use a big mallet to punch set holes in big metal plates. The best thing about it was dinner times, when we used to go over to Carrow Road and play football...on the car park!'*

Brewing

Original Bullards sign by Alfred Munnings, c.1909

At the end of the 1950s the City's brewers employed 900 people. Norwich was a natural site for the industry being situated at the centre of an area which grew some of the best malting barley in the country. It also had the advantage of having access to good-quality water, essential to the brewing process, from the chalk that underlies much of the City.

In the 1940s Norwich was home to four breweries: Steward & Patteson (S&P) operated on Barrack Street; Bullards had a site on Westwick Street; Youngs, Crawshay & Youngs (Youngs) together with Morgans were located on King Street. The breweries owed much of their value to their tied estates, which it is estimated amounted to some 80% of their total assets and encompassed more than 1500 public houses, the majority located in Norfolk.

Similar to other local industries they also did war work: supplying the USAAF, which had 18 airfields in the surrounding countryside! Morgans Old Brewery was the only one to be badly damaged during the hostilities. In 1946 the firm started rebuilding its plant. Like other firms in the same position, up-to-the-minute technology was incorporated into its design. This was particularly apparent in the new brew-house. It was seven floors high. Each floor was some 60ft square, and had to support heavy plant. Using new techniques, the reinforced concrete floors could be suspended on meshed steel. As a result, there was no need for extra supporting columns so leaving the floor area clear of obstruction.

By 1950, the firm was back in production, in a building that Sir Robert Bignold (chairman) believed was big enough to brew for Norfolk and Norwich. Sadly, and somewhat ironically, Sir Robert was correct. After a series of takeovers (which began in 1958 when S&P and Bullards took over Youngs) the 'big four' all went out of business. By 1970 this wonderful new brewery, a sign of prosperity in the 1950s, was the only one still operating in Norwich. By then, along with 95% of the City's pubs, it was owned by Watney Mann.

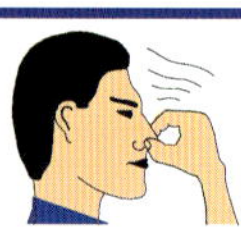

50s Memories

Roy Cracknell explains why you could tell where you were in Norwich by the smells – good and bad: *'Along Chapelfield a lovely aroma of chocolate wafted from Caleys, whilst on King Street you could catch the very distinctive odour of yeast and hops drifting across from the breweries. Around St George's you couldn't miss the whiff of leather which came from the shoe factories. Whilst on Davy Place you caught the enticing smell of coffee from Dakins.*

'Barrack Street was home to a tannery which absolutely stank. Another horrid smell was the whiff of sulphur fumes which came from the old gas works based on the corner of Palace Street and Bishopsgate. Then of course at the weekends when hundreds of animals were herded through the City on the way to the Cattle Market, you really couldn't miss the "eau-de-cow".'

St James Mill, Jarrolds print works, 1949

Of the 2000 workers employed in the City's printing trade around 50% were employed by Jarrold & Sons Ltd. By 1904 the business, which was first established on London Street in 1823, had transferred all of its printing operation to St James Mill (Whitefriars), where it continued to flourish.

In 1942 the firm had a lucky escape. It was hit by incendiary bombs but saved by the prompt action of the works' trailer-pump team, who used water from the adjacent river to douse the flames. As part of the war effort, the firm printed millions of pay books for both British and American forces. It was later claimed that: 'Probably every man in the British forces and most American airmen carried at least one piece of Jarrold printing.'

After the war, the firm invested heavily in new technology, including the installation of the largest four-colour litho plant in the UK. This, along with the company's highly skilled craftsmen and in-house research team, all contributed towards the firm earning an international reputation for its quality of colour printing. As the country recovered from war, this put it in a perfect position to meet growing demand for a range of items, including holiday publicity brochures, picture postcards and souvenir booklets. Other specialities included children's books, fine art publications, mail-order catalogues and calendars.

The World of Work

A combination of legislation, changing social attitudes and the decline of manufacturing trades, have all contributed to a change in the typical Norwich workplace.

In the immediate post-war era many of our youngsters left school at 15 and were then thrust into a strange, often dangerous world, full of alien smells and sounds. If you were a lad, at 18 you would have been called up to do national service – another big shock to the system.

This was an era when the words 'politically incorrect' had not been heard of, when sexism was rife and little more than lip service was paid to the words 'health and safety'. However, this was also a time of paternalistic employers, when entire families worked for the same firm and when your social life revolved around work.

Equality at Work

The attitude towards women in the workplace was very much of its time. It is very easy to criticise now, but it merely reflected what was happening across society as a whole. This was an era when there was a widely held belief that a woman's place was in the home looking after her husband and children. But that's not to say that women never took the opportunity to redress the balance.

The threat and outbreak of war gave women more opportunities. For instance, it was only in 1937, on a day known internally as 'Black Monday', that women were first employed in the Life Office at the Norwich Union. The incentive to change was the growing likelihood of the war and the inevitable call-up of men to the armed forces. However, with peace, men returned from the forces and it was all change again. Michael Brett, whose family owned Loose's (the china and glass specialist store on Magdalen Street) describes what inevitably happened across the City: 'During the war our young men were called up. We had a chap working for us, called Mr Mallett, who was too old for conscription, and so he ran the business with a number of ladies. The ladies were entrusted with buying what they could, countersigned by Mr Mallett. Most of the ladies remained with us after the men returned from the forces, but they moved back into the shop, and stepped aside from any senior buying roles. It was a cultural attitude of the time.'

Historically, in the manufacturing trade jobs were very gender specific. For example, Rodney Barker recalls that at Jarrolds print works women tended to do the non-skilled, non-apprenticed jobs, such as stacking and sorting paper. Similarly John Rumball notes that: 'In the bookbinding department, not one man worked on a sewing machine. All what we would call the semi-domestic jobs, like folding, creasing, cutting

All-female machine room at Norvic Shoe Company, St George's factory, 1952

and pasting, were done by women.' Similarly if you take the City's largest employer, the shoe industry, factories were divided into departments, known as rooms, where specific tasks were undertaken by either men or women. For example, in the clicking room men cut leather uppers, whilst in the ladies' machine room the uppers were prepared and sewn. Put simply, jobs were regarded as either men's or women's work. This did lead to behaviour that today would be frowned upon: and often the women were the worst. It was said that young men took their lives in their hands when they entered the machine room, it was a real rite of passage. Especially at Christmas there were stories of young lads losing their trousers, whilst Martin Miller recalled: 'On the first floor of the Norvic factory was the closing room which was staffed by 200 women machining uppers. In the room were big baskets on wheels which were used to transport the sewn uppers to the making room. On odd occasions when the forewoman, who was an absolute disciplinarian, wasn't looking, some of the women would pounce from behind on any young chap who had gone into their domain, and bundle him into a basket.'

Even when it came to office work, jobs were designated as men's or women's jobs. For example, when Barbara Miller joined the Norwich Union as a secretary in the late 1940s, she worked for a person called the lady superintendent who was in charge of all the women who worked there. She explains 'There were certain rooms where only women worked, such as the typing pools, which were overseen by very formidable ladies, most of whom were unmarried. A few women did work in other departments alongside men, such as in accounts, but they would probably be unmarried, quite old, and been there a long time and slowly worked their way up.'

A similar stance was taken in the police force. When Maurice Morson joined the City Police in 1956 there were just six WPCs working there. They did totally different jobs to the men. They weren't allowed to walk the beat nor do nights. Their job mostly involved patrolling school crossings, looking after children and interviewing women who'd been victims of indecent assaults. Behaviour reflected what was considered the norm in society. Maurice is in no doubt that in the late 1950s: 'The force was very hierarchical and had an element of bigotry. Applying today's standards, you'd have to describe male officers' attitudes to their female colleagues as chauvinistic. I wouldn't say it was any worse than any other workplace, it was very much in line with attitudes of the time.'

Would this happen today?

Roy Cracknell explains: *'My wife, Jean, worked at the Norwich Union, I met her there in 1944 just before I joined up. We were both at a works' dance. I can still recall asking if I could write to her whilst away on national service. We eventually got engaged in 1946, and were married in 1948, on my 22nd birthday. In those days at the Norwich Union it wasn't quite the thing to marry so young. I was even sent for by the chief of staff who disapproved, he said: "I was married at 25, and that was thought to be very young." I didn't take his advice to put off the wedding, but neither did I take umbrage. I think in those days you just accepted those sorts of things. We married in Thorpe St Andrew Church and had our reception in the upstairs room at the Samson & Hercules. We hadn't been married very long and we were spotted walking though the office premises arm in arm. We were both told off separately, me by the chief of staff and Jean by the lady superintendent, because it was not the "done thing" for couples to fraternise on company premises.'*

An article that appeared in the 'Eastern Evening News' (1959) announcing the opening of a new nurses' school at the N&N seemed to be more concerned with the pupils than the facilities: *'My introduction to those now christening the school was on a brilliant summer afternoon....I met a bunch of fine, healthy-looking girls, many in shorts and shirts, returning from physical exercise. In no time at all the 23 of them had changed into their even more becoming uniforms.'*

Nurses enjoy some Christmas fare, 1954

Health and Safety

During the 1950s employers took a different attitude to health and safety than they do now.

As early as 1945 the Central Office of Information and Nationalised Industries had started to produce educational films and posters which promoted safety in the workplace. Subsequently, regulations were introduced on an ad-hoc basis. This resulted in a confusing mass of legislation which quickly became outmoded and cumbersome when new technology was introduced.

In the shoe factories industrial accidents were a way of life. The noise in the factories was cacophonous, but no one wore ear muffs. One of the noisiest machines was the pounder, which was used to flatten the pleats around the bottom of a shoe after the upper had been shaped around a last. It was a wheel with washers on it. You'd hold the shoe against it as it rotated around at a terrific pace and it vibrated onto your hands. Lenford Laband, who worked in the industry from 1946 until 1990, recalls that you could stand in Colegate and hear their 'dreadful scream' from the Norvic factory on St George's. Even worse, after the operatives finished working on the machines their hands continued to vibrate because it had stopped the blood circulation. Eventually its use was banned. Meanwhile the press room, where operatives cut soles and heels, was one of the most dangerous rooms in the factory. The press room at Edwards & Holmes new purpose-built factory, opened in 1948, was located on the ground floor. Peter Metcalf, who worked at the factory, explains why the procedure was so dangerous: 'We used around ten huge revolutionary presses which were about ten-feet across. They were shaft driven with one motor driving a number of machines. To do this each press had a whopping great turning wheel on the side which had a big belt running around it to the shaft. The press was operated by a foot treadle which ran along the length of the machine. The press knives, which operated on the same principle as pastry cutters, were made from forged steel and were about six-inches deep. When the press came down they were pushed through the material below. The quickest way to cut the soles would be to cut one, then the next etc. and allow them to build up inside the press knife. When it was full they would be pushed out. The number of men who had lost fingers and thumbs in that room was unbelievable. This was because they were trying to get the work out as quickly as possible and they'd press the treadle when their fingers were still under the knives. It all relied on foot-hand coordination. They were also incredibly noisy places.'

At Jarrolds print works John Rumball doesn't recall any major problems with industrial injuries. Although many of the machines didn't have protective guards, major accidents were averted, because like the clicking presses (below) they could only be operated using two hands.

In the News

In Norwich there is evidence that the City Council took workplace safety seriously. In October 1952 the Norwich and District Industrial Accident Prevention Council gave prizes to local industrial firms in the 'Better Housekeeping Week' (dubbed 'Tidiness and Safety Week' by the 'Eastern Daily Press') – incidentally the winner was Reckitt & Colman.

Would this happen today?

Arthur Holmes worked as an accountant in the shoe trade at the Start-rite factory: *'I remember going into the press room in my early days [1950s] and saying to a chap: "You've lost the top of your finger." He replied: "Yes, everybody who works here has lost the top of their finger." I looked around and they really had. You see they used to put the knife under the press then as the press came down they tried to adjust it and caught a finger. They did it once and they never did it again.'*

In the 1950s clicking presses were introduced to cut leather uppers. The new machines were much safer as they could only be operated using two hands, which meant that one could not be under the press as it came down.

Presses used to cut uppers, clicking room, Bally, 1959

Although, because of the danger of fire, smoking was banned at the print works, employees often flouted the rules. John recalls the day this stopped: 'John Jarrold was on inspection and he went into the gents' toilets in the binding department. He could smell smoke, and knocked on the door of the one locked cubicle: "Come out," he shouted, "you're smoking in there." The guy, Ray, came out. He'd flushed his cigarette butt down the loo and was trying to look innocent. John Jarrold just looked at him and said, "Go to personnel. Get your cards. Wait at security. We'll have all of your stuff at the security gatehouse in 15 minutes." Ray actually sobbed. We were all shocked, because we all went to have smokes in the toilets. Talks went on for a fortnight between management and staff. Ray was reinstated after a fortnight, and he worked at Jarrolds until he retired, but after that none of us smoked in the loos.'

Would this happen today?

Arthur Houlston in his new 'Octopus' lorry, c.1950

One of the perks of working at the one of the City's breweries was the availability of the beer. *Arthur Houlston started work at Morgans in 1947 when all employees had an allowance of a pint a day drunk at around 10 o' clock. The drivers were often out delivering, and so missed this treat, but it wasn't a problem as they were normally offered a complimentary pint at each pub they visited. Arthur explains: 'The story goes that some had no problem driving their lorries back to the yard, but couldn't get on their bikes to cycle home.' Not so at the Crown Brewery, where John Beaumont started work in 1956, he recalls one Christmas Eve, when a drayman overloaded his lorry: 'The dray crashed into [the garage entrance] and took out the door. There was glass everywhere. The driver was disciplined, that was all.'*

Starting Work

The 1944 Education Act raised the school-leaving age to 15. Many youngsters left without qualifications and immediately entered the world of work, often relying on parents to get them jobs. Workplaces were very hierarchical, and so as the new boy or girl, you soon knew your place.

This was an age when it was very easy for young people to find a job. Avis Brown's experience was not untypical: 'I left school in 1957 when I was 15, and went to Caleys chocolate factory. After a few months someone said that they were paying more at Harmers, so a group of us went over there, but I only lasted two weeks because I was put on the hot press, which I didn't like. I knew about the shoe trade because my mother was in it. So I left Harmers and walked up the road to Edwards & Holmes and found myself at the age of 15 on my third job!'

Working conditions in factories were often a shock to the system. This was discovered by John Rumball who can still remember back to 1953, when he started work in the bookbinding department at Jarrolds – and not in a good way: 'The smell of the adhesives was pungent and pervaded the factory. A big motor with a long shaft and belts running from it operated five noisy guillotines which stood along the wall. The folding machines were massive, they were 15-foot-wide, the size of a small room. It was a dark afternoon, a dismal day, and I thought to myself, "What have I let myself in for?" It was noisy, it was smelly, it was dark, it was busy – it was daunting!'

Similar to many youngsters Rodney Barker relied on his father, Sidney, to get him a job. Like John, he still recalls his first day at Jarrolds when he was just 15 years old: 'I must have been the shortest person working there at the time. Thinking back I probably looked about 12. You had to buy your own boiler suit, your own work shoes, your own gloves, and all of that sort of stuff. The problem I had was that the smallest boiler suit I could get, was still miles too big – the crotch came down to my knees.' Reg Kilburn, who started work at 15 at the Barfield and Richardson shoe factory, had a similar challenge. Being only 5ft 2in tall he couldn't even reach the cutting board, but this problem was soon overcome when he was given a box to stand on.

Like most girls in her school, Sylvia Buxton left with no academic qualifications. This did not prevent her getting a job, and in 1956 she started work at the Bally shoe factory on Tombland, where she stayed until 1967: 'When I first started I was a runabout. I'd do things like take the samples down to the office. I used to go to the Tech [on St George's] one day a week: all newcomers did. I ended up working in the machine room, where I did a variety of jobs...it was piecework and so you had to earn your money. Of course, the older women who'd been there donkeys' years always picked the best jobs, and so us young girls had to work twice as hard.'

But of course not all school leavers went to work in the City's factories. Barbara Miller left Norwich High School in 1947 when she remembers: 'The girls leaving school generally took one of four options. A few went to university, some went onto nursing and others to secretarial college, whilst lots of girls went to train as teachers.' Meanwhile Glenna St Quintin's first job was as a telephone operator at the Eaton Exchange. 'In those days you couldn't dial anyone direct, you'd dial zero, to get through to an operator on a switchboard, where an operator would say, "number please". We'd have a board in front of us, dial the code for them, and plug them into the connection. If no one answered at the other end, I'd say: "Sorry we can't connect you." It's so different to today when everyone has a mobile phone. Then most people had to go to a telephone box. We weren't supposed to listen to any conversations, but of course we did. At times it was a bit like a soap opera... complete with instalments.'

During the war and throughout the 1950s, work was interrupted for many young men whilst they completed their national service. Roy Cracknell, joined the Norwich Union (NU) in 1942 when he was 15: 'I didn't have the faintest idea what I wanted to do. However, I had a cousin working at the NU, and so my father said I should get a job there as well. It was seen to be a good steady job: a job for life. It wasn't well paid. I started on £50 a year, but on top of that we were given a free lunch every day, and also we finished at 4.30pm. At the time you were paid according to your level in the company, irrespective of which department you were in. We got a little increase every year. It was a job that carried a certain status, even if it was only because you were wearing a tailored suit rather than a boiler suit.' In 1944, Roy was called up to the air force, after completing his national service he returned to the NU, and worked there until he retired, and so it really was a job for life.

Would this happen today?

Rodney Barker recalls his early days at Jarrolds: *'I can't count the number of times I was clipped around the ear or on the back of my head or kicked up the backside. It wouldn't be allowed now, but it happened then. If you didn't take it and made a noise about it the senior men wouldn't tell you anything about the machines or the jobs, and that was the only way you learnt what to do, and so you had to take it. But nobody worried about it, in fact there was a brilliant atmosphere in the print works.'*

Jean Woods started work at Norvic in 1956, she trained at their shoe factory on St George's: *'One of my supervisors was lethal. If you were just a little bit out, even when you were learning, she'd prod you really hard. She really did lay into you, I still remember how painful it was. But they could do that then. You didn't go home and tell your parents... they'd just say you probably deserved it anyway.'*

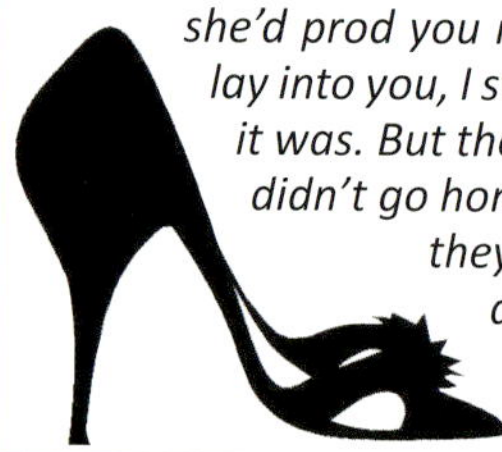

Diss telephone exchange, c.1960

Paternalism and Loyalty

Through the 1950s many of Norwich's leading firms were family owned and led. This often translated into close relationships and loyalties in the workplace.

To avoid confusion, 'the family' members were known by their Christian names, but a note of deference was added by preceding these with a title. John Rumball explains: 'John Jarrold was the Managing Director, his office was in St James Mill [print works]. His sons had specified roles: Peter Jarrold, was in charge of the print works; Anthony Jarrold, the youngest, was in charge of Jarrolds Publishing; Richard Jarrold, was the director in charge of the shop on London Street. The directors were called Mr John, Mr Peter, Mr Anthony and Mr Richard. They were a terrific family to work for, very supportive of staff.'

If you were a good worker and loyal to a firm this would be rewarded. One of the major perks was being able to get a job for your relatives, and so in the same way families ran a firm, families also worked for them. In 1958 when Barry Berwick was 15 he was taken on at the Steward & Patteson (S&P) brewery as an apprentice cooper where he joined his grandad, father and uncles. He recalls: 'Grandad Billy was a foreman; my dad, Ernest, and Uncle Alfred all worked in the fermenting department; Uncle Leonard was an engineer; Uncles Albert and George were in transport; Uncle Billy was in the boiler room. All of them worked there for over 40 years and my grandad and Uncle Billy made it to 53 years apiece."

Loyalty was a two-way street. Loose's china shop on Magdalen Street was owned by the Brett family. When the premises were destroyed in WWII, Michael Brett has no doubt why the business both survived and later flourished: 'Despite our near destruction during the war, with the commitment of my father and a tremendously dedicated loyal staff, Loose's recovered to become one of the top ten specialist china shops in the country. In the 1950s, and through all my time there, the firm had tremendous loyalty from our staff which, as owners, we reciprocated.'

Berwick family, S&P's Pockthorpe Brewery yard, c.1950

However, this support and loyalty extended beyond the family-owned firms. In 1942, when Caleys was bombed, its owners, the Halifax based firm of John Mackintosh & Sons Ltd, continued to pay their employees for a time afterwards, to help tide them over. When the directors suspended employment of their Norwich workers, they pledged 'We hope that one day Caleys will once again be in full production and that we shall be able to offer them employment again. In that event their time away from us will not be considered as a break in length of service.' The latter was an important concession, as some company benefits were based on length of unbroken employment.

Similarly, Roy Cracknell has very fond memories of his time at the Norwich Union, where he started work in 1942: 'Whilst I was there, the Norwich Union was definitely a paternal company to work for. They were very concerned about staff welfare, in turn there was a lot of loyalty to the company amongst staff. That loyalty extended from the company, through the agents who sold the business, all the way through to customers.'

Camaraderie in the Workplace

Fun in the workplace, the social club, the works' outing, and Christmas, were all very important to working life in the 1940s and 1950s.

All the major firms had social clubs. These were often housed in a substantial building with extensive grounds where employees would meet to dance, to drink, to play sport and generally enjoy themselves. As such, the re-establishment of the clubs went hand-in-hand with post-war rebuilding programmes. Take Caleys (Mackintosh), for instance. By 1949 the social club had been reformed. In the same year their premises, the Elms Pavilion on Unthank Road, had been reopened by Lord and Lady Mackintosh. It was reported in the staff magazine: 'We had a grand week of entertainment to mark the occasion. The Saturday night Crazy Dance which concluded the celebrations was the gayest and most exciting of any show ever staged at the Elms.' Although the smaller factories didn't have the same facilities, they still hosted social events. Shorten & Armes, the shoe manufacturers, didn't have plush facilities, but this didn't stop the girls who worked there getting hold of a record player and organising dances in an old building next door to the factory.

Social events were not always organised at the works' social club. In the 1950s dinner dances were very popular, and these were often held at one of the City's ballrooms, in particular at the Lido on Aylsham Road or the Samson & Hercules on Tombland.

There was great excitement when local firms played host to *Workers' Playtime* (a radio variety programme transmitted by the BBC from a factory canteen 'somewhere in Britain'). First produced in 1941 it had originally been intended as a wartime morale-booster, but it was so successful that it continued to run until 1964. The show certainly went down very well when it was presented in Reckitt & Colmans canteen at the Carrow Works in 1947 where the 'clapping, cheering, whistling and screaming of the audience rose to a pitch approaching hysteria'.

During the summer, one of the most important events of the year was the 'works outing'. As Betty Barnard, who worked in the shoe trade in the 1950s, explained: 'We were like big kids: we used to look forward to it all year.' In the shoe factories, fairly typically the entire factory would go, and the day would consist of an outing to the coast, complete with a meal and a visit to a show. But this wasn't always the case. At Jarrolds print works, John Rumball recalls the trips as being more akin to a lad's day out. He recalls: 'Outings were arranged by individual departments. For the men it didn't really matter where we went, the trip basically depended on having enough crates of beer, and so we went to places like the Tottenham Working Men's Club. They were good days.'

Then, of course there was Christmas, when employees' children were invited along either to a party or to the pantomime. In 1954 around 750 children attended Caleys Christmas party, where they enjoyed: live entertainment, a film showing of Mickey Mouse and 1600 sausage rolls. So many children attended, they had to employ two Father Christmases! In the same year the firm booked two full houses for the whole of the staff and their families to see the pantomime, *Sleeping Beauty*, at the Theatre Royal. Interestingly, in the staff magazine particular mention was made of the cast being presented with chocolates – 'a return to the pre-war custom made possible by derationing'.

In the News

The owners of Frank Price, the Magdalen Street store, were renowned for their paternalistic approach, epitomised by the number of long-serving staff who worked there, as reported in the 'Eastern Evening News' in 1954: 'The doyen of these is Miss Agnes Towler – 72 in March, and still giving valuable service to the firm in a semi-retired capacity. She started in 1898, and for many years was head cashier working in close touch with the first Frank Price (who died in 1922), his son the second Frank Price (who died in 1946) and with Mr Roy Price in the current regime. Constancy of individual service seems somehow symptomatic of the consistent policy of the firm through these many years.'

50s Memories

***Stephen Hindes, whose family owned Bonds, recalls**: 'It was a family business with a terrific staff. I particularly remember a lady who worked in the restaurant who joined Bonds around 1931. She was a pastry cook called Blanche Russell. She lived to be over 100. In the restaurant we had dumb waiters, and she used to like to tell the story of the day when I was born, when a message came down this chute announcing: "It's a boy." Blanche used to make me a birthday cake every year. It was always a Madeira cake in the shape of a number.'*

Welfare in the Workplace

After WWII it was inevitable that the demand for social change would impact on the workplace. In the same way that post-war rebuilding facilitated the improvement and modernisation of production methods, it also enabled Norwich businesses to update the facilities they provided for employees. This was very much epitomised at Curls department store. When they reopened in 1956 they put great emphasis on the facilities they offered their staff. These included: 'Up-to-date amenities only to be found in a modern building – light and spacious workrooms, a fully equipped clinic for the treatment of accident and illness, a bright staff canteen... well-equipped cloakrooms, a ladies' powder room and comfortable lounges.' The firm also employed a welfare supervisor to look after the interests of their employees.

Similar facilities were being offered in workplaces across the City. For example, in August 1949, the *MC Monthly News* (Machintosh-Caley staff newsletter) proudly announced the opening of Caleys new Welfare Department, which contained such features as rest rooms, a new canteen, a surgery and treatment rooms. But was the provision of such facilities purely altruistic? A clue comes in the conclusion of the article: 'Our high standard of health and our efforts to keep it should produce a happy healthy family. There should also be little loss of time when attending the Welfare Department.' Clearly time means money, but more than this, industrialists were very aware that eventually legislation would be passed enforcing minimum standards of welfare: it made sense for them to stay ahead of the game.

Firms also recognised the need to attract workers. This was particularly true of skilled, female machinists who worked in the shoe and clothing industries. Any shortfall was partially solved by using outworkers who stitched uppers in their own homes, and also by opening satellite factories in the villages and towns around Norwich. For example: Edwards & Holmes had premises at Sheringham and Holt; Start-rite operated at Wymondham and King's Lynn; and Harmers opened at Watton and Fakenham. But it was also important to attract City workers, and so when Harmers rebuilt their factory on Havers Road (Mile Cross) they not only placed great emphasis on the Personnel and Welfare Department and their 'very nice canteen where staff can buy a mid-day meal for 10d', they also heralded the introduction of their new hairdressing section – believed to be the only one of its type in Norwich. Here the girls but not, as already noted, the men, were able to make appointments every two weeks as part of their normal working day. In 1957, Miss Wilmott (the firm's personnel officer) extolled the benefits of the service not only as a staff perk, but of maintaining standards in the workplace: 'The job calls for girls who are neat and tidy and take a pride in their appearance....We don't have many girls with "ironmongery" [curlers] in their hair here, and if they turn up like that we tactfully suggest a visit to the hairdressers.'

Improved production methods, also had an impact on working conditions and staff welfare. When W. H. H. Clarke opened its new Apex Works on Sussex Street, the *Evening News* ran a glowing article on the high standards set in the new shoe factory which included the installation of 'high-efficiency dust extraction and air purification; and the use of thermostatically controlled heating'.

Elsewhere, in 1955 'the City's newest industrial canteen' with accommodation for 500, came on stream at LSEs Gothic Works. The canteen embraced 'the most modern hygienic ideas in the preparation of food and in coping with the formidable aftermath of washing up'.

Of course, older factories also installed new facilities. For example, Barnards, converted a disused part of their premises and paint store at their Norfolk Ironworks on Coslany Street into a new canteen and at the same time updated their washing facilities. Interestingly, in 1951, the firm's personnel officer noted that the new facilities were much more popular with their younger, rather than older, employees.

Also, new factories were continually modernised. Take, for example, Edwards & Holmes Esdelle Works on Drayton Road. Although the factory was relatively new, around 1958 Mr Forrest (Director) decided it was time to review the facilities. Avis Brown remembers the event well: 'Mr Forrest decided he was going to build a new ladies' toilet – we even had an opening ceremony. I think that he must have been on holiday somewhere posh because when it was unveiled, hand painted in pastel colours across the top of the door was written the word "Boudoir". Well of course it was something new to us. We were quite excited. We all went in for a look. In the first section across one side there was a full-length mirror with a shelf. I remember him telling us that it was for us to put our handbags on. There were seats all around and ashtrays on stilts, so that we could sit and have a smoke. In the next piece there were the hand basins and then the loos. I can tell you now that in all of the factories I've ever worked in I've never seen such posh toilets!'

50s Memories of a Chocolate Factory

Heather Trower, c.1958

In the mid 1950s, at the age of 16, Heather Trower left the Notre Dame School to start work in the display department at Caleys. At her job interview she had taken along her O Level art portfolio, it was so good she was asked why she wasn't going to art school. Sadly, she had to explain that she had already stayed on an extra year at the Notre Dame, and in her family further education was not an option.

Heather worked alongside six male colleagues. When she started she spent a lot of time washing brushes, clearing up and making tea and coffee. She was also entrusted with the job of collecting large tubs of poster paints from Bayliss Wright on Prince of Wales Road.

The display department was responsible for creating a range of advertising material, including displays for trade fairs and shop windows. They were ingenious in their approach. One colleague, an engineer, was also a skilled woodworker, and so one of his jobs was to make models of chocolates out of boxwood. Other workmates created plaster models of chocolates, some of these were painted or wrapped for display purposes, whilst others were used for making chocolate moulds. Paper sculpture was often used to create elaborate and large displays.

After six months the firm paid for Heather's enrolment at Norwich Art School. One day a week she attended day classes in painting, drawing and printing. She spent an additional three evenings studying graphics, lettering and commercial displays. Whilst there she was particularly thrilled to be taught by the renowned artists Leslie Davenport, Geoffrey Wales and Noel Spencer.

Because she had lovely hands and nails she was often used as a photographic model. Close-up pictures were taken of her holding or selecting chocolates which were then used in magazine adverts or reproduced in posters. She also posed as Miss Sweetly standing next to Major Quality – the couple who featured on Quality Street advertising/ packaging.

There were several perks to working at the factory. In particular, at the end of the week you could buy bags of waste (seconds) for two shillings each: which were especially good when Easter eggs were in production. Then at Christmas every member of staff was given a large box of chocolates and two weeks' wages as a bonus. The firm also hosted a dinner dance each year at the Samson & Hercules Ballroom. It was Heather's responsibility to produce all the table decorations, a job which introduced her to flower arranging. All the attendees were given beautiful cardboard hats and cigarettes were freely available on the tables.

There was one aspect of the job Heather did not enjoy: despite working in offices next to the laboratories (overlooking Chantry Road), well away from the production lines, her clothes always reeked of chocolate. Even today, she is not fond of its smell.

The Consumer Society

The 'Back' of Norwich Market, 1949

Shops and Shopping

Background

In the late 1940s shops were very different to today: the high street was dominated by small independently owned stores; self-service was rare; there were more specialist outlets; shop hours were significantly shorter; stocks of goods were low and limited.

One of the biggest factors influencing the retail sector in the years immediately after WWII was rationing. Any hope that the end of the war also meant the end of rationing was soon quashed. Why did it continue? The conflict had cost Britain around 25% of her national wealth. In order to repay a colossal level of foreign debt, the government were faced with the challenge of boosting exports, improving the balance of trade and stimulating the economy: this all had to be done whilst controlling inflation. Rationing encouraged manufacturers to export goods and reduced the demand for imports, both of which had a beneficial impact on the country's balance of payments. At the same time it had the effect of curtailing domestic demand which in turn reduced the possibility of inflation caused by too much money chasing too few goods. Although consumer rationing of clothing, furniture, petrol, soap and many foodstuffs was abolished by the end of 1950, it was maintained on some food items until 1954. As rationing ended shops were once more piled high with wonderful things to buy.

As the 1950s progressed other factors also affected how we shopped. Stores that had been bombed were rebuilt – often bigger and better than before. At the same time there was a discernible increase in the number and size of national chains, and a corresponding reduction in locally owned outlets. As importantly, there was a feeling of affluence in the country, fuelled by a buoyant economy and high levels of employment. What is more, the lifting of restrictions on personal loans and HP meant shoppers didn't even have to save to buy the new, exciting goods they saw in the stores: the consumer society had arrived.

Magdalen Gates, Magdalen Street, c.1950

Shopping in Norwich

The *City of Norwich Plan* noted that the City's central shopping area was focussed on Gentleman's Walk, London Street and the immediate vicinity. Although the Plan did not 'aim at any alteration thereto', it envisaged an expansion of retail outlets in surrounding areas, including All Saints' Green and Timberhill Street.

Like other cities, many shops located in this prime-retail area were local, specialised and small. However, it also encompassed some of the City's major stores, including Chamberlins (the Market Place), Curls (Orford Place), Buntings (Rampant Horse Street), Garlands (London Street), Greens (Haymarket), Bonds (All Saints' Green) and Jarrolds (London Street). These outlets formed a very clear hierarchy. Thus, for example, Garlands and Chamberlins concentrated on luxury goods, in the middle were Curls and Buntings whilst Greens stocked cheaper lines. Positions in the rankings did change, for example when Bonds reopened its new store in 1951 they began to concentrate on the top end of the market. As it did not sell clothes at the time, Jarrolds stood apart from the others.

The evolution of these stores through the 1950s was very typical of what was happening across the country. Of particular note was the loss of our independent retailers and post-war rebuilding.

Memories

Despite Chamberlins being regarded as Norwich's pre-eminent store, as a young man, Roy Cracknell took advantage of war-time restrictions to make a very large purchase there*: 'One of the issues we faced when we married [1948] was how to buy furniture. When you wed, you could buy a certain amount of what was known as Utility furniture. You were sent a catalogue which listed all the things you could buy: they were stamped CC41. It didn't matter which shop you went to, you could only pick from one catalogue. You were given coupons which allowed you to get enough furniture to set up home, like a three-piece suite, a bedroom suite and one carpet. Jean and I went to Chamberlins. It was an expensive store, but since we were buying Utility furniture from a standard catalogue, it didn't matter where we shopped, because all the stores supplied and charged the same. And so we thought we might as well go to Chamberlins! It was actually jolly good furniture; it was very well made.'*

Chamberlins (left side of picture), Guildhall Hill, Market Place, 1950

National Takeovers

Across the country independent stores were increasingly being taken over by national firms: a pattern that was mirrored in Norwich. By 1950, although they continued to trade under their family names, Curls, Garlands, Chamberlins and Buntings had all been absorbed into the national group, Debenhams.

The first to go was Curls, which had been taken over in the 1920s. Garlands was bought out in 1942.

Meanwhile, Buntings, despite been badly damaged during the 1942 Baedeker Raids, managed to both maintain its independence and to keep trading on the ground floor of its Rampant Horse Street store (the upper levels were taken over by the NAAFI Club for service personnel). Then in 1948 the premises were bought by Marks and Spencer (M&S), for what was reputed to be the highest price ever paid for a commercial property in Norwich. By the time the new M&S store opened, what remained of the Buntings business had been bought by Debenhams who opened a new Buntings store on London Street next door to Garlands.

Around the same time, 1949, Chamberlins was also taken over. For years it had been the City's pre-eminent store. Roy Cracknell recalls: 'When I married, Chamberlins was Norwich's most upmarket shop, it was a bit like Grace Brothers which featured in the comedy *Are You Being Served?* When you entered you were met by a floor walker and people expected to be served sitting at the counter.' Despite the new owners assuring loyal customers that there would be no changes to the store's name, in December 1954 it was rechristened Marshall and Snelgrove.

Recovery and Growth

Post-war rebuilding gave owners the opportunity to build bigger and better stores. Across the City shops were extended and improved. From 1945 to 1960 the journey to affluence is exemplified by the evolution and redevelopment of many City's shops, including Curls, Bonds and Loose's.

The three were amongst the many buildings bombed on the nights of 27/28 and 29/30 April 1942. During these so-called Baedeker Raids Norwich was devastated; they marked one of the lowest points in the history of the City. Roy recalls: 'The next day when I went back to work at the Norwich Union, a group of us went up to the flat roof that topped the Westlegate building. From there we looked straight across to Rampant Horse Street where Curls and Woolworths had gone. Further across, we could see the ruins of Caleys. As you can imagine, it was a scene of devastation. We were amazed; we could hardly believe it.'

Buntings and the NAAFI Club, 1947

Bombed remains of Curls, 1946

Curls Department Store

Following the raid Debenhams, which had owned Curls since the 1920s, acted quickly to secure its survival. They took over a shop in Exchange Street to house the furniture department whilst the women's fashion department moved to Westlegate.

It would be another 14 years before the shop reopened on Orford Place. Over that period the site of this once fine store served as both a static water tank and a car park.

When Curls finally opened its doors in 1956, it was a milestone: war and austerity were behind us, good times were ahead.

But why had rebuilding taken so long? The delay had been principally caused by disputes on how this prime site should be developed. In particular, the Council wanted to take the opportunity to widen Brigg Street, Rampant Horse Street and Red Lion Street. Unsurprisingly, as such a scheme would have reduced the size of the site by 1.5 acres, it did not find favour with the owners. Eventually, compromise was reached and work commenced on the new four-storey building (plus basement) with a floor-space of 97,000 square feet. Once complete it was described as 'dominating the shopping area of Norwich as the Norman Castle...once dominated East Anglia.' The new store had window displays

Curls site as a car park, 1952

Rebuilding Curls, 1954

which stretched to some 430 feet which 'reminded shoppers that they can buy anything from a party dress to a paint brush'. All goods were displayed on the principle that customers should be encouraged to see and handle them. But most impressive of all was the introduction of escalators to carry customers up (but not down) through the store, the first in East Anglia. These escalators were particularly loved by small boys; for many youngsters the main highlight of a trip to the City was visiting the store and running down them. The new store was air-conditioned and wired for announcements: maybe more worrying was the pride the company took in its asbestos ceiling blocks! But it was not only the design of the store that was impressive, here you could purchase an array of goods that clearly showed we were all feeling wealthier. Rationing was a thing of the past. Newly weds were no longer restricted to buying Utility goods, in fact the whole of the second floor was devoted to furniture, where shoppers could see exhibitions of rooms and related schemes.

Customers loved it. At its opening the new store was swamped by expectant shoppers. Despite having enough tills to deal with 40,000 transactions a day extra tills had to be brought into service to deal with the ever-lengthening queues.

Andy Anderson sums up local feeling at the time: 'I was thrilled to see Curls reopen in 1956. It did restore the whole centre really. I found the rebuilding exciting. To me it felt like Norwich coming back to life.'

Rebuilding Curls, 1955

Rebuilding Curls, 1955

Similarly, Bonds not only recovered after its premises was bombed, but it rose from the ashes better than before.

On 27 June 1942 the store was destroyed. Stephen Hinde, Ernest Bond's grandson, recalls: 'At the time my grandparents had moved in with us, and so had been able to store surplus stock at their house on Newmarket Road. This meant that they had enough goods to keep trading, but they needed somewhere to trade from. Undeterred, my grandfather bought some old buses which he put in Bonds car park, and within seven days he was back in business. He even set up a makeshift restaurant in an old corrugated-iron building. This story featured in an article in a national magazine entitled "The Spirit That Hitler Would Never Beat". The wreckage took a week to cool down. The day after the bombing someone asked when the salvage sale would be held, only to be told that there would be no sale because everything in the store had been destroyed.' Subsequently, the company took over empty premises throughout the City, including a building on Red Lion Street, now occupied by Barclays.

In the austerity years after the war stock was hard to come by. However, as observed by Stephen Hinde, this did not deter his father (Eric Hinde): 'We sold quite a bit of second-hand furniture. My father would go to sales and auctions around Norfolk with a cheque book and a Bonds van, and he'd buy merchandise to sell in the shop.'

When Eric (who was married to Ernest Bond's daughter Marjorie and appointed MD in 1949) returned from the war, he was responsible for overseeing the construction of the new building. The eye-catching store with the distinctive rounded end (which still characterises the building today) was designed by the architect Robert Bond. It had already featured in the *City of Norwich Plan,* as part of the proposed redevelopment of All Saints' Green. Construction started in 1946. The building took nearly five years to complete. When it opened it was hailed as Norwich's first modern department store.

In the 1950s as more items became available on the home market, Bonds positioned itself as an up-market store which sold top-quality goods and gave first-class service. The firm flourished through the 1950s and in 1960, when Greens closed, Bonds was in a strong enough position to take over their stock and goodwill.

Bonds, 1955

Loose's

Another much-loved local store (owned by the Brett family) was Loose's. After their shop (23 - 25 Magdalen Street) was destroyed during the Baedeker Raids, they temporarily moved to 43 Magdalen Street. At the end of hostilities a new property, incorporating modern features, was built on the site of the original store. The new outlet, which was opened in 1951, was larger than its predecessor which at a time of austerity gave a minor problem, as noted by Michael Brett: 'When we built the shop after the war we considerably extended the floor space. When we opened in 1951 we had very little stock, which is clear from photographs taken at the time [see below]. The staff had to disperse it in a way that made the shop floor look attractive and not too sparse.'

Loose's, 1951

The progression from deprivation to affluence in the post-war years is typified by the business in several ways.

Firstly there was a change in the company's wholesale business. In particular, as more people could afford holidays, there was a noticeable increase in its hotel, pub and restaurant trade. Likewise, its hire business was booming. Most noticeably, in 1953, the Coronation year, the firm had a massive 50,000 pieces of crockery on hire throughout the county.

There was also the question of merchandise. Michael Brett sums up the position: 'Immediately after the war when the priority across the country was to export to repay the National Debt, it was very difficult to buy stock. You could sell it easily, but you couldn't buy it.' As the 1950s progressed, not only could the business buy merchandise, but designs changed: 'We'd had the austerity period in the 1940s when crockery was white and utilitarian and the only decorated ware was what they called export rejects. In the 1950s we saw a return of highly decorative tableware for the home.' In fact, in 1954 the shop had tea-services in over 150 patterns together with an 'unrivalled' selection of dinner services all on display in 'glitteringly attractive showrooms'.

By 1955 the shop, which specialised in 'equipping the table, the kitchen and the pantry', had a large array of wares and was proud to describe itself as East Anglia's leading store for china and glass. An article in the press illustrates how times had changed. Abstinence and shortages were a thing of the past, by now the store represented 'the proud housewife's vision of the promised land'.

Loose's, 1951

Jarrolds Department Store

With one exception, all the independent department stores that served Norwich in the 1950s have been closed or taken over. However, Jarrolds has not only survived but flourished.

The Jarrold family first opened a store in 1823 on the opposite side of London Street to today's building, primarily to sell the books they printed and published. The first portion of the building on the present site was opened in 1840 and from that time onward other premises have been added and the facade altered.

Through the 1950s, alongside their popular restaurant, Jarrolds sold a range of merchandise, including books, toys and household goods. During this period they regularly promoted kitchenware in a series of 'Home Needs Exhibitions'. Meanwhile, in the toy department, Father Christmas made an annual appearance; in 1958 he met children in the 'Land of Nursery Rhymes', that same year their seasonal toy fair was described as the largest in East Anglia.

It was only in 1965, after purchasing and renovating the neighbouring Corn Hall, that the store started to sell ladies fashions. Since that time it has continued to expand, innovate and adapt.

Coronation decorations, Jarrolds, 1953

Home Needs Exhibition, Jarrolds, 1947

Book Department, Jarrolds, 1951

Kitchen Display, Jarrolds, c.1953

Display, Jarrolds, c.1958

Notable Shopping Streets

Although they were located outside the central shopping area designated in the *City of Norwich Plan,* St Stephen's Street, Magdalen Street and St Benedict's Street were all important retail areas in the 1940s and 1950s.

St Stephen's Street

Prior to WWII St Stephen's was one of the busiest thoroughfares in the City. Not only was it lined with an eclectic array of shops, it was one of the major roads into the centre. It was also very narrow and not suited to the age of the motor car. In the 1930s the Council began investigating how they could widen the road but could not decide which side of the street should be set back. They had a conundrum. On the east stood two medieval buildings: the Boar's Head Inn and Crown & Angel public house. To the west stood Buntings and (on Red Lion Street) Curls. Their problem was solved somewhat drastically following the Baedeker Raids, when three of the four buildings were destroyed: only Buntings survived.

The *City of Norwich Plan*, proposed that the road should be redesigned as a dual carriageway with pavements 15ft wide. Furthermore, and somewhat controversially, it stated: '[St Stephen's] should not be lined by shops, with customer's cars and delivery vans impeding the traffic; it is recommended that no more shops should be allowed to be built on this street and that those already established there should be gradually replaced by offices.' Although in 1953 a start was made on widening the east side of the road at the City-centre end (the scheme was completed in the early 1960s), as is now obvious, the plan for a 'shop-free' street never came to fruition.

Daphne Way enjoyed visiting St Stephen's before it was widened: 'We used to shop on the old narrow St Stephen's. We loved going to the Co-op, my mother was a real Co-op lady. I went there until it closed. Over the top was the Co-op social club. At the top of Bull Lane was their butchers, they even killed animals there. Proctor's the butchers [later Dewhurst's] was further down St Stephen's, they used to sell lovely sausages, and we used to get delicious cakes from Ashworth's who were bakers. Then there was the Maypole Dairy who sold butter, they'd make pats with wooden paddles.'

Looking along St Stephen's with the Co-op on the left, c.1960

Looking along St Stephen's with M&S on the right, 1953

A hole in St Stephen's about to be filled and become the site of Saxone (now part of M&S), 1954

Magdalen Street

Although well away from the central shopping area around Gentleman's Walk and the Market Place, if you lived to the north of Norwich in the 1950s, going 'down the City' usually meant going to Magdalen Street. Despite its popularity it was somewhat drab. However, in 1959, as the beneficiary of a 'Town Improvement Scheme', the street was given a welcome face-lift. These were the days before the Magdalen Street flyover split the street in two and ruined the ambience of this historic thoroughfare.

Roy Cracknell remembers the street well: 'You could buy anything. Sainsbury's, Woolworths and Frank Prices, were all there. You also had bike shops, fishmongers and butchers, and the list goes on. There was even the Thirty Shilling Tailors, where you could buy a suit for 30 bob – made to measure of course!' Similarly it was a favourite haunt of Lynn Preston and her family: 'There was Thirkettles, a pork butcher, the Dolls' Hospital and "Little" Woolies [Big Woolies was on Rampant Horse Street] where I bought lots of stuff for 6*d*. Also Peacocks – a cheap store that smelt of mould. The shops were not glossy and streamlined like today, and I guess there wasn't much to buy, but my childish impression was not of dullness but of bustle, people, noise and smells.'

In the 1950s, one of the most popular shops on Magdalen Street was the Frank Price department store. Through its long life, it was held in great affection by the people of Norwich. An article that featured in the *Eastern Evening News* in 1954 had nothing but effusive praise for the family-owned store: 'The example of service to the public set by Frank Price is conspicuous even among the dedicated endeavours of the other firms of comparable tradition and repute. The urge to serve is the driving force... that dictates everything that Frank Price undertakes.'

Prices had more than 30 departments, including clothing, footwear, furnishings, linens and hardware. In the days before the internet, the company devised many means to sell goods to customers who were unable to visit the store. For example, shoppers could write in with their requirements and a van was dispatched with a range of items from which they

Magdalen Street after the 'makeover', 1959

could select their purchases. They also put on fashion parades at a range of venues, including the Norwich Industries Club and Caleys. If a girl expressed an interest in a particular product, it would be delivered the next day.

Despite its impressive fittings which included a wrought-iron staircase, mahogany balustrade and a basement with parquet floor and oak panelling, Prices was well down the City's shopping hierarchy. Yet, it stands out as a local shop which was held in great affection in the post-war era.

There are several examples of the owners being very innovative. Take, for example 'The Draw', which was run like a lottery. Agents sold tickets, one of which was selected each week, and the winner was given £5 (equivalent to around £120 today) to spend in the store in their own 'shop currency'. They were also forward thinking in the field of staff welfare. For example, employees took part in profit sharing, and could always put forward their views in an open forum, where they would be sure of a hearing.

As people became more affluent and competition increased, Roy Price (governing director) continued to innovate. In September 1958 he even hit the local headlines when, in response to HP charges being slashed in shops across the City, he took the unprecedented decision to offer interest-free deals. At the time he proudly announced that the store could offer customers five methods of paying for goods: cash; a personal credit account with eight months to pay; a personal credit account which was constantly maintained at eight times the amount of a predetermined monthly payment; hire purchase; and using the firm's 'currency' which had been won through 'The Draw' system.

In 1963, having survived the Blitz, the store was demolished to make way for the Magdalen Street flyover and Anglia Square. A sad end to a much-loved shop with a policy still highly relevant in the 21st century: 'We strive always to give service and civility, We believe in personal service for every customer for every purchase. We want new customers to become regular customers.'

Frank Price, had frontages on Botolph Street (pictured) as well as Magdalen Street, 1948

Larger shops in St Benedict's Street included Walter Mace Footwear and Greens, c.1950

Just as Magdalen Street was favoured by communities that lived to the north of the City, St Benedict's was popular with those who lived to the east.

Although the *City of Norwich Plan* deplored the narrowness of St Benedict's, especially the angled junction with Westwick Street, it acknowledged that it was a good shopping centre. It could have been very different; in 1942 the area around St Benedict's Gates was reduced to rubble during the Baedeker Raids, but luckily the City end emerged almost unscathed.

As these pictures show, the street contained an eclectic range of shops, where you could buy practically anything. Although perhaps not considered an up market-destination, St Benedict's had several speciality shops such as Bretts furniture shop and a men's and boys' outfitters owned by Greens. But primarily it served the local community, with a diverse range of small traditional shops and, of course, more than its fair share of pubs.

Muriel Chilvers often visited St Benedict's: 'After passing Greens, which was a gent's outfitters [42 and 44], you'd come to a special sort of butcher's called the British & Argentine Meat Co. Ltd [40], which as far as I could tell sold nothing but beef. Jarvis [55], was a department store, you almost went into the shop then you turned a corner and there was another little alleyway with an arcade – we thought it very posh.

The Brett family had several shops on St Benedict's Street, c1950

The majority of shops on St Benedict's were small outlets, c.1950

'Moores on the other side of the road [21-23], weren't so big. They were drapers and sold all sorts of things like clothes, curtains and linen.' Meanwhile, Pauline Bell's parents had their own favourite: 'Mother always bought her hats from a wonderful shop called Flori Coopers....At Cookes, which sold musical instruments, my father would be invited to come and try out any new pianos.'

Moores, drapers and outfitters, St Benedict's Street, c.1950

50s Memories

Barbara Miller recalls the Fifty Shilling Tailors on the Haymarket (in the 1950s it became John Collier Tailors): *'My father was very dismissive of the clothes they sold. Eventually I asked him what was wrong with it, and he replied: "They don't measure you for a suit, they just stand you up against the wall and chalk it out around you!"'*

Muriel Chilvers recalls: *'There was a definite pecking order in the City shops. I used to like to go to Curls, because it lay between the really posh shops, which I couldn't afford, and the rather tatty shops, which I didn't like. To me, Curls was quite nice, you could get all sorts of things there.'*

Glenna St Quintin remembers buying a television: *'We bought it from Carrs, a shop which also sold bikes and radios, on Golden Ball Street. For some reason Jock Carr always wore a plastic neck tie.'*

On Sundays, evenings and Thursday afternoons many City-centre shops were closed. This gave rise to an interesting pastime, as Albert Cooper explains: 'Although my mum and dad rarely went into the City to shop, the big thing for them was window shopping. All shop lights would be on until around 11 o'clock at night, and mum and dad would say, "We're going window shopping this evening." They'd just go for a walk around, and look at the things they would have liked to buy if they could've afforded them.'

Window shopping wasn't exclusive to the older generation. Avis Brown recalls wandering around the City with her sisters and friends in the evenings and it being full of people just looking in the shop windows. The same happened on Sundays when Sylvia Buxton and her friends followed a very specific route: 'We started outside the Castle Museum and then walked around the top of the Castle Mound and down Prince of Wales Road. The shops were shut, but we enjoyed window shopping. There were shoals of us. We rounded off the day with a trip to the cinema.'

Stump Cross, c.1955

Food, Glorious Food

Shortages and Rationing

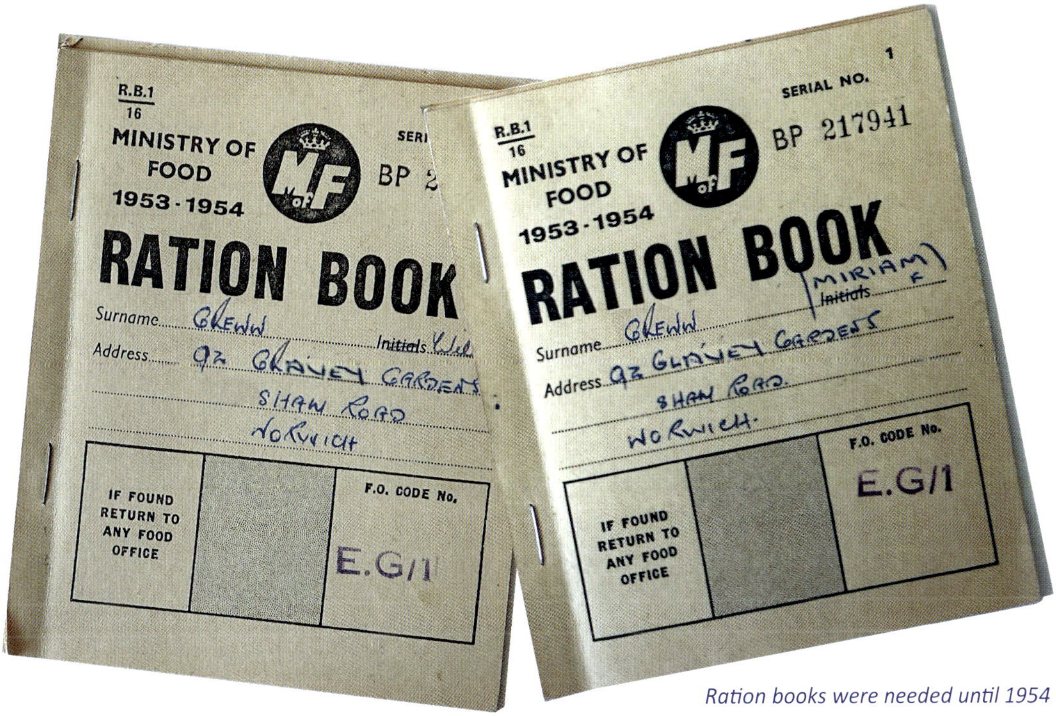

Ration books were needed until 1954

The good news is that in 1950 the British diet was pretty nutritious; in fact, many dieticians argue that as a result of rationing the nation's eating habits were amongst the healthiest they had ever been. Food rationing, which was not abolished until 1954, resulted in the average diet containing sufficient (but not excessive) protein and energy, whilst being relatively low in sugar and fat.

The bad news is that for 14 years the country had been put on an enforced diet. The position was so bad, that donors from America and Canada began sending food parcels to Britain. Sylvia Buxton recalls that '...getting a food parcel was a real treat. We had things like sweets, tins of fruit and stuff like that. We saw them as luxuries.'

It is particularly disheartening to know that food rationing ended in Germany on 6 January 1950. Not only did it continue in victorious Britain for another four years, but in some cases it became worse. Take, for example, bread. It had not been rationed during the war, but in July 1946 bread rationing was introduced and it remained in force for two years. The *Daily Mail* reported that it was 'the most hated measure ever to have been presented to the people of this country'.

Later, following a dispute with Argentina, the source of much of our imported beef, the meat ration which had been set at one shilling and sixpence in 1945, was slashed to eight pennies in 1951.

Adaptation was the name of the game, and there were lots of tips on how to make the best of what was available. Barbara Miller's mother was always on the look-out for suggestions: 'There were endless recipes where scarce ingredients were swapped for something which wasn't rationed, and you were told how to cook it to make it taste like something you couldn't get. Offal wasn't rationed, and I still remember a recipe for ox heart, which said if you soaked it overnight in milk and then fried it gently, it would taste like duck. I can you tell now...it didn't. It tasted like ox heart!'

To combat food shortages homeowners were encouraged to 'dig for victory'. In Norwich, as elsewhere, gardens were given over to vegetable patches, the more enterprising also kept animals. Muriel Chilvers benefitted from having a father with green fingers: 'Our family didn't really experience any hardship through food rationing. Dad was a milkman, and so we always had our milk. We lived in a council house on Ripley Close, off Elizabeth Fry Road, where we had an eighth-of-an-acre garden, and my father was an accomplished and enthusiastic gardener, which meant that we always had fruit and vegetables. He also kept rabbits and chickens, and so we always had a ready supply of meat and eggs.'

Arthur Holmes soon found out about rationing when he returned to Norwich from his wartime national service: 'When I first came home [1946] there was very little in the shops: you especially noticed it at Christmas. One of the first shocks I had was when my mother asked what I'd like to eat and I said that I'd love a cheese sandwich – I hadn't had any cheese for a couple of years or more. She gave me the sandwich which I enjoyed very much and after I finished it she said: "Did you know that you've just eaten a week's ration?" That gave me a real jolt! People seemed to take rationing for granted. They'd got used to it and just got on with it. I didn't notice much in the way of a black market, but if people heard that something was available in a shop, they flocked there.'

Unsurprisingly, the nation rebelled. The Tory propaganda machine, aware of the public's anger and frustration, featured a match-box sized meat ration across its posters in their 1951 election campaign. There is little doubt that rationing contributed to the subsequent defeat of the Labour Government. Women were particularly fed up with ration coupons, and the interminable queueing they generated, and they turned against the Labour Party in huge numbers.

In 1953, the Food Minister, Gwilym Lloyd-George, made derationing a priority. In that year, he took sweets, eggs, cream, butter, cheese, margarine and cooking fats off the ration books. The following year, restrictions on the sale and purchase of meat and bacon were lifted, and then on 4 July 1954 the BBC could report that members of the London Housewives' Association had held a special ceremony in Trafalgar Square to mark 'Derationing Day'.

Would this happen today?

Sylvia Buxton's mother was a very good cook, but would her money-making venture pass today's health and safety rules?: *'When apples came into season mum used to make sticks out of a bit of kindling and make toffee apples. All of the kids used to queue up in the street and buy them for threepence each. Her toffee wasn't like that old sticky stuff you often get today, it was hard, and crunchy. There was always a big blob on the end of the apple – the kids got plenty of toffee...they loved that.'*

Memories

Avis Brown, lived in a new council house on Woodcock Road (Catton Grove), and her family never went short of meat: *'Our back garden was full of animals that we reared for food: we had things like rabbits, chickens and cockerels. My brother, Brian, even brought home a little pig once, but my mother made him take it back. It was a massive back garden and we had hutches all the way down both sides, and there were chickens at the bottom. We all looked after them. I had a favourite, a rabbit which was mine. Then one day I came home and it wasn't there! Brian waited until we were eating our dinner then said, "You're eating your rabbit." I started to cry, and mother said, "No it isn't. Your rabbit died. This is not your rabbit." But of course, years later when I was grown up she admitted that it was my rabbit. My friend Brenda's father, who lived two doors down, slaughtered the animals for us. We all used to sit in the kitchen plucking the chickens into a big metal tub. We never threw out the feathers they were all used to stuff pillow cases. Many of our neighbours also kept chickens and rabbits, which unfortunately meant that we were also plagued by rats.'*

Barbara and Martin Miller married in 1951 when rationing was still on, but they did not let it spoil their day: *'The hotel had a certain amount of food coming in and they used to say whether they could do an event or not and let you know how many you could invite. Food was far less elaborate. I mean for a wedding you'd have ham and salad probably followed by a fruit salad with Ideal Milk, plus, of course, a wedding cake.'*

During rationing one of the biggest hardships for many children was having to do without sweets. Albert Cooper recalls: *'I used to cut a Mars bar, my ration for the month, into tiny slivers to make it last.'* ***Meanwhile, Avis Brown was more devious:*** *'When mum wasn't looking I'd dip bread into the sugar bowl. Because sugar was also rationed I got into trouble if she saw me. I was sweet crazy, but I think that you always are for something you can't have.'*

In the post-rationing era there was a huge choice of sweets, Stephanie Brooks was given half-a-crown on a Friday evening: *'I'd use this to buy a bottle of Corona for one and threepence from the Corona delivery man. I'd then go round to the sweet shop and buy black jacks, flying saucers, sherbert dabs, rhubarb and custard or pineapple chunks.'*

Grocery Shopping

The change in shopping habits is clearly illustrated in how we bought groceries. In 1945 self-service stores were few and far between. Instead, in most food shops customers queued up to give an order to an assistant who fetched their purchases.

There is some dispute as to when and indeed which organisation opened the first British supermarket. One of the earliest pioneers and advocates was the London Co-operative Society, which opened a self-service shop in 1942. Subsequently, in 1948 they launched what is reputed to be the UK's first full-scale supermarket in Manor Park, London. The new store, which followed the lead of American food stores, would have seemed very alien to shoppers who were not used to helping themselves. The main pros and cons of the new style of shopping were outlined in the *Advertising and Marketing* magazine, where it was noted: 'From the point of view of the customer the chief advantages of self-service shopping are the speed with which shopping can be done and the ease with which one is reminded of things needed....It seems to be generally agreed that these advantages substantially outweigh the disadvantages of not getting the personal attention of the assistant.' The public agreed, and throughout the 1950s more food chains introduced supermarkets: Sainsbury's (Croydon) in 1950, Waitrose (Streatham) by 1955, and Tesco (Maldon, Essex) in 1958. In 1956 there were only 3000 self-service grocery shops in Britain, by 1967 there were 24,000.

Amazingly, even at the end of the 1950s Norwich did not have one supermarket. However, we did have 'multiple grocers', with some self-service counters. Amongst their number was Sainsbury's, which had stores on both the Haymarket and Magdalen Street. Albert Cooper often visited the Haymarket store: 'It was a wonderful shop. You entered a huge hallway with big marble counters which stretched the full length down both sides. You'd have all the different trades, including the butchers, the bakers and the fishmongers. At the dairy counter they'd pat your butter up, and then wrap it up; it wasn't pre-packed.'

Another 'multiple grocer' was the International Stores. This chain had a number of premises located around Norwich, including London Street, Magdalen Road and the Haymarket. Similar to Sainsbury's, not only did shoppers queue at different counters to buy goods, they paid at each one as they were served.

The International Stores, Haymarket, 1956

Alongside such stores there were many more specialist food shops than we typically have today. These included Mac Fisheries, the fishmonger, located on the Haymarket next door to the Curate House restaurant. Martin Miller recalls it well: 'The front of the store, where they put their display, was all sloping marble. Underneath was a water tank, where they had fish, particularly eels, swimming around.'

Also, we must not forget, that this was a time when Norwich Market was a provision market. Of the approximately 200 stalls, about 80 sold fruit and vegetable, whilst a general assortment of other traders sold goods such as groceries, flowers, fish, drapery and books.

At a time when few households had fridges many people shopped every day for perishable items, and so local shops thrived. More goods were also delivered, as observed by Roy Cracknell: 'You didn't do huge shops at a supermarket, like you do now. You used to do "small shopping". Most of the terraced streets had corner shops....You also had quite a lot delivered, such as milk and bread.' Albert Cooper goes on to say: 'I lived on William Street. The area I lived was bounded by Heigham Road, Earlham Road, Grapes Hill and Dereham Road. In that big square we had everything. We had corner shops, where you could buy almost anything, and so like other people we did most of our shopping locally.'

Would this happen today?

Although we may now decry excessive health and safety legislation around food handling, in 1951 a series of allegations was made to the Norwich City Council which illustrate why rules are necessary.

The Council were particularly concerned that it was becoming commonplace for food handlers to smoke whilst working. They noted the danger of nicotine poisoning caused by them both coughing over food and from the alternate handling of cigarettes and foodstuffs. They recommended putting up notices asking food handlers not only to wash their hands but also not to smoke on the job; interestingly, they did not seem to consider asking the handlers not to cough over food. Obviously it was well before the enlightened times when it was known, 'coughs and sneezes spread diseases'.

Looking at a more isolated case, the Council also discussed the 'shocking conditions under which some lollipops were made...[We found] one shop where if a person returned 20 lollipop sticks he was given a free lollipop.' It is good to note that the Council's Health Committee confirmed they were going to stop 'that sort of thing'.

Corner shops, West Pottergate and Laurence Street, undated

Eating In

As rationing came to an end food became more plentiful, but meals were often monotonous. Barbara Miller sums up the position: 'Both during and after the war food was boring. A main meal was normally meat and two veg.'

This was also the era of spam fritters, commonly eaten with chips and mushy peas. For tea (evening meal) sandwiches of tinned salmon followed by tinned fruit with evaporated milk was a rare treat. Crisps came in one flavour: plain. You were even left to add your own salt, from a little blue bag found in the packet.

But times were changing, as epitomised by the new 'celebrity chefs'. One of the first food broadcasters was Marguerite Patten. In her early career she worked for the Ministry of Food, where she taught the nation's housewives how to create, wholesome, thrifty recipes out of rationed ingredients, including such delicacies as powdered eggs and spam. However, as the 1950s progressed, rationing eased, incomes rose, and recipes became more inventive. Now Marguerite began to teach the British public how to bake such novelties as quiche and baked Alaska. New presenters arrived on our screens, including Fanny Craddock who encouraged cooks to be flamboyant and adventurous. Meanwhile, as more exotic ingredients, such as aubergines and garlic, became available, the cookery writer Elizabeth David rose in popularity. It was under her influence that the British were introduced to the delights of Mediterranean food.

Memories

Lynn Preston's main meals were typical of many families: *'We had the same dish on the same day each week and so it's easy to remember: Sunday was a roast; Monday, cold meat with potatoes, gravy, tinned processed peas; Tuesday was always fish and chips, which we bought at Brighties at the bottom of Livingstone Street; Wednesday, we had meat pattie with mash and gravy and probably cabbage or shepherd's pie (always with mince); Thursday, the meal varied but we had a lot of pig's fry or other offal like liver, chitterlings or pork cheese. Food was nourishing and tasty but not what we would eat today.'*

Eating Out

Takeaway food in the 1950s was almost exclusively fish and chips. There were many such outlets around Norwich, amongst the most popular was a small chain owned by the Valori family.

Dining out was a luxury in terms of cost, rather than the quality of the cuisine. This meant that restaurants were rare, on the other hand cafés were commonplace. Having a meal in a pub was not an option: you went to a pub to drink not eat. However, as time moved on eating out became more adventurous.

This was partly in response to an expanding youth market, which in turn was influenced by American trends. Initially there was a growth in coffee and milk bars, then in 1954 the country's first Wimpy Bar was opened. It is somewhat surprising, that this American import first opened in a very British institution: Lyons, the well-known café chain that operated Corner Houses across the country. Although originally set up as a fast-food section in Lyons, they proved so successful that soon independent Wimpy Bars appeared.

Valoris, Dereham Road, looking up Grapes Hill, c.1959

The following year the country's first Berni restaurant was opened in Bristol. Here, diners could splash out eight shillings to enjoy the delights of prawn cocktail, followed by steak and chips, finishing with Black Forest gateau. Another Bristish icon was launched in the 1950s: the Little Chef. It was in 1958, inspired by the American roadside diner, that the caravan maker Sam Alper set up the first Little Chef Restaurant in Reading: it later grew to be the largest roadside chain in the country.

But were the people of Norwich enjoying such culinary delights?

Amongst Norwich's most popular cafés was the Lyons Tea Room on Gentleman's Walk. As a young girl Lynn Preston was a regular visitor: 'The ground floor sold cakes and upstairs there was a café. The cakes were awful – synthetic cream and very sickly – but I loved the café with its art-deco design, great big mirrors and a lovely staircase.' Stephanie Brooks used to go with her mother every Saturday morning: 'It was a good old-fashioned tea shop. You'd go upstairs, and there'd be these waitresses in their little white hats and pinafores, over black dresses. They'd write your order on a pad with a little pencil that hung on a string from their waist. You'd give your order for your drink, then they'd wheel up a tea trolley with all these cakes on it: it was a wonderful array. You'd pick what you wanted and the waitress would serve it to you on a little plate; she didn't pick the cake up with her fingers, she'd use little silver tongs.'

Another very popular café was Lamberts Oriental Café (LOC), which was located on London Street in the basement of Lamberts confectionery and tobacconist shop. Until 1960 the LOC was a male-only preserve. Even after women were accepted, they were reportedly made to feel unwelcome by the regulars. The café was particularly popular with local businesses and professional firms, many of whom met here to cement business deals.

Lyons Tea Room, Gentleman's Walk, c.1960

A number of the City's department stores, including Jarrolds and Garlands, also had cafés. Unsurprisingly, a very definite hierarchy evolved, as recalled by John Chilvers: 'There were some fascinating social nuances, in that my nanny and grandad on my mum's side would take me into Woolworths for a cup of tea and a cake, but my mum and dad never would, they saw it as a little bit down-market, they could afford to do better, and so went to Jarrolds. Just occasionally if nan and grandad were feeling flush we'd go to Buntings, but only if mum was able to give me a real treat would we go to Garlands. As a lad, the quality of the cakes was very important to me.'

Of course the youngsters had their own cafés where they used to hang out. To the City's older citizens, the new teenage cafés represented the youth culture and were not favoured. The Boundary Buttery (Aylsham Road), was seen as a nuisance by locals, but was very popular well into the 1960s as a rendezvous for teenage motor-cyclists. Colin Buxton met his pals at the Blue Bat, on Upper King Street: 'That's where all the Teddy boys used to hang out. Next door was an amusement arcade. Some bikers came in, but they mostly went to the Boundary Buttery Café. It wasn't rough in the Blue Bat, we used to go there to drink coffee and listen to records on a juke box. It was just a social meeting place.'

In 1957 what is believed to be Norwich's first Wimpy hamburger was sold at Paul's Espresso Coffee Bar. Then in 1959 the Soochow was the first Chinese restaurant to open in the City. Interestingly, both ventures were located on Prince of Wales Road. Like today the street was vibrant. Maurice Morson recalls: 'In my day, even before I joined the police force, Prince of Wales Road was known as the chicken run, because the girls used to go down one side and the boys down the other. Then the Chinese restaurants came: now that livened things up. It was a big event for Norwich, having a Chinese restaurant.'

IN THE NEWS

In November 1956 the 'Eastern Evening News' informed its readers about a new form of party which was catching on fast: 'Simple to arrange and cheaper than cocktails, it is sure to be popular at Christmas. Instead of cocktails or sherry... give a wine and cheese party'

The article gave much helpful advice to prospective hosts, including such gems as: 'Don't worry too much about marrying off the wine and cheese; like the father of daughters, be not particular.' The writer seemed more concerned about presentation than matching flavours, advising hosts that: 'The cheeses look well on straw mats or lettuce leaves garnished with cucumbers and tomatoes. Slices of French bread should be ready in wicker-work baskets – there is no need for plates and forks.'

Did You know?

The Wimpy brand was created in 1935 by Edward Gold when he opened his first location in Bloomington, Indiana. The name was inspired by the character of J. Wellington Wimpy who featured in the Popeye cartoons.

Corner of London Street and Exchange Street, c.1960

The 1940s: Austerity

RAF personnel waiting to be demobbed, 1945

As WWII came to an end, what did people look like? How did they dress?

One of the noticeable changes in attire during the conflict had been the number of people wearing uniform. It is estimated that around 25% of the British population was entitled to wear one, either as part of the armed or women's auxiliary forces or as a member of the many voluntary organisations that proliferated at the time. Increased demand for uniforms, coupled with general shortages in supplies put a huge pressure on the country's textile and clothing industries. In June 1941, as a means of introducing both a fair distribution of clothing and improving the availability of garments in the shops, clothes were put on ration, and they stayed on ration until 1949.

Rationing worked by allocating each type of clothing a number of 'points' which in turn were based on how much material and labour went into its manufacture, for example, 11 coupons were needed for a dress and two for stockings. Initially, each 'standard' adult was given 66 points, but in both 1945 and 1946 the basic allocation was reduced to 24 coupons per year, which was just sufficient for a man to buy one pair of trousers, a shirt and a pair of shoes. Although extra coupons were given to selected groups, including children and some manual workers, inevitably new clothing was at a premium. In response the Government launched a 'Make-do and Mend' campaign, giving advice on the care of clothes, how to renovate your existing garments and also how to make clothes. Whilst rationing remained in place people became quite ingenious: old clothes were recycled, furnishing fabrics were used for dressmaking (until these too became rationed), blackout material, which wasn't rationed, had many uses. Barbara Miller recalls: 'During rationing, many people refurbished and trimmed up old clothes to give them a new lease of life, I even made a skirt out of my father's old grey flannel trousers. When I was first at the Norwich Union I can remember seeing ladies knitting. At the time (*c*.1948) balls of wool were on ration but darning wool, which was cut into pieces about three foot long, wasn't. So women knitted entire jumpers out of these short lengths, because that was all they could get. Of course, it took forever to sew the ends in.'

Rationing did not make clothes cheaper. Each item had the same points value, regardless of price and quality. Wealthier shoppers could afford to buy well-made garments which would last, those on lower incomes did not have that luxury. To address this issue, in 1942 the Government introduced Utility clothing which offered consumers a range of well-designed, practical, durable, mass-produced clothing. The Government even used high-end fashion designers to create the clothes. The Utility scheme did not end until 1952, it was a product of the war, but like so many other enforced changes it impacted society for years to come. In particular, it gave consumers the confidence to demand value for money and also led to consistent standards in materials.

50s Memories

Whilst working at the Fifty Shilling Tailors (the Haymarket) Albert Cooper soon found that there were ways of working around rationing: *'The cheapest suit you could get after the war was £4 10s. Because of rationing you also needed coupons. We had one assistant who was just like the spiv, Private Walker, in "Dad's Army". Some customer would come in and say: "Ooh, I can afford it, but I haven't got enough coupons." So this guy would say, "Don't worry about that; I can sell you some." He'd always have a supply in his top pocket. You see, people would sell on their coupons, and so he was a bit like a broker. Every one made a little profit each time they changed hands. There was a lot sold on the black market in 1948. The assistant used to come in with supplies of food, such as butter, and we'd all form a little queue at the top of the stairs down into the cellar to buy it.'*

The 1950s: Prosperity

In the 1950s a series of events revolutionised clothes and the way they were bought. Change became the order of the day, not just for the rich and titled, but also for the 'ordinary' man (and woman) on the street. After years of deprivation, Brits of all ages lapped up the new fashions.

One of the most important factors influencing the fashion scene was the introduction of new materials. Artificial materials had been known about for some time and had been essential to the war effort, but in the 1950s they were produced on a large scale, which dramatically increased supply and lowered costs. Many of these new materials offered huge advantages over natural products, in particular they were often cheaper and easier to style and wash, especially if households had electric washing machines and irons. Take, for example, nylon. Nylon was first made in the 1930s, but during the war its main use was for military equipment, including parachutes, ropes and tyres. Although nylon was synonymous with 'stockings', the advantages of nylon underwear were soon recognised: its easy-washing, shrink-proof, hard-wearing qualities were all promoted. Another increasingly popular material was Terylene (Dacron in the USA). Like nylon it was easy to wash and was crease resistant, but it could take permanent pleats which meant it didn't need to be ironed. The cloth was lightweight but warm, making it ideal for men's tailored items, particularly suits.

At the same time, the days of bespoke tailoring were drawing to a close. Mass-production techniques and processes, which proved so effective in wartime to fill bulk orders for clothing, were now used to meet domestic demand. Faced with the growing importance of the ready-to-wear market, manufacturers started to offer the standard sizes and better quality which people had become used to with Utility clothing. Mass-production also brought down costs at a time when the country was moving to a period of relative prosperity. Glossy magazines and films promoted the new fashions, which were now affordable. People began to believe they really could dress like their movie idols.

Did You know?

Utility clothing was subject to 'austerity' regulations, which restricted how much material was used. For example, a maximum length was prescribed for men's shirts, whilst a ban on turn-ups for men's trousers was introduced.

Fashion show, Tivetshall, 1955

Ladies' Fashions

Fashion model, Chamberlins, 1951

In the late 1940s the basic outfit for a lady was a knee-length dress or suit. In 1947, Dior's 'New Look', typified by full skirts and slim-fitting bodices, was launched and continued to influence many designs through the 1950s. However, there were many variations on the theme with new designs – complete with gimmicky names – constantly appearing on the high street. These included: the tight-fitting sheath dress; the trumpet coat, which clung down to the knees and then flared to a mid-calf-length hemline; and the uninspiringly christened sack dress. First appearing in 1957, the sack started the trend for straighter, waistless shift dresses. There was some consternation in the Norwich press when the design featured in Garlands autumn fashion show of the same year when a dismayed reporter wrote: 'The fashion dictators have caught up with the women of Norwich. "The sack line" has arrived in the City.... Audiences are always unpredictable. Yesterday they regarded the sack line nervously, hesitantly. But, say the despotic fashion designers, women will be wearing it tomorrow. And the day when the sack, in all its glory, will be seen on the streets of Norwich and Norfolk, is not far distant.'

IN THE NEWS

May 1955: *A fashion parade was held at Garlands store when a reporter from the 'Eastern Evening News' declared that beachwear had 'never been more gay and amusing'. Denim featured in a variety of guises, including 'a well-cut sun-top, a button-through dress tailored in green...[and] a clerical grey town dress smartly pleated and trimmed with white.' Meantime, the use of nylon went from the sublime to the ridiculous when it featured in both 'practical summer housecoats' and 'softly striped in grey for a "special-occasion" frock with a floating full skirt'.*

November 1956: *The 'Eastern Evening News' proclaimed, 'Pleats are for everyone.' Although they extolled the washing qualities and attractiveness of 'pleated permutations', the article held a note of warning: 'Gathers around the midriff look well on a 23-inch waist, but for one of more ample measurements a cummerbund which is folded in lateral pleats is far more slimming.'*

March 1959: *There was particular excitement for the fashion conscious when the local press announced that Dior hats were in Norwich for the first time. The hats, which featured in Garlands Spring Fashion Show, included: 'A turquoise turban of straw and veiling, trimmed with a white rose low on the right cheek, and an off-the-face cap made entirely of pure-silk poppies in bright nasturtium colours.' It was also reported that favourite colours of the season included 'nasturtium, apricot, pumpkin and orange sherbert'.*

Would this happen today?

On 11 September 1951 the 'Evening Eastern News' carried this advert from Chamberlins store for a promotion of furs:

'Mannequins will model the latest styles daily. The autumn collection of furs especially created by our London furriers will be displayed in our windows and salons and many interesting Utility models will be featured...During the week an expert furrier will be in attendance to give free advice and estimates for the remodelling, renovating and redyeing of your own fur.'

Fashion Tips

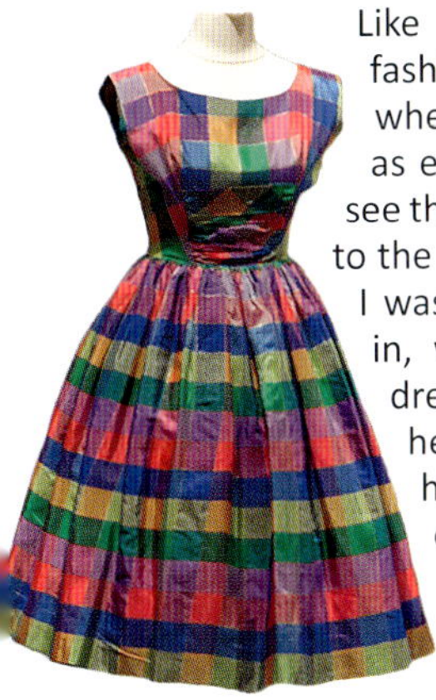

Like today, keeping up with the fashions was not always easy, but where there is a will there is a way, as explained by Avis Brown: 'We'd see the outfits in films when we went to the cinema, and copy them. When I was 15, because rock 'n' roll was in, we had the flouncy, bouffant dresses with full skirts which were held out by petticoats. I wore half a dozen petticoats under one dress, because that was the in-thing at the time. The petticoats were made out of net and the more you had the more your dress flowed out, almost like a ballerina. Although starch would make the netting stiff, it wouldn't make it stand out how we wanted. So our mothers used to mix up sugar with hot water, then they dipped the netting in the mixture and hung it on the line to dry. After that it really did stick out and you could arrange the netting just how you wanted it. We all used to laugh when we went out and said: "Don't sit on the grass, 'cos if you do all the ants will come after the sugar in your petticoat."

'After the flouncy dresses, we wore what I called the smart fashion, with very narrow pencil skirts which came down to the calf of your leg. They were really tight. We had jackets to match, and so the outfit looked like a suit. We didn't wear hats, but I never went out without a pair of earrings. I had millions of button earrings, of all different colours. We wore matching gloves and shoes and carried walking umbrellas. I had loads of walking umbrellas, which I dyed to match my outfits. I hardly ever put them up, I used them more like a walking stick. I'd mince up the street with the umbrella, wearing a pair of gloves and matching shoes, looking all posh. I must say, we used to have one heck of a job getting on the bus, because the step up was quite high and our skirts were very narrow. You couldn't step forward onto the bus without hitching your skirt above your knees, and of course you weren't going to do that, and so you used to have to get on sideways. So you can imagine the problems we had going upstairs!

'We thought that we were very sophisticated and elegant, but my mother wasn't impressed. When she saw me walking up the road, she used to say that I looked like a little Japanese woman, because the skirts were so tight at the bottom I could only take half a step at a time. But I didn't care because I wanted to be in all the fashions.'

Horrockses Dress

Founded in 1946, throughout the 1950s Horrockses Fashions was one of the most respected ready-to-wear labels. The company concentrated on the production of superior women's wear and children's attire. They put great emphasis on high-quality cotton fabrics printed with patterns designed by contemporary artists, such as Graham Sutherland.

Swimwear

In 1946 The French engineer Louis Reard invented the bikini. Rather crassly he is believed to have named it after the Bikini Atoll in the Pacific – the site of a nuclear bomb test in 1946 – because he hoped its impact would be as explosive. However, most women in the 1950s continued to wear all-in-one swimwear: wearing a bikini was seen as very daring.

Manufacturers were aware that as swimsuits became more revealing, women were demanding garments that enhanced their shape: many women had no intention of swimming in their costumes – they wanted to look good on the beach. Just like today costumes of the time often incorporated tummy control panels, boning and bra cups, but they also incorporated a zip – either in the centre back or up the side. They were basically designed as a corset.

Glenna St Quintin, 1955

Ladies' Shoes

In the 1950s, a number of styles came and went.

As skirts became shorter, heels became higher and decorated with embellishments, such as jewels, stitching or lace. In particular, it is the decade which witnessed the birth of the stiletto heel. The shoe designer Ferragamo is usually credited with the introduction of a steel support in a synthetic heel that facilitated the very small steel tip essential to a stiletto, but early versions of the heel combined wood with steel. In Norwich, Bruce Rampley recalls that the shoe manufacturer, Edwards & Holmes, introduced a variation on this theme – with questionable success: 'When stilettos first came out plastic heels weren't available, so they were made of wood. Wood isn't as strong as plastic so the stiletto heels often broke. Somebody sold the manager the idea of copper plating the heels, which we did for our shoes and also for other firms. It worked, but eventually the heels got a little spiky and had to be ground down!'

Another style introduced in the decade was the winklepicker – the bizarre name derived from its resemblance to the pointed tool used to pull winkles from their shells. Although the style reached its height of popularity in the 1960s, in the 1950s it was a favourite with youngsters who enjoyed rock music.

In addition to such extreme styles variations on court shoes were a staple, whilst ballerina shoes were popular with all ages. Also, as more people went on holiday, casual shoes and sandals became an important part of a lady's wardrobe.

Alongside new designs, up-to-the-minute materials were used to create a variety of styles. These included lurex – a glittery, unbreakable, untarnishable thread – that was incorporated into evening shoes.

Many Norwich manufacturers made high-quality fashion shoes. Some of the finest were made by Edwards & Holmes. The firm had a number of gimmicks to promote their wares, amongst which was a display called 'the magic birdcage', for which the company made special shoes which were exceptionally attractive, but were hardly wearable. It used to travel around the country to the major department stores which sold their footwear.

Examples of beautiful shoes made by Norwich firms, are pictured here. Further examples are on display in the Museum of Norwich at the Bridewell.

In the 1950s many shoe shops X-rayed customers' feet using a pedoscope with the aim of ensuring well-fitted shoes. They were only phased out when the dangers of radiation were held to outweigh the benefits of comfortable footwear.

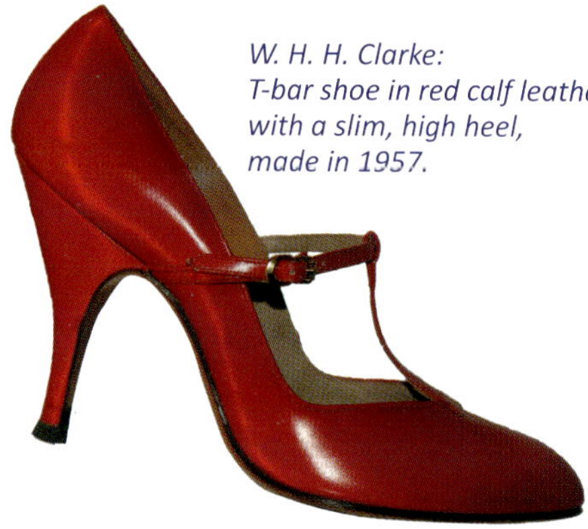

W. H. H. Clarke: T-bar shoe in red calf leather with a slim, high heel, made in 1957.

Edwards & Holmes: Court shoe in blue and purple with bow containing cut beads, made in the late 1950s.

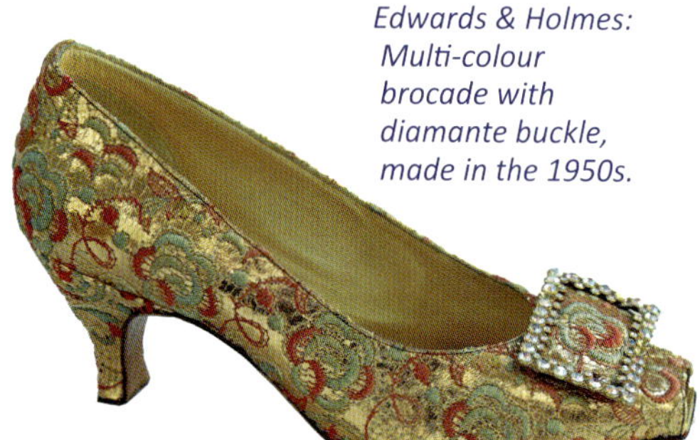

Edwards & Holmes: Multi-colour brocade with diamante buckle, made in the 1950s.

James Southall: Sandal in gold leather, made in 1950.

Men's Fashions

In 1950 a basic outfit for most men consisted of a suit, shirt and tie. For less formal occasions the suit may have given way to jacket and flannels and maybe a sleeveless jumper, but a tie was still normally worn. The usual garb for outdoors consisted of a knee-length macintosh or heavy coat paired with a trilby hat or flat cap. Such outfits were even worn for leisure activities, such as an outing to the seaside (in which case it was allowable to roll trousers up), or for a trip to Carrow Road, as observed by Sylvia Buxton: 'When I lived down Mariners Lane (1942 to 1960) and there was a football match on a Saturday, I'd look out the window and see loads of men on their way to see the Canaries. They were all dressed the same: in the old-fashioned macs and caps, maybe with a scarf. It was as though they were in a uniform. It was really a sight to see.'

As the decade progressed, light-weight suits in pastel shades made in synthetic fibres became increasingly popular. In 1955 in an attempt to promote such a modern range, Harmers, the Norwich-based clothing manufacturer, laid down the gauntlet to the local journalist known as the Whiffer, when they challenged him to be photographed on London Street wearing a pair of their new range of trousers. This doesn't sound too daunting, until it was reported that the garments in question were made of rayon gaberdine and produced in either 'bra pink' or 'sky blue'. It is unclear if the Whiffler rose to the bait, despite being offered a pair in a 'more sober grey or brown' as a reward.

Not all men conformed to such stereotypes; young men, especially teenagers, wanted to express themselves more flamboyantly.

Roy Cracknell (left), dressed for the beach, Cromer, c.1950

Teenagers' Fashions

The 1950s saw the birth of the teenager: for the first time this group of young people had spare cash from paid work to spend on non-essentials. They set their own agenda and wanted to separate themselves from the world of adults. They took their lead from popular culture: rock 'n' roll heroes such as Elvis Presley and film stars like James Dean. Teenage style was expressed in many ways,: particularly in the clothes they wore.

Sylvia and Colin Buxton step out in style in the 1950s

Young men may have dressed as 'greasers', wearing jeans and biker jackets, a look inspired by Marlon Brando in *The Wild One* (1953). Others sported the Teddy boy look. The Teds wore long draped jackets, often with velvet trim collars and pocket flaps, drainpipe trousers, waistcoats and narrow ties. On their feet they sported Day-Glo coloured socks and suede 'brothel creepers', with thick crepe soles. Their elegantly coiffed hair would be styled into a D.A. (see page 140) and they finished the look with long sideburns. First spotted in London's East End in 1952, the following year it was the *Daily Express* that christened followers of this fashion 'Teddy boys', the name deriving from their Edwardian-inspired clothes. Although sometimes seen as bad boys, many young Teds, like Colin Buxton, just enjoyed dressing up: 'I was a sort of Teddy boy, though I had more of an Italian style. I had a powder-blue suit, with drainpipe trousers and a long jacket which I had made by a tailor in Old Palace Road – it didn't have the velvet lapels, or anything like that. I wore it with a white shirt and a shoestring tie. I was also rather proud of my suede shoes and of course I had my hair cut in a D.A. As a young lad I thought I looked very smart.'

Young girls may have adopted a 'preppie' look. Preppies were exceptionally neat. Their wardrobe ranged from a full dirndl skirt, worn with T-shirts or sweaters with large appliqués, to tight-fitting blouses tucked into 'Capri' pants or 'pedal pushers'. Short ankle socks and scarves tied around the neck completed the ensemble.

50s Memories A Norwich Tailor

Albert Cooper *is well-known in the City as an entertainer, but back in 1948, when he was 15, he started work at the Fifty Shilling Tailors (on the corner of White Lion Street and the Haymarket). Albert explains: 'When I started I was "the boy". Even then I had to wear a black jacket and striped trousers, like a solicitor. I had to sweep the floor, card up the cloths, brush the shoulders of the jackets, and just do the mundane jobs like get the coffee for the men. As time moved on I learnt to measure: I'm still pretty good at it now. I can shorten trousers, sleeves: you learnt things like that.*

'I liked the Teddy boys. I used to measure them up for their suits. They'd come in looking for bright colours, with contrasting velvet collars and pocket trims. We tended to use the same cloths that we used to make women's costumes [suits].

'We measured up in the shop, but the suits were made in our Leeds factory. We did do alterations and "customise" suits. Dealers often came to us to put big chamois leather pockets in their jackets. It was where they put their money, and so they needed them made out of something that wouldn't wear out.

'The company made suits and slacks (we never called them trousers) for ladies. For men, the two or three-piece suit was always the favourite. There were various jacket and trouser designs, but the trousers were normally 21 inches wide across the hem; for Teddy boys the width was reduced to 14 inches. The Italian look became very popular after Perry Como became famous. Then men wanted box jackets, a "Norman Wisdom" jacket if you will, but quite full. Everyone dressed so much smarter then. Men all wore suits, or a sports jacket and flannels for the week ends.

'I loved the rag trade. I did it for 17 years. The end came with jeans. Stores like the Fifty Bob Tailors didn't keep up with the times, and many shops like that just went out of business. '

The Fifty Shilling Tailors, 1950

Children's clothes

Children were typically dressed like 'mini-adults'.

Paul Warr describes a typical boy's outfit: 'As lads we were dressed up in our finery on a Saturday to go to the City. For us, finery constituted a short pair of trousers, a cap, a shirt and tie, a tank top, polished shoes, and a pair of socks which came up to our knees.' Even when they went out to play, grey shorts, a shirt and tank top were often the order of the day, although after 12 you'd progress to long trousers.

Girls would typically wear dresses and a cardigan, or a skirt and jumper. For their Sunday best they may have had a smart coat and matching hat and for parties a pretty frock. If they were lucky beach wear for girls was a ruched swimming costume, if they weren't it was knitted. As many soon found out woollen swimwear had a major design fault – it drooped when it was wet!

Lynn Preston in her Sunday best, c.1954

Eileen Page Dance School, 1947

Lynn Preston (front row, second from the right) and friends dressed for a party, c.1954

Children's party, City Stadium, 1950

Hairstyles

Through the 1950s both men and women experimented with new styles. They were often influenced by celebrities, especially American film stars. A permanent wave, as favoured by Elizabeth Taylor and Queen Elizabeth II, was particularly popular amongst the more sophisticated – helped on its way by the introduction of home perms.

Meanwhile, the new teenagers took their lead from their rock 'n' roll heroes. The girls sported ponytails, and the boys crew cuts, whilst those with a rebellious streak favoured greaser comb backs or a D.A.

The introduction of new hair-styling products had a huge effect on fashion. As improved hair lacquer sprays and plastic rollers came into general use, women were able to create more complex hairstyles, including backcombed bouffants, beehives and French pleats, without an expensive visit to a hairdresser as explained by Sylvia Buxton: 'I had long hair in the late 1950s that I used to wear in a big bouffant style. I had loads of pins in my hair when I had it up. It took hours to get ready. I worked with a girl at Ballys, who used to do my hair for me, she was brilliant at it. When we had a break we used to nip in the cloakroom and she did my hair before I left off. It also needed a gallon of hair lacquer, but there again they never had the aerosols like you get today. We used to buy sachets, which you put in a squirty, plastic bottle to spray it on. It was only like sugar water really, but it did the trick.'

Men's hairstyles ranged from the regular haircut (side-parted with tapered back and sides) to the high-quiff pompadour style favoured by Elvis Presley and James Dean, a variation of which was the 'Duck's Arse' or simply the D.A. The D.A, involved the hair being brushed back around the sides of the head, a comb was then use to define a central parting that ran from the crown to the nape: the resulting style resembled the rear of a duck, hence its name. Rodney Barker sported a D.A. in the 1950s: 'I went to a barber called Joe Fisher, which I believe was on Rupert Street. It was basically a room in a terrace house, with chairs around the sides. All these fellas were crammed in, they were all smoking, and so the mix of the heat and smoke was overpowering. He gave the best Boston D.A. [a variation on the standard D.A.] in Norwich. You needed lots of grease to hold your hair in place, hence my excessive used of Brylcreem. We thought it made us look debonair. I remember an advert jingle which went along the lines of: "Brylcreem, the girls will all pursue you, they'll love to put their finger through your hair." I don't know why they would, it was like having lard smeared on your head. You'd get a lump of thick, greasy, cream in the palm of your hand, you'd then rub your hands together and rub it into your hair. I used jars of it every week!'

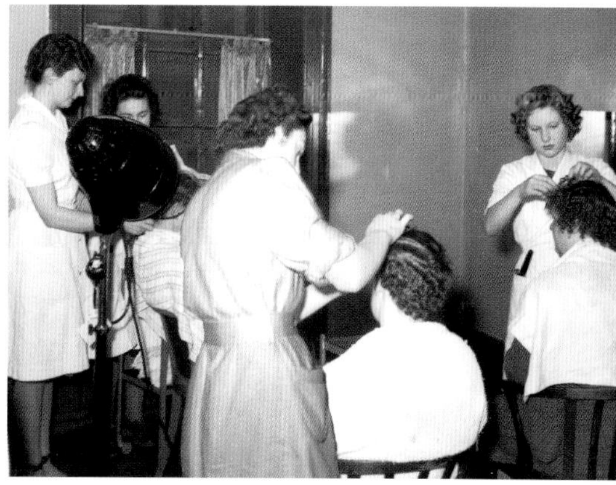

Eugene School of Hairdressing, Bank Plain, 1948

Fashion Tips

Colin, impeccably coiffed, as a teenager, c.1956

***Colin Buxton** describes a few home-grooming tips from the 1950s: 'My mother used to bleach her hair, and sometimes I used to comb the bleach though mine to give it sort of highlights, it was a bit hit and miss, but at the time I thought I was very trendy. When I was around 11 and still living in the prefabs, we all had quite long hair, but crew cuts were starting to come into fashion, and my mates all decided to go to the barbers and have the new style. I didn't have the money, and so I went home and just chopped all of mine off, and then I found I was the only one who'd had it done. Luckily, the next day they did follow suit.'*

Transport and Holidays

The Snails at Great Yarmouth's Joyland may not be the most efficient form of transport but they have been popular with many generations of Norwich holidaymakers, c.1960

Transport: The Rise of the Motor Car

The National Picture

The motor car was one of the greatest symbols of post-war prosperity. The rapid increase in car ownership was proof that the austerity and deprivation of the post-war era had come to an end.

Immediately after the war cars were in short supply. Like other sectors, as a means of improving the country's balance of payments, the government put pressure on UK manufacturers to export and simultaneously prohibited the import of foreign cars.

At a time of austerity these measures did not have a huge impact on the average family, car ownership not being high on their list of priorities. For the vast majority, public transport and bicycles were their main form of transport. Others invested in a motorcycle combination, i.e. a motorcycle and sidecar. In fact the 1950s were the high point for British motorbike manufacturers, including BSA, Triumph and Norton.

However, through the 1950s, as personal wealth grew and trading restrictions were removed (including the lifting of petrol rationing in 1950), both the demand for, and the supply of, cars increased. Between 1950 and 1960 the number of private and light goods vehicles licensed in Britain expanded from 2.3 million to 5.7 million.

British-built cars of the era included the Morris Minor, which was first produced in 1948 as a two-door saloon. Two years later a four-door model appeared, this was followed by a wood-framed estate car christened the Traveller. With a fuel consumption of over 40mpg and a price tag under £400, the Morris Minor was a favoured family car. Meanwhile in 1953 the American-owned Ford Motor Company, updated the old 'sit up and beg' Anglia to produce the cut-price, very basic Ford Popular. Costing around £390, the price compared very favourably with the cost of a motorcycle and sidecar (in 1955 a 600cc side-valve motorcycle and sidecar cost from £270 to £300). Although the financial gap was too great for many would-be buyers, it did encourage motorcyclists to trade up to a second-hand car.

Did You know?

The impact of the motor car was summarised by the economist Sidney Pollard:

'The motor car was...a product of advanced technology and mass production, a luxury which had become a necessity....A "consumer durable" which permitted a distinct widening of personal experiences, as well as an increase in the comforts of those possessing it....It was typical in that it was often bought by means of credit before it could be afforded.'

Morris Minor Series II, built c.1954
Image created by Simon GP Geoghegan

As more vehicles were licensed it became progressively clearer that the country's infrastructure was woefully inadequate. In 1945 we had no motorways, and few dual carriageways: London's A4 Great West Road and A40 Western Avenue being notable exceptions. Even in major conurbations roads were typically narrow whilst car parks were relatively rare. Also, safety procedures had failed to evolve, as evidenced by the increasing number of fatalities. Through the 1950s all these issues were addressed.

As car parks, shopping centres and pedestrian precincts were gradually introduced, city-centre authorities started to assess the negative impact of car ownership. In 1958 the country's first parking meters were launched in Mayfair, in the same year the first parking tickets were handed out. Spearheaded by the Royal Society for the Prevention of Accidents (RoSPA), authorities also began to address the question of road safety. Key initiatives included the introduction of a cycling proficiency scheme in 1945 and the 1953 launch of Tufty Fluffytail, the road safety squirrel who featured in stories that gave clear safety messages to children. Other initiatives by the Department of Transport encompassed the introduction of 'zebra' crossings flanked by Belisha beacons (1951).

As early as 1946 a map was published showing a projected English motorway system. However, it was not until 1958, with the opening of the 8.3-mile Preston bypass (since incorporated into the M6), that the country had its first motorway. Although largely successful, amongst major problems was the unprecedented number of breakdowns; the result of enthusiastic drivers taking full advantage of the road having no speed limit, resulting in many a blown gasket and overheated engine. Additionally, the bypass attracted more traffic than had been anticipated, and within six months it had to be closed for reconstruction, including the addition of an extra lane in each direction. The following year, 1959, the first 60-mile stretch of the M1 opened. Looked upon as the London-to-Birmingham motorway the road ended at Watford Gap where the country's very first motorway service station was launched.

By the end of the decade around a quarter of households in the UK owned a car. 1959 was a high for the industry. In this one year four classic designs were launched: the new Ford Anglia, the Triumph Herald, the Jaguar Mark 2 and the Mini. All were popular, but it was the iconic Mini (voted the second most influential car of the 20th century) that had the most impact. The newly emerging youth market wanted a car that was small and fun, and the Mini, just 10-feet long, fitted the bIll perfectly. The vehicle's revolutionary design, which incorporated a transverse front-wheel drive engine (i.e. compared with conventional design it was rotated by 90 degrees) allowed 80% of the car's floorplan to be used for passengers and luggage. A vehicle of the 1950s, the Mini set the scene for the Swinging Sixties.

Would this happen today?

To keep the price of the Ford Popular down various modifications were made. Of particular note, the windscreen wiper (just one) was powered by the vacuum created by the engine. Unfortunately the vacuum dropped when the engine was labouring, and so the wiper tended to slow down when the car was driven uphill or when overtaking.

Ford Popular built c.1955 and the Morris Mini Minor built c.1960 Images created by Simon GP Geoghegan

Norwich

Prince of Wales Road, c.1960

Today, the streets of Norwich are dominated by motor vehicles: not so in the 1940s and the early 1950s. For many people, their most redolent memories of the era are of the waves of cyclists arriving and leaving factories, not just in the mornings and evenings, but also making the obligatory journey home and back at lunchtimes. The position is summed up by Maurice Morson, who vividly recalls being a PC on point duty at St Benedict's Gate: 'There was a forest of cyclists when all the shoe factory workers arrived and left. You'd turn around to look, and you'd see an armada of cycles hurtling towards you.'

As the 1950s progressed, motorised transport increasingly replaced the pushbike. Arthur and Audrey Holmes were typical of many couples: 'First we got a tandem, then we got a motorbike (an Ariel Square 4) and then finally in 1948 we got married! Later, when our son David was born we attached a sidecar with a single seat to it, and then when our son Roger was born a sidecar with a double seat. Like many other families it was our main form of transport until we managed to afford our first car: a second-hand Ford Anglia.'

As car ownership expanded, Norwich City planners faced the same problems as their counterparts across the country: the City's roads had not been designed to cope with huge volumes of motorised traffic.

The need to cater for motor vehicles was not new. In the interwar years it had become clear that the City's road network was not suitable for the car. Although Barrack Street was successfully widened in the 1930s, other schemes had been mired in controversy as they involved the destruction of buildings of architectural interest. During the war such projects had been put on the back burner, but the *City of Norwich Plan* brought them back to the fore. Developers were aided by the Baedeker Raids which had led to sections of the City being razed. As a result, in 1953 the Council were able to go ahead with the widening of St Stephen's (see page 116 for details). But what about another major project? The construction of an inner ring road.

The Boar's Head, 1934

Policeman on point duty, St Stephen's, 1951

The Plan contained two proposals for the route of an orbital road, one in the main text the other in an addendum added by City engineer, Horace Rowley. Although neither proposal went ahead in its entirety, an adapted version of Rowley's scheme was accepted in the 1960s which resulted in the construction of what is regarded by many as the City's greatest eyesore: the Magdalen Street flyover.

When assessing such schemes planners also considered more strategic options, as explained by David Percival, City Architect, in 1956: 'The question has to be faced as to whether the centre of the City will survive or succumb to traffic congestion. If the traffic problem cannot be solved, one approach would be to move activities out of the centre, as is being done with the Cattle Market.'

John St Quintin with his Singer Roadster, 1951

This was a time when City-centre car parks were few and far between. In the years before rebuilding started on Curls department store, the bombed site doubled up as a car park, but this was one of the few. It wasn't until 1961 that the City had its first pay and display car park, which opened on Pye's Yard (St Martin at Palace Plain). However, John St Quintin recalls that motorists had few problems in the late 1940s: 'If you did have a car, you could drive wherever you wanted: up and down any road. Streets were normally quite narrow; places like Grapes Hill were only just wide enough for a car. You could also park anywhere, there were no restrictions.' By the late 1950s parking bans were being imposed, but Maurice Morson recollects some quite strange regulations: 'Rose Lane, for example, had different parking restrictions depending on whether it was an even or odd date. The night-duty man had to get a pole from the police box at Thorpe Station and flip over a pointer, which indicated the rules for that day. If a month had 31 days and he hadn't remembered, he was in trouble, because of course there were then two consecutive odd days.'

Policeman on point duty in distinctive box, c.1960

Being very aware of the challenges, the Council started to investigate a range of options. In 1956 Norman Tillett, Chairman of the Norwich Town Planning Committee, was part of a 'fact-finding mission' to Coventry, he reported: 'The car shopper in Coventry is compelled to leave the car some distance from the centre, and walk to and from it...for those of us beginning to think in terms of excluding all private cars from the centre of Norwich, the experiment will be watched with interest.'

In the News

In December 1951 the 'Eastern Evening News' reported that members of the Norwich City Council objected to the introduction of Zebra crossings in Norwich on the basis that they would constitute a 'danger to the public'. A Mrs Hardy was particularly vociferous in her objections having noticed: 'Particularly in twilight or dull weather, a pedestrian wearing dark clothes merged into the stripes.' She suggested that instead the Council should install all-white crossings: she was overruled.

Would this happen today?

Maurice Morson recalls the challenges of being a policeman in the late 1950s: *'When I started [1956], there was no such thing as putting a parking ticket on a windscreen. When we saw a car in a time-restricted space we'd record it in our books. If it was still there when we came around again and it had exceeded its allotted time, we'd wait for the driver who inevitably said that he hadn't been there the whole while. There was one PC who had a simple way of getting around this ploy. He had a piece of chalk which he used to draw around the wheels on the road. Then, when an innocent-looking driver claimed, "I've been and come back." He'd respond, "No, you haven't," and point to the chalk marks.'*

In the 1950s point duty (traffic control) was a routine part of a police constable's day – a task which became more challenging as the 1950s progressed. It was only in 1964 that traffic lights were installed at the St Stephen's, Rampant Horse Street, Westlegate and Red Lion Street intersection, before then traffic was controlled by Maurice Morson and his fellow officers in the City Police: 'Initially the policeman on duty just stood in the middle of the road, he then progressed to an orange box purloined from the nearby Empire Fruit Stores. Eventually, a member of the force with some carpentry skills manufactured a skeleton box, to which was later added black and white stripes. In that box you were all mighty. You were omnipotent. You could just crook your finger, or call a halt and all those vehicles did your bidding. It could be very entertaining, in fact the girls from Norwich Union used to come out in their lunch break to watch. Some of my colleagues were real characters. PC Gilly Potter used to bang on the roof of cars that didn't stop quickly enough and articulate: "I-told-you-to-stop". And the blokes in the cars responded: "I-am-sorry-officer."'

The many changes made in Norwich to cater for motorised transport, both in the 1950s and beyond, mirror what has happened in cities across the country. Emphasis is now given to keeping cars out of urban areas: we have shopping centres on the outskirts, park-and-ride schemes, pedestrianised streets and shopping malls. Most interestingly, attempts are now being made to promote cycling as a healthy, environmentally friendly option. We may never again see the swarms of cyclists commuting, but maybe we still have something to learn from the 1950s.

Memories of the Vespa Club

The Vespa made its debut at the 1946 Milan Fair: it came of age in the 1952 movie, 'Roman Holiday'. However, it was not this film that brought the scooter to Philip Armes' attention: 'I'd been thinking about getting a BSA Bantam, then one day outside the City Hall I saw four girls demonstrating a Vespa and I thought "This is it". It looked so safe, although it wasn't. Because the engine was on the side of the back wheel it was unbalanced, also it would suddenly stop, and so you had to take the plug out and kick start it. Despite these shortcomings, I bought one from the local agent Maud's, based on Prince of Wales Road.

'I started a Vespa Club. Maud's sent me the names of people who'd bought a Vespa and I invited them to come to a meeting I'd set up at the Assembly House. That's how I met my wife Gill, because amongst those first members was Gill's brother. As a club we used to go off on trips and had lots of social events. Once we had a tramps' supper, and dressed appropriately we drove our Vespas to a field and cooked a meal around a campfire. Gill and I somehow got stuck at the traffic lights where we got some very funny looks – obviously people didn't associate tramps with Vespas!

'In 1953 we went on a trip to France taking the bikes on Silver City Airway's Bristol Superfreighter, which ran cross-Channel flights. The front opened up and you could drive vehicles on. After we landed we rode into Paris: the only problem we encountered was when the clutch went. In fairness, thinking back It shouldn't have surprised us, when you think that we expected a 125cc bike to carry the two of us along with all of our luggage!'

Setting out from Norwich, c.1953

Time for a break on the way c.1953,

Always something that needs fixing, c.1953

Vespas on display outside Norwich City Hall, c.1952

Gill (second from left), Miss Vespa competition, c.1952

Transport: Trains

Trainspotting at Thorpe Station, c.1955

By the end of WWII there had been years of under-investment in the rail network; their fall into decay had been accelerated by overuse and damage during the war. In 1948, in a bid to improve the country's infrastructure, the government nationalised the railways. British Railways, known from the 1960s as British Rail, was formed from the amalgamation of the 'Big Four': London North Eastern Railways (LNER), London Midland and Scottish Railway (LMS), Great Western Railways (GWR) and Southern Railway (SR).

The rationalisation of the railway system was counterbalanced by the progressive replacement of rail journeys by road travel. This had been a pre-war development, only interrupted by the conflict. However, in the 1950s as both motor vehicles and the road network improved, the trend quickly resumed: every year saw a transfer of traffic from rail to road.

Reform accelerated after 1955 when the Government presented a modernisation plan designed to take Britain's railways from the 19th to the 20th century. Its far-reaching proposals included: replacing labour-intensive steam engines with diesel, updating obsolete coaching stock and signalling systems, and the closure of loss-making lines. This was the forerunner of Dr Richard Beeching's 1963 report, 'The Reshaping of British Railways', which recommended the closure of a third of passenger services and more than 4000 of the country's 7000 stations.

The 'Big Four' rail companies: London North Eastern, London Midland and Scottish, Great Western and Southern

Norwich

Victoria Station,Queen's Road, c.1900

City Station, Station Road, c.1900

In 1951 British Railways was one of Norwich's biggest employers. Its workforce was spread between the Crown Point maintenance depot (Trowse) and three stations: Thorpe Station, Victoria Station on Queen's Road, and City (Midland) Station on Station Road.

Three stations were not needed in a city the size of Norwich. They were a legacy of the many independent railway companies that had served the City since the 19th century. At the time of nationalisation:

- Thorpe Station was owned by LNER. Services from Thorpe included routes to London and across East Anglia, including lines to the Norfolk coast.
- City Station had been fully owned by LNER for 12 years. Before then it had been run by the Midland & Great Northern Line (M&GN), affectionately known by some as the 'Muddle and Get Nowhere' railway. M&GN lines ran from Lincolnshire to the west, through Melton Constable and onwards to Great Yarmouth and Lowestoft in the east. Trains which ran on the former M&GN network (controlled by LNER from 1936) came into Norwich at City Station. The main station buildings had been badly damaged during the war and had been replaced by 'temporary' buildings adapted from LNER sectional concrete huts.
- Victoria Station only dealt with goods traffic. It had been established by the Eastern Union Line in the mid-19th century as the terminal of a line running from Colchester via Ipswich. After 1916 all passenger trains were diverted to Thorpe.

Rationalisation was inevitable. In fact, if war hadn't intervened, many believed that LNER would have already discontinued the M&GN routes. However, in 1958 the public were shocked when a plan to close most of the former M&GN network was announced. Protests proved futile, and on 28 February 1959 around 180 miles of track were erased. City Station remained open, but now only dealt with freight traffic.

Alongside the rationalisation of networks, this period also saw the modernisation of the trains themselves.

In 1952 the 'Broadsman' express was introduced on a two-hour schedule between Norwich and London, and by 1959 there were four two-hour trains in each direction. The first diesel railcars (a train consisting of a single coach with a driver's cab at one or both ends) were introduced in 1954 and rapidly took over most of the services between Norwich, Wells, Yarmouth and Lowestoft. Although steam vehicles ran from Norwich throughout the 1950s, diesel traction quickly became established and the last scheduled steam engine left Norwich in 1962.

By the end of the 1950s Thorpe was the City's sole-surviving passenger station. During the decade it had been improved by the addition of platform six in 1954 and a new booking hall the following year. It has changed significantly since the 1950s when 400 people worked there, including 80 guards, 50 signalmen and 50 porters who were employed to carry luggage and to load/unload parcels. There was a hierarchical staff structure, encompassing some 40 different grades of employee, most of whom earned from £7 7*s.* to £10 10*s.* a week.

In the News

In February 1959 the 'Eastern Evening News' ran the headline 'Norwich to have share of £16m Loco Order'. *The industrial correspondent went on to report: 'Of the 266 diesel locomotives which have been put in hand – the largest order placed since the railway modernisation plan was made public in 1955 – 137 will have diesel-electric transmission equipment made by Crompton Parkinson Ltd. Messrs' Laurence, Scott & Electromotors [Norwich's largest single employer] will be co-operating with Crompton Parkinson in the manufacture of electric equipment on the new main line locomotives.' Mr E. Yeeles, LSE's Works Director, described the job as being, 'A very useful contract.'*

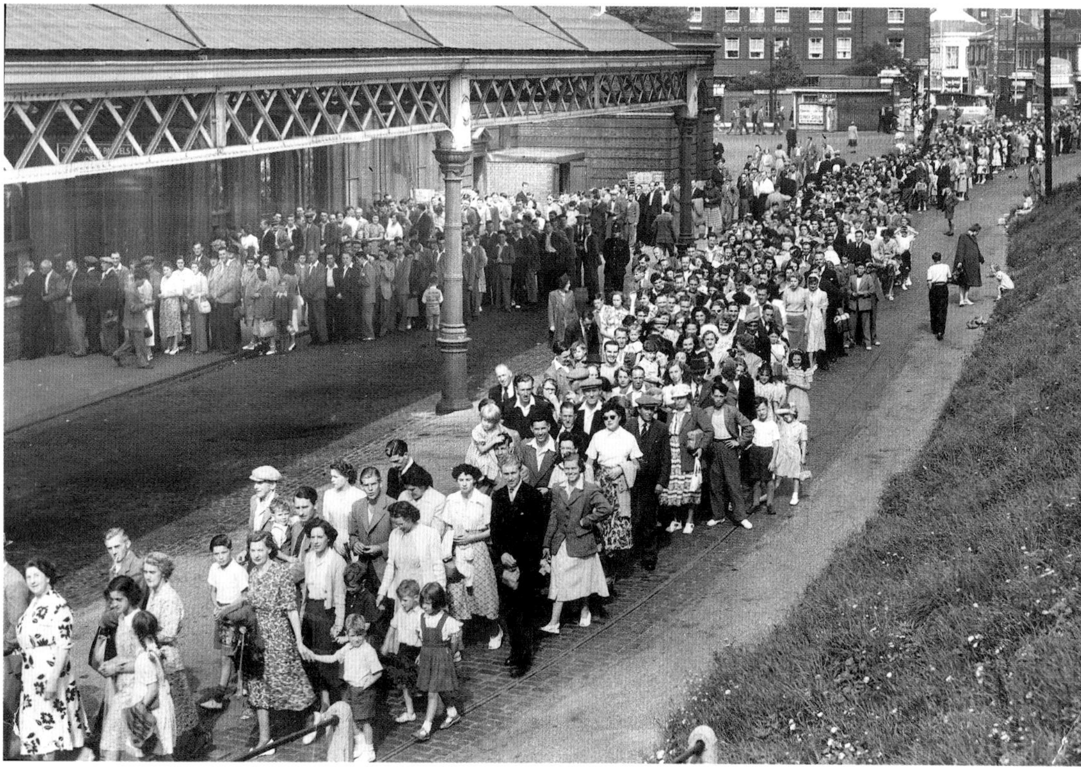

Bank Holiday queues at Thorpe Station, c.1955

Despite the rise in car ownership, on summer Saturdays during the 1950s more than 20,000 holidaymakers travelled from Thorpe Station using up to 260 passenger trains a day. In addition, there were the Bank Holiday outings, still recalled by Stephanie Brooks: 'On the Heartsease Estate most people worked in factories, and so they had the first two weeks in August off. On Bank Holiday Monday many of us flocked to Thorpe Station where we took the train to Yarmouth: you can just imagine the size of the queues. When we got there, we headed towards the market for our chips, mushy peas, jellied eels, chitterlings – the lot. Then we'd walk down Regent Street on the way to the beach and Joyland. It was a special day because money was tight, and it really was a treat for us to go out. We never had a holiday where we stayed away, and so we really looked forward to our day in Yarmouth.'

However, in the late 1940s through the 1950s the importance of Thorpe Station extended well beyond its role as a transport hub: it was the setting of some of the most poignant scenes in the City's history. It was here in 1959 that thousands gathered to greet Norwich City players travelling back to Norwich having lost the semi-final of their magnificent FA Cup run. Despite the defeat, the City wanted to gather to celebrate an outstanding achievement and to show their support for the players. But there had been even more emotional displays in October 1945, when the first local servicemen who had been held as prisoners in the Far East returned by train to Norwich. One can just imagine the scene described so evocatively in the *Eastern Evening News*: 'At about 9.30pm a train approached, and the crowds waved and clapped, only to hear that the train carrying their loved ones had been delayed. Then came the voice of the announcer, but this time it had lost its calmness: "The train now arriving is the London train..." Then her voice was drowned by cheering. Mothers, wives, children and sweethearts ran along the platform and embraced their menfolk.'

A steam train at Thorpe Station, c.1955

Holidays and Days Out

After WWII holidays gradually became affordable for the average family. A major factor behind this was the provision of the 1938 Holiday Pay Act, which expanded the number of workers with guaranteed paid leave. Where did holidaymakers go?

British Seaside Resorts

In 1947, despite post-war restrictions (particularly rationing), slightly over half the British population took a holiday of some kind. 'Staycations' were the order of the day. Few people had cars, and so if you were going on a long journey you'd take the bus or train, maybe to one of the traditional Victorian-era seaside resorts. Others preferred cycling and camping holidays, or they may have treated themselves to one of the new holiday camps epitomised by Butlins.

Billy Butlin had opened his first camp in Skegness in 1936, by the end of the war he had control of five large camps. He had a talent for recognising what war-weary Britons wanted. He offered fun, colour and entertainment. Everything from 'Knobbly Knees' competitions to opera was organised by an army of Redcoats, who became synonymous with the brand. In 1948, Muriel Chilvers went with friends and family to the Clacton camp: 'Accommodation was in wooden cabins which were like beach huts. Although rationing was still strict, the food was good. We had three meals a day: a cooked breakfast, a two-course lunch (three choices for main course) and a lighter tea with cold food. There was entertainment every evening, often a variety show with dancing and singing. There was also a fortune teller. There was an outdoor swimming pool and you could swim before breakfast – but we only did it once! The Redcoats worked hard organising all the entertainment, fun and games, for both adults and children. The TV show *Hi-De-Hi* was accurate in the way it portrayed Butlins – we even had the wake-up call!' By the late 1950s nine Butlins camps were welcoming 60,000 guests (known as campers) every week.

Families living in Norwich often holidayed at the Norfolk coast. Fairly typical was Peter Watson's family: 'Laurence & Scotts, where my father worked, used to shut down for two weeks in August. Every year, until I was about 12, we spent that fortnight having a holiday in Gorleston. We stayed in a B&B, in a house near to my aunt's. Every day we played on the beach, whether it rained or not it never made any difference. We used to go in the swimming pool at the Floral Hall, and we'd sit and listen to Eddie Yates, the blind organist. My mum, dad, aunt and uncle used to dance, us kids stayed in the swimming pool.' Similarly, every year Michael Holmes headed off with his mum, dad, grandparents and brothers, for their annual holiday at the Speedwell Caravan Park in Hopton: 'We stayed in a caravan owned by the chimney sweep who lived a few doors down from us on Woodcock Road. There was no swimming pool but every day we would swim in the sea whatever the temperature. An unusual treat was being allowed to go into the clubhouse with the adults, instead of waiting outside the pub with the obligatory orange squash.'

Often trips were arranged by the local Sunday school, for some children this was their only holiday. Avis Brown's sister, Margaret, was very involved with the local Methodist church: 'I used to have to go to Sunday school because Margaret was my teacher and I couldn't get out of it! We used to go on little day outings organised through the church. Then one year Margaret got a bungalow which was next door to Robinson's café in Hemsby, and she took the Sunday school pupils on holiday. We all had to sleep on the floor. Roy, her husband, who was her boyfriend at the time, was responsible for the boys. We had the boys sleeping up one end and the girls at the other. There was never any "hanky panky" at that age, we were just mates. Roy and Margaret were in charge, and so we had a lovely few days. We went on the beach and just played. There wasn't a lot down there, but it was wonderful.'

Peter Watson with Mum and sister Mary, c.1952

Memories of trips to the seaside

Many families still couldn't afford holidays, and instead had days out to the coast which was reached by train, bus or even bike. These would be arranged independently, or maybe by the local pub landlord or even by the Sunday school teachers.

One of the few times in the year that Paul Warr's family went to the seaside was on the August Bank Holiday weekend, when they went to Yarmouth for the day: *'We travelled by train and went to Joyland, where our favourite rides were the Snails, which you can still go on today, and the cake walk. One of my clearest memories is my dad getting dressed up to go to the beach. Father and my uncle would have their suits on: grandfather went one better and wore his suit and cap. They dressed up immaculately just to sit on a deck chair. Of course, looking back there was always a point in the day when the menfolk left mum, nan and me on the beach, and that's when they went off to a pub.*

'I did go on a few other excursions as a child. One was a trip to go cockling at Wells, organised by the landlord of the Park House (Catton Grove Road). He arranged a charabanc outing once a year for local families.'

On her day trips to Yarmouth, Stephanie Brooks discovered that you did not need to go abroad to encounter exotic animals: *'Going down Regent Street we passed a monkey sitting in front of a shop: every single year I had a photograph taken with this monkey sitting on my shoulder. Then one year we went and he wasn't there, instead there was a snake, and so that year I had my photo with a snake curled around my neck.'*

It was not unusual to pedal to the coast, as recalled by Peter Watson: *'At the weekends we'd regularly cycle to Sea Palling or Hemsby and meet up with an uncle who had a car. When we lived at Rackheath I'd sit on a little seat on the back of dad's bike. When my sister came along, he made what was a little sidecar for my sister, and he'd pedal all the way with us as his passengers.'*

Although Michael Holmes' family normally spent their annual holiday at the Speedwell Caravan Park at Hopton, one year they had a change: *'Instead of hiring a caravan we bought roundabout tickets which enabled us to travel anywhere we liked on the buses for a week. As the Cromer bus passed by the top of our street [Woodcock Road] that was a popular destination, but Lowestoft was always a favourite. A swim in the sea at Children's Corner followed by the Punch and Judy Show was mandatory, and then after lunch we took the long walk up to Kensington Gardens where parents and grandparents were surprisingly pleased to see a long queue for the electric boats. They flopped onto the deckchairs round the boating lake and read the newspapers in the sunshine while my brothers and I queued. When the queue was very long, we could never understand why they encouraged us to have a second ride!'*

Stephanie Brooks, Yarmouth, c.1958

Terence, Michael and Robert Holmes, Cromer, 1952

Travelling Abroad

In many ways the 1950s witnessed the swansong of the British seaside holiday, because this was also the decade which saw the emergence of the overseas 'package holiday', which made foreign travel accessible to the mass market.

In the late 1940s around 3% of the population holidayed abroad, the vast majority of these were wealthy and went no further afield than the Mediterranean or northern France. However, you did not need to be rich. Glenna St Quintin's father may not have had much money, but what he did have in abundance was a spirit of adventure: 'My dad came from a very large and poor family, but he always had a car. He worked hard to get on. Just after the war he took us abroad on holiday in a shooting brake. We went with my uncle and aunt and nanny. We all crammed into this car. We took the ferry to the Hook of Holland, where we stayed overnight. We'd then do what I'd call an American tour of the Continent, we covered miles in a week, with my father steaming around. We went to Germany and nobody would speak to us, it was horrendous. It was unusual to go abroad in those days, but my father would do things like that.'

In the days before the Channel Tunnel, there were other ways apart from a slow sea crossing to take vehicles abroad. In 1948 Silver City Airways ran their first car ferry flight between Lympne (near Hythe) in Kent and Le Touquet on the French coast. As already explained, in 1953 Norwich's Vespa Club, organised by Philip and Gill Armes, were some of the many who found the service very useful when they took their scooters on a trip to France. The service was popular through the 1950s, and in 1960 the airway transported around 90,000 vehicles and 220,000 passengers across the Channel.

Glenna's nanny on the Hook of Holland ferry, c.1948

After sustaining trading losses, Silver City failed in the 1960s. By then a new affordable holiday was available. It was in 1950 that the foreign package holiday was born with the launch of Vladimir Raitz's Horizon holidays to Corsica. Within four years the choice of destination had been extended to include both Majorca and the Costa Brava. By the end of the decade airlines had introduced economy fares. Falling prices allied with more choice and rising prosperity all contributed to a change in the holiday aspirations of a nation. By 1960, 2.25 million Britons went overseas for their vacations, increasing to 5 million by 1967.

Silver City Airways, 1953

At the Seaside

A crowded Gorleston, c.1955

The Holmes family, Sea Palling, 1958

Entertainment and Sport

Black Anna and Albert Cooper at the Jolly Butchers, late 1950s

Television

The National Picture

The 1950s marked a revolution in how we spent our leisure time. Until then we went out to be entertained, maybe to the cinema, to the pub or the theatre. A night in would probably consist of the household sitting in the living room listening to the radio, the children playing, mum knitting or ironing and dad reading. But this was the decade that the television came of age – and life would never be the same again.

It is impossible to underestimate the impact that television had on the way we lived in the 1950s: the layout of living rooms changed; aerials 'sprouted' on houses; adverts raised our expectations and encouraged spending; and, maybe most importantly, rather than go out we spent our evenings at home watching the television.

The world's first regular television service had been launched by the BBC in November 1936, when it transmitted around four hours of programmes each day from Alexandra Palace to owners of sets in the London area. However, it was slow to catch on, and on 1 September 1939, when the service was suspended for the duration of the war, there were fewer than 20,000 sets in operation.

Transmission resumed in 1946, and by 1960 10 million sets were being watched by approximately 50% of the population. The growth in popularity can be credited to several factors, including:

- A flourishing rental market (although sets had fallen in price over the 1950s, at £70 they were still above most household budgets).
- The transmission of the Coronation in 1953, which gave a boost to sales: it is estimated that the event was watched by around half of the British population, with an average of seven people watching each set.
- The 1954 Television Act which broke the BBC's monopoly and paved the way for a second channel. In 1955 six commercial franchises were awarded in London, the Midlands and the North of England. More followed, although we had to wait until 1959 for the launch of Anglia TV.
- By 1960 around 90% of the country was within range of both BBC and ITV transmitters.
- Technological improvements which made it easier and cheaper to record programmes rather than showing them live. This also meant broadcasters could buy and sell the recorded shows.

All of the above contributed to an increase in the choice and quality of programmes, which in turn made television more attractive, and meant more households bought or rented sets.

Many of the most popular TV programmes of the era had transferred across from the radio, including *Hancock's Half Hour* and *Listen with Mother* (reinvented as *Watch with Mother*). Other favourites included *Sunday Night at the London Palladium* with Bruce Forsyth and *Take Your Pick*, where Michael Miles would try to entice contestants to say either 'yes' or 'no'. Youngsters were entertained by such series as *The Adventures of Robin Hood* and *Zoo Quest*. The latter was presented by David Attenborough at the start of his distinguished career.

The BBC 'angel' or 'bat wings' logo, 1950s

Test Card C was first broadcast in January 1948.

Norwich

The development of television in Norwich was relatively slow. It was not until 1955 that the BBC was able to regularly relay a local service from a transmitter based at Talconeston. The following year, when a permanent transmission station was opened on the site, reception further improved. At the same time enhancements were being made to television sets. In the second half of the 1950s major differences included better sound quality and reliability. The design of sets also became more sleek. Now, at a 'moderate' additional cost, rather than be housed in an 'ugly square box', sets could be slim (a relative term) and portable, or even housed in a 'handsome' cabinet.

Such improvements contributed to a significant increase in the number of households in the Norwich postal region with a TV licence. Over the second half of the 1950s numbers increased from *c.*13,000 to *c.*51,000.

For most of this time television viewers in Norwich only had access to one channel, but in 1959, in a blaze of publicity, Anglia TV was launched. The new independent channel built a 1000-foot transmission mast at Mendlesham, Suffolk (which at the time was the tallest structure in Britain) and established its studios in Norwich in the former Agricultural Hall (renamed Anglia House). The station went on air at 4.15pm on 27 October 1959, immediately displaying its local credentials with a filmed tour of the region, entitled *Introducing Anglia*. Other programmes transmitted on that first evening included *Emergency Ward 10* and *The Violent Years,* a drama of romance and tragedy.

The rise of television inevitably had an adverse impact on other forms of entertainment in the City, particularly the cinemas. The position is summed up by Avis Brown: 'We usually went to the pictures on Fridays and Sundays. That all changed when the number of channels increased, and programmes got better. Then, as more people got a television we all stopped going out. Years ago, before TV, we had less money, but we went out more.'

In the News

The following advice on how to care for your television set was given in the 'Eastern Daily Press' in 1959:

- *Never jar the cabinet when the set is switched on, or within five minutes of switching off, when the red-hot filaments in valves and tubes are at their most fragile.*
- *Avoid over-heating either by proximity to a source of heat or by blocking the channel for the very necessary draught of air from ventilation louvres in the base or the back panel.*
- *Handle all controls gently and turn them on slowly.*
- *Do not forget to switch off when viewing ends, in any case give the valves ten minutes to cool down after three hours continuous viewing.*

Anglia House, c.1980

Radio

A 1950s radio, Gressenhall Farm and Workhouse, 2016

Before TV became widely available most people received their news and entertainment from the radio (often called the wireless). This was an era when you would be more likely to talk about what you had heard rather than what you had seen.

In the 1950s there were three main BBC radio stations: the *Light Programme*, the *Home Service* and the *Third Programme.*

The *Light Programme* transmitted popular music and light entertainment in the form of comedy, drama and variety shows. Its programmes followed a traditional pattern. Typically the day started with the breakfast news, followed by programmes such as *Housewives Choice*, *Mrs Dale's Diary* and *Music While You Work*. Popular series included *Educating Archie* (which had a bizarre radio star – a ventriloquist's dummy) and *The Goons*. The *Home Service* broadcast general entertainment, and was also the main channel for news, regional programmes and 'more demanding' dramas. The *Third Programme* was openly highbrow, its transmissions included classical musical, poetry readings and educational talks.

Such channels did not appeal to listeners who favoured pop music, particularly the new breed of teenagers, who much preferred to tune in to Radio Luxembourg.

Unlike today, radios were a large piece of kit: they were not portable, and would often hold pride of place in a living room. Typically, families would spend the evening sitting around their radio listening to a favourite programme. However, following the invention of the transistor in 1947, the radio underwent a dramatic technical revolution, which also proved to be its saviour. Transistors meant radios could be smaller, less fragile, cheap and transportable. By 1960 affordable transistor radios were on the market. Thus, despite competition from television, the radio continued to flourish: 'trannies' appealed to all age groups, particularly the newly emerging youth market.

Memories

The radio would often be blaring out all day in the City's shoe factories. *Jean Smith worked at Edwards & Holmes: '"Music While You Work" was a real favourite. We used to pay sixpence and then write the name of a song on a piece of paper and put it in a tin. If your song came up you won all of the money.' At Norvic they went one better and their club room, which was located at 54 Pitt Street, played host to 'Workers Playtime' (a variety programme transmitted three times a week on the radio by the BBC between 1941 and 1964, from a canteen 'somewhere in Britain'). Mike Quinton recalled: 'We had people such as Charlie Chester perform there. When the show was transmitted the social club was packed with around 400 people.'*

Norvic Social Club, Pitt Street, 1938

Lynn Preston's family did not own a radio: *'We had a 'radio relay' where programmes were piped to us. There was a control switch screwed to the window sill. We paid a set amount each week for the service.' 'Radio relay' was quite common in the 1950s. The quality of transmission was high and listeners did not need to purchase a set. However, unlike a radio where many stations were available, with a 'relay' choice was normally limited to the three main channels.*

The Cinemas

The National Scene

Although radio survived the TV revolution relatively unscathed, it brought about a serious decline in the fortunes of Britain's cinemas and theatres.

It all started well: 1946 was a peak year for the industry, with more than 16 billion cinema tickets sold across the UK. A trip to the 'pictures' remained a popular pastime, and even at the start of the 1950s it was one of the country's main forms of entertainment. This was an era when it was common for adults to go to the cinema two or three times a week, whilst on Saturdays most cinemas ran special clubs for children. To meet this demand programmes would change up to thrice weekly. However, as television improved and more families had access to sets, cinemas fell in popularity.

Because TV pictures could only be transmitted in black and white and were often fuzzy, the cinemas rightly believed they offered a much better on-screen experience. They did not rest on their laurels, and understood the need to innovate. In particular, in 1953 the introduction of Cinemascope significantly increased the size of screen images. However, despite all their efforts, over the 1950s cinema audiences fell. As a result, revenues plunged and in this one decade around 30% of the country's 4500 cinemas closed.

The Haymarket Picture House, 1934

Norwich

Until 1954 Norwich cinemas seemed to be bucking this trend. It was one of only nine conurbations with a population of over 100,000 where cinema-going had increased over the previous 12 months, and was the only one which was neither a seaside resort nor a big seaport. Whilst on average people in Britain went to the pictures once a fortnight, in Norwich the average was once in every 10 days.

Why? Put simply, Norwich had still not felt the full impact of television: in 1955, 75,000 Norwich households had a wireless licence, only 17% of these also had a TV licence. Local cinema owners remained bullish that they could withstand the competition: 'Many people prefer to have a night out, especially the young fellow with his girlfriend. He does not want to sit at home and look at TV.'

How wrong could they be? As the quality of local television improved, cinema audiences fell. Between 1956 and December 1961 seven Norwich cinemas (Regal, Mayfair, Gaumont [Haymarket], Theatre de Luxe, Capitol, Norvic and Ritz) plus the Hippodrome Theatre closed. There were several reasons for their decline. Of course, a major factor was falling

The Carlton, All Saints Green, 1935

audiences, rightly attributed to the growth of television, but owners were also faced with increased costs. Entertainment tax was often quoted as a factor, together with the expense of investing in new equipment.

The nationally owned cinemas did better than the local independent venues; in this period the only one that closed was the Gaumont on the Haymarket. The nationals had the edge over both television and the local establishments because their interiors were more opulent. As Andy Anderson recalls, they could add a touch of glamour to your life: 'If, like me, you lived in a nice but humble house, there was something magical about going to the top-tier cinemas. You'd walk into rooms with carpeted floors, a luxury we didn't have at home. The old Odeon on Botolph Street was a great place: it was really quite plush, as was the Carlton.' The Regent on Prince of Wales Road, part of the ABC chain, was similarly impressive. Of particular note was the large fountain and goldfish pool that graced the foyer and the ornate auditorium, complete with boxes either side of the stage. The independents didn't have the same allure. Take, for example, the Theatre de Luxe (pronounced 'de-Loo'). Although famed for being the only Norwich cinema which served tea in the afternoon, that was the nearest they came to opulence. Albert Cooper was a frequent visitor: 'They always called it the Ranch House, because it showed lots of westerns, or the Flea Pit, because they used to come around and spray disinfectant over the audience.'

ABC, Prince of Wales Road, 1984

Odeon, Botolph Street, 1938

Not only did the smaller, independent venues tend to be less attractive, but they screened lower-quality films and did not have the same economies of scale as the national firms. Typical was the Regal on Dereham Road. When it closed in 1959 the *Eastern Evening News* reported that audiences were dwindling, but even when there was a full house the maximum profit the cinema could earn was £56. This was a sad end for what was once a very popular venue. In the mid-1950s Christine Perfect was a frequent visitor: 'It was just a few minutes walk from where I lived on William Street, and so as kids we went there for Saturday morning pictures. We were allowed to cross Dereham Road on our own, because obviously it wasn't so busy then. Going to the cinema was a lovely thing to do. It was a sort of escapism from everything else in the world. I'd have been six when I first went. I'd meet up with a bunch of other kids on the corner of William and Valentine Streets, outside Pestell's bakery, and from there we'd set off together. My favourites were the cowboy films.'

Of course, in the face of falling audiences the cinemas fought back with a variety of strategies. These included showing X-rated films, installing improved facilities and screening foreign movies: all to no avail. For example, despite being one of the first cinemas in Norwich to introduce Cinemascope (1954), by the late 1950s the Norvic (Prince of Wales Road) was in decline. It went on to screen vintage classics and even foreign art-house films, but it still could not attract audiences, and closed on 30 September 1961.

Despite the doom and gloom, there was some good news for cinemagoers in the 1950s when the 272-seat Noverre Cinema opened in a converted ballroom in the Assembly House. The programme at the Noverre featured good rather than popular cinema and appealed to 'that discriminating section of cinemagoers to whom the biggest and most expensive of films are not necessarily the best'. Like the nationals, it offered the discerning cinemagoer a well-appointed venue in a wonderful building, which together with its niche programmes enabled it to successfully compete for a dwindling audience.

The 1950s was a devastating decade for the City's independent cinemas. Clearly they did not share in the country's 'prosperity', instead they were victim of it. Audiences were no longer going out because they had nothing to do at home, they now wanted to experience something better than they had at home.

Norvic Cinema, Prince of Wales Road, c.1950

In the News

On the night the Theatre de Luxe closed (10 February 1957) vandals wrecked the auditorium. *The following April one young man, James Clarke, was brought before the magistrates. He protested his innocence, explaining that he had merely 'put his feet on the seats in front of him and they had broken...it was an accident'. The magistrate did not believe him. This may have been something to do with the fact that alongside the £3 he was fined for vandalism, he had to pay a further £1 for firing a gun within 50 feet of a highway, £2 for carrying it without a licence and £1 for causing damage to a street lamp!*

In 1957 police were called in to the Regal on Dereham Road to deal with lively fans who danced in the aisles during a Saturday night showing of 'Rock Around the Clock' featuring Bill Haley and the Comets. *When they emerged they were confronted by rows of police. Some of the boys rocked parked cars and danced in the street, only to be chased away by the officers. Although not much of a riot, it is an event which has become part of the City's folklore. Sylvia Buxton recalls seeing the film there: 'We all got up and danced in the aisles. It was noisy, but in a good-natured way, there wasn't any trouble. Afterwards loads of us got a taxi back, it was great.'*

Theatre de Luxe, St Andrew's Street, 1934

The Regal, Dereham Road, 1938

The Norvic ceased trading on 30 September 1961 after showing Elvis Presley's 'Wild in the Country'. *The intention had been to close at 10.30pm, but after hearing of planned 'vandalism' by a group of Teddy boys (and being aware of what had happened at the Theatre de Luxe just four years earlier) management closed early. When the gang arrived at 7pm they discovered a locked, empty building. A sad end, for a popular venue.*

In 1957 the Noverre hit the headlines when the Lord Mayor, Arthur South, objected to the programmes shown: *'If a film is shown in a small cinema it is dirty, if shown at the Noverre it is art.' In reply, the cinema's trustees pointed out the cinema had shown only six 'X'-rated films in the last year: 'We were picked out as if we were showing pornography,' they responded, 'though in fact we have the opportunity of hiring 50 "X" films if we wanted to.'*

Memories

For those people of a 'certain age' who can recall going to the cinema in the 1940s and 1950s, the following may sound familiar:

Status of the Venue: There were two main classes of cinema. The top tier consisted of the national chains which would typically show a new release as a single programme for six days and then on Sunday screen a rerun of an earlier release. Below them were local cinemas, which showed older films and would normally have programmes running Monday to Wednesday, Thursday to Saturday, and a one-off Sunday programme.

Cost: Although prices varied considerably, going to the cinema could be relatively inexpensive. In general, the local independent cinemas were cheaper than the nationals. In the mid-1950s the lowest-priced Norwich venue was the Mayfair (Magdalen Street), where you could get in for ninepence. In contrast, the most expensive seats in the Gaumont (Haymarket) peaked at four shillings.

The Programme: This was typically made up of a newsreel, trailers, adverts, and a support and main film. All the cinemas had 'continuous performances', which meant that the cinema was never cleared at the end of the programme. You could literally sit there all afternoon or, as explained by Albert Cooper: 'You'd often enter in the middle of a picture, then you'd sit through the programme until you eventually got to the point where you came in, and then you'd leave.'

Commissionaire Jock, outside Theatre de Luxe, c.1957

The 'Sixpenny Rush': In addition to the adult programme, most cinemas had a Saturday club for children, they normally cost sixpence to get in, hence the name. The Regent (owned by the ABC chain from 1929) had a thriving Saturday club, much enjoyed by John Chilvers: 'I started to go to the cinema by myself when I was seven, and the Regent was one of my favourites. I really enjoyed the westerns, partly because of the goody-baddy stuff. I particularly liked Roy Rogers and Gene Autrey.' Michael Holmes also enjoyed going to the Saturday club, known as the ABC Minors. 'You were given a card (like a cigarette card) when you went in and you could collect all sorts of sets. My favourites were those linked to space travel, such as creatures from different planets. As we often got "doubles", before the film started we'd pass the time wandering around the aisles seeing if anyone wanted to swap.' Stephanie Brooks and Paul Warr can still sing, word perfectly, the club song:

We are the boys and girls well known as
Minors of the ABC.
And every Saturday all line up
to see the films we like and shout aloud with glee
We like to laugh and have our sing-song,
such a happy crowd are we.
We're all pals together.
We're Minors of the ABC.

The Commissionaires: These gentlemen, controlled the queues: they reigned supreme. Albert recalls: 'You'd see them outside in their smart uniforms, complete with peaked military-styled caps, braided coats and white gloved. You'd be stood in the queue and they'd shout out something like: "I've got one 1/3d and one 1/11d. You'll have to sit separately, but you might be able to join up later." The most famous commissionaire was called Jock, who worked at the Theatre de Luxe (St Andrew's). Dear old Jock was a rough Scotsman. He was big, loud and full of life. He was a rough man but a great character.'

In Conclusion: At the end of the last performance, there would often be a rush for the doors, because after the house lights had been turned up the National Anthem was played, and woe betide anyone still in the auditorium who did not stand to attention for its duration.

The Norwich Theatres

The 1950s was also a difficult period for Norwich's theatres: the Theatre Royal, the Hippodrome and the Maddermarket. Like the cinemas they were faced with dwindling audiences and high costs. To survive they had to successfully compete with television.

They appealed to different audiences: The Theatre Royal concentrated on plays and musicals; the Hippodrome favoured variety – often 'risqué'; the Maddermarket put on classical plays. By 1960, the Maddermarket was the City's only live-theatre venue.

Norwich Theatre Royal

The first to fail as a theatre was the Theatre Royal. In the late 1940s all seemed good, as audiences flocked to see an eclectic selection of shows. These included plays and reviews, an annual pantomime and even the odd circus – complete with live animals. However, like other provincial theatres, in the early 1950s attendances began to fall. Around this time Roy Cracknell, with his wife Jean, often went: 'We used to get the cheapest seats which were in the back four rows and a long way from the stage, they cost 1s. 9d. It was rather funny really, because they often had repertory theatre on in the summer, and the "one-and-nine pennies" were packed, and in front of us there'd be a big sea of empty seats.' It was becoming increasingly clear that live professional performances were not financially viable in Norwich. Touring musical shows, which did attract audiences, had become too expensive to bring here without a subsidy. Increasingly, travelling companies and performers were loathe to come to a city where so many productions flopped.

In 1956, after a short period putting on variety, the owners threw in the towel. The lease was taken over by the Essoldo cinema circuit, a Newcastle-based operation that owned around 190 cinemas across the country. Initially, Essoldo introduced a programme of 'ciné -variety', when shows were staged early evening, often featuring big stars such as Billy Cotton, Lonnie Donegan and Max Bygraves. These were followed by a separate programme of feature films. However, as audiences fell for the variety acts, film programmes became 'continuous daily'. Although live shows were staged periodically, the reputation of the Theatre Royal as a centre for drama was, albeit temporarily, lost.

The Theatre Royal, c.1960

The Hippodrome

The Hippodrome (St Giles) suffered a similar fate. It had prospered during the war, taking full advantage of a new audience: single servicemen stationed on the many airbases within easy reach of the City. During this time it staged revues with saucy titles such as *Strip Please* and *Follow the Girls*. Post-war, it put on variety shows, which attracted first-class acts such as Laurel and Hardy (1954). It also hosted big radio shows, including *Opportunity Knocks* with Hughie Green, and the *Goon Show*. However, in the 1950s, as audiences fell, revues at the Hippodrome became increasingly bawdy. Then in March 1958, despite what had happened to the Theatre Royal, the owners took a huge gamble. They rechristened the venue the 'Norfolk Playhouse' and reinvented it as a permanent repertory theatre. With 1000 seats to fill, it soon became clear that the enthusiasm of the cast and owners was not matched by the general public. They also had a stroke of bad luck. Just when they needed to generate large audiences, they had another competitor, the Canaries, who had embarked on their incredible cup run. One theatregoer, Elizabeth Cave, sadly wrote to the *Eastern Evening News:* 'I suppose a relatively small fraction of the support given to the Canaries would substantially ensure the life of such an enterprise as the Playhouse.' Unfortunately such support was not forthcoming, and in March 1959 the theatre temporarily shut down, announcing that crowds had been hit by a combination of 'icy roads, fog and football'. The company regrouped and reopened in April for one final attempt to make a success of the venture. Sadly they failed, and in June 1959 the Hippodrome was one of six theatres across the country to shut down within a few days of each other. In December 1959, trying to recover some of their losses, the owners followed the path of the Theatre Royal and converted to a cinema. Sadly the Hippodrome was not so lucky. Without national backing, the strategy proved unsuccessful (takings on its final day amounted to £3) and the venue closed for good on 27 April 1960. It was eventually demolished in 1966 and the site redeveloped as the St Giles Car Park.

Interior of the Hippodrome, 1960

Memories of the Hippodrome

Even today, more than 50 years after its demolition, Silvia Buxton is amongst the many theatregoers who still remember the Hippodrome with affection: *'I loved going there. We went as a family on a Saturday night: it was a real treat. Sometimes my father went on the stage when they asked for volunteers. I can remember him going up, and he had to burst balloons between him and one of those leggy showgirls, I really cringed then...but he enjoyed himself. We saw all the old singers. They used to have cards up at the sides to tell you who was coming on, a bit like an Old Time Music Hall. They started to get in those nude models, but they did it very respectful like. They had a net curtain at the front of the stage, and so you couldn't really see anything. My uncle, who did the curtains, said the models were covered in strategically placed sticky tape, and so it wasn't so glamorous after all.*

'When I went with mum and dad we always sat downstairs, where the seats were quite plush. Later, when I went with friends, we sat in the unallocated seats right at the back. We used to run up the stairs like crazy to try and get the best ones. The seats there were on platforms made out of planks of wood – they were so poorly made you could feel people's feet in your back. I think it was a terrible shame it was pulled down: it was a lovely building.'

Amongst the shows put on at the Hippodrome in the mid-1950s was Carroll Levis 'Top of the Towns' Talent'. *Levis was on a '...nationwide search for stars' and invited local teams to compete for £1000. The show, a very low-key version of the X-factor, also featured B-rated performers.*

Albert Cooper at the Jacquard with cherubs, c.1965

Albert Cooper recalls: 'When the Hippodrome was demolished its fittings were sold off at ludicrously low prices: the light pendants and mirrors in the bar fetched only six shillings whilst the carpets were sold at 30 shillings a piece. Me and my brother Tony rescued two golden cherubs. We put them on show at the Jacquard Folk Club which we ran at the Mischief Tavern on Fye Bridge Street.'

Memories of the Madddermarket

Barbara Miller was a member of the Norwich Players, the amateur group that performed at the Maddermarket, when both were presided over by Nugent Monck: *'I loved acting and was in lots of plays at school, and so one of the teachers who was very active in the Maddermarket Theatre, offered to recommend me – in those days that was the only way you could perform there. Eventually I was invited to have tea with Nugent Monck, and was pleased to be accepted as one of the Norwich Players.*

Nugent Monck, undated

'Nugent Monck was internationally known. He didn't put on plays because they would be commercially viable, but because he thought people ought to see them. Thus we did Ibsen, Shaw and all Shakespeare's plays. Every year he put on the main GCE examination texts as plays. This meant that children, having taken them to pieces line by line in the classroom, had the chance to watch the whole thing, and understand what it was really about.

'I knew Nugent Monck well. He wasn't very tall, in fact he was quite short. I always thought he was a marvellous actor, because he would say "I know nothing about money", whereas he was very shrewd, and knew exactly what he was doing. He never remembered people's names that well, and he would get in an absolute temper with you, but it went as quickly as it came. It wasn't personal for him, it was always about the play. One month you'd have a walk-on part, the next you'd have a good speaking role. He was a hard task master, but only because individual actors weren't important. That was why he never put anybody's name in the programme, or allowed curtain calls, because for him the play was the thing. It was all very *different from today's celebrity culture.'*

Barbara Miller, c.1950

In the News

In the late 1950s the 'Eastern Evening News' received a number of letters complaining about the shows staged at the Hippodrome. *These included a missive from Jennifer W. Fleming Smith in April 1957: 'Until yesterday I thought that Norwich was a city of beauty and culture, but I made a discovery last night that disillusioned and disgusted me. In search of light entertainment I went to the Hippodrome. I understand that the current show is typical of the Hippodrome's presentations. I have rarely seen a more revolting spectacle than the semi-nude poses of the girls, who are presumably deluded into thinking that it is "art". Let me say here that I do not condemn the girls on the stage. Given good lighting and sets they can be breathtakingly lovely, but as in the whole performance these acts were clumsy and lacked finish.'*

Three months later it was in the news again, after having the temerity to include the word 'Sexciting' on bills advertising a revue. *Arthur Spencer entered the debate, writing to the 'Eastern Evening News': 'Is this word any more shameful than, for instance, such words as "exotic", "daring", "nude", or any of the other "luring" words one reads on almost every show bill these days....Everyone is entitled to his or her own taste, and the less fuss made over nudism the better, and perhaps the sooner it will again be able to take its rightful place among the truly great arts....One sadly recalls the great shows which visited Norwich in the pre-war days....There were nudes, but just one little item sandwiched in a well-balanced programme.'*

The Maddermarket Theatre

Interior of the Maddermarket Theatre, 1930s

Despite financial difficulties, the Maddermarket Theatre survived the decade unscathed. It had several advantages over the other two venues:

- It was a relatively small venue and, like today, had an amateur local cast – both of which reduced overheads. They did not need to attract the same size of audience to remain viable.
- Nugent Monck, the original owner, had many influential connections in both the world of theatre and locally. These proved invaluable when it came to fund raising. Supporters included John Gielgud, whilst in 1954 the Queen Mother came to the theatre to support a special fund-raising matinee.
- It operated in a niche market, and was renowned for putting on classics and plays chosen for their quality as much as their popular appeal. This approach proved successful and audience figures held up, notwithstanding the growth of television.

In Conclusion

By 1960 the City had no professional theatre. Theatre lovers were appalled, but the situation was summed up in a letter to the *Eastern Evening News*: 'Do not throw blame upon the public for enjoying the type of entertainment that is convenient; if the live theatre cannot compete then unfortunately and inevitably it must close. This is the end of an era, the end of families trooping religiously to the cinema week after week, the end of live theatre, which although pleasantly enjoyed in the past, is now on the threshold of a serious and inevitable decline.'

The Circus

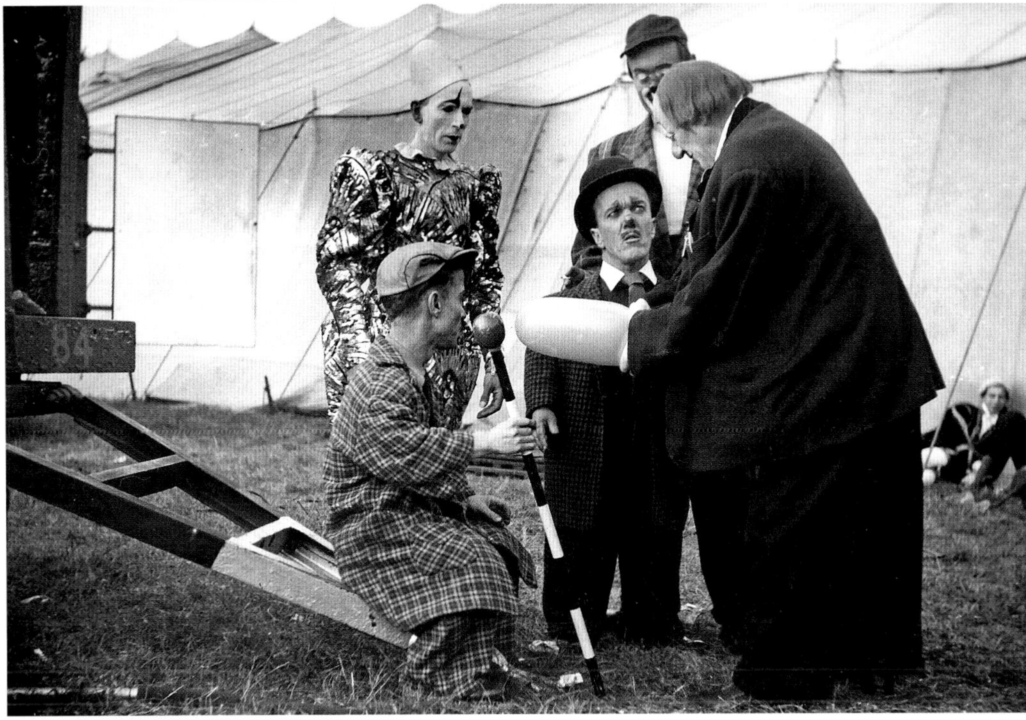

Bertram Mills Circus, c.1954

Thousands of people attended the circus in the years after the war. Touring shows were put on at an assortment of venues, including the City's parks and the Theatre Royal. The excitement started when, after arriving in Norwich by rail, the animals paraded through the streets on their way to the show. Rodney Barker was amongst the many youngsters who joined in the fun: 'Whenever the circus came, we'd go to Eaton Park and watch the massive trucks arrive. The animals walked there, all the way from Thorpe Station. The big top always looked huge when it was up, but I was always amazed how small the circus ring was after it had been taken down.'

In April 1948 the Bertram Mills Circus delighted crowds at the Earlham Road Recreation Ground, performing in their big top which seated more than 3000 spectators. Animal acts were particular favourites as reported in the local press: 'Many people who saw the six elephants on their way to the fairground from the station would hardly believe that they could [perform] "ballet". There are several other animal acts, including performing lions, and the clever dogs of Louise who ride ponies....The equestrian displays provide great entertainment, with the Cumberlands providing thrill after thrill as they ride and perform acrobatics.' When the company returned in 1954 to put on their show at Eaton Park, they again received rave reviews for their acts which included jugglers, clowns, performing animals and the Condoras, 'three flying trapezists whose daring leaps are complicated by somersaults in the air, leading up to a blindfold jump to a swinging partner'.

Although the Theatre Royal was a much smaller venue it still hosted acts which thrilled and entertained audiences, even if they did not always go to plan. This was discovered by a reporter from the *Eastern Evening News* who reviewed Gilbert's International Circus in 1955: 'Kandy, the elephant, is a sure favourite...Publicity does not worry her: she has just appeared in a film, *Charlie Moon*, with Max Bygraves. Not everyone shares her immunity to the footlight's glare: Pat Freeman's llama for instance. He was either shy last night – or was he trying to join the orchestra every time he dashed out of the ring?'

Another challenge of being in the City centre was exercising the animals. Andy Anderson, a policeman in the 1950s, discovered that when the circus was in town it was not unknown to see unusual, not to mention large, creatures strolling along the City's streets: 'One morning when I was on point duty on the crossroads on St Stephen's, outside Marks & Spencer, I saw an elephant with a man sitting on its back coming down past Woolworth's towards me: they were performing in a circus at the Theatre Royal. I was probably being paranoid, but I could have sworn that the elephant had its beady eye on me, and I had visions of being hoisted aloft.'

Norwich Pubs

Norwich pubs have changed significantly since the 1950s.

Today, pubs are associated with food as much as alcohol. In the 1950s you would be lucky to get crisps and peanuts. Even the choice of drinks was very different. In particular, with over 95% of the premises being tied to one of the City's breweries (Steward & Patteson, Bullards, Morgans or Youngs, Crawshay & Youngs) beer choice was severely restricted. Wine was not served in any Norwich pub until well into the 1960s, and so the variety of alcohol on offer was not great.

Going to a pub before Sunday lunch was very common; often the men went by themselves, leaving their wives to cook the roast. In the days before mobile phones it could be difficult to get the menfolk home, and so children would be sent out to get their dads. In Paul Warr's household more extreme measures were frequently called for: 'Father was always at the pub at Sunday lunchtime. There were invariably rows when dinner was put on the plate and father had not made it home. Many a day I remember mum and nanna marching down to the pub to drag out my dad and grandad. One day, my mum stormed down to the Park House pub [Catton Grove Estate] with the dinner on a plate, and she slapped it on the table in the bar in front of him.'

This was a time when pub hours were generally restricted to eight hours trading (in some cases nine) from Monday to Saturday, and just five hours on a Sunday. In addition, an afternoon break in service was compulsory. Unsurprisingly, landlords became quite adroit at flouting the rules. However, as explained by Maurice Morson, who joined the police force in 1956, the 'City's finest' was on their case: 'Pubs were well patronised. Every so often, probably once a month, a sergeant would come up to you and say: "Come on boy, we have some pubs to do." Off we'd go and duly visit pubs, which he'd mark off as checked in his register. The reason you went was to catch them infringing the licensing laws. It used to be a big thing. After closing time, normally 10.30pm, they were allowed 10 to 15 minutes drinking-up time. We were very suspicious of pubs that had curtains drawn very tightly so you couldn't see inside – we'd stand outside listening for the chink of money. In fact, once a sergeant was checking on the Magpie, on Magpie Road, and was peering through the keyhole when someone opened the door and fell over him. I don't know who was most shocked. It became a game in a way. Could you catch them and prove they were serving after hours?'

Despite such limitations on opening and the increasing popularity of television, the local pub was often the heart of the community.

Bullards sign above the Orford Arms, Red Lion Street, c.1960

The New Pubs

Premises were generally smaller than today. Many City pubs were run from very old buildings consisting of a bar that was little more than a front room. However, change was afoot. Newer pubs, which tended to be larger and more luxurious than their predecessors, were opening. Typically, they were built for one of two reasons: either to replace those that had suffered damage during the war or as newly licensed premises designed to serve housing estates on the outskirts of the City.

War-Damaged Premises

Many public houses had been bombed during WWII: in April 1942 alone 120 premises were either destroyed or damaged. Apart from the obvious, if a pub had been demolished the landlords were faced with a problem: they knew if they did not reopen within a short period their licences would be forfeited. However, because of war shortages they were unable to rebuild. But, like the manufacturing and retail sectors, landlords faced the problem with resilience and resourcefulness. Take the case of the Little John on the corner of Northumberland and Armes Streets which was wrecked in the Norwich Blitz. Undeterred it reopened a few months later in a wooden hut which it occupied until 1957 when a new pub was built. Walter and Gertrude Whitmore took over in 1943 and ran the premises until 1979. Like so many pubs, throughout the 1950s it was at the heart of the community. Despite the somewhat humble premises the Whitmore's presided over a range of activities, including a fishing club, darts teams, outings and musical entertainment. In 1957 they transferred to brand-new premises complete with a snug, a bar and a lounge.

The Little John's new lounge, 1957

The Trafford Arms (Grove Road) suffered a similar fate. On the night of 27 May 1942 the building was reduced to a burnt-out shell. When the licence was suspended on the 15 October 1942 because of 'war circumstances' the end seemed nigh. However, the spirit which carried so many people through the war gave inspiration. On August 1943 the new tenants, Cecil and Doris Clarke, reopened the Trafford in a temporary wooden building converted from a large broiler house which was nicknamed the 'Chicken House'. They traded from there until autumn 1955 when the first half of the present building was completed. The pub closed one evening in the 'Chicken House' and reopened the next morning in the new wing (no pun intended) which later became the bar. The 'Chicken House' could then be dismantled and the second wing, which fronts onto Trafford Road, could be built. Finally the two halves were joined with an ornamental doorway and the resultant passage became the snug.

Trafford Arms, half rebuilt but open, 1955

Trafford Arms, 2011

The Tuckswood pub was built to serve the growing estates of Lakenham and later Tuckswood, 1933

Estate Pubs

This was an era when people did not have cars, and so they did not travel far. When they went out for a drink they went to their 'local'. This fact was recognised when Norwich's council-house building programme began in the 1920s. From the first, pubs were incorporated into the new estates.

Often, as houses and pubs were demolished in the City centre as part of the Council's slum-clearance programme, the licences were transferred from very small pubs to brand-new premises. For example, the rather grand Tuckswood pub, which opened in Lakenham in 1931, took over the licence from the Butchers' Arms on Ber Street.

Similarly, in 1935 the licence of the King's Head on Barrack Street was passed across to the Woodcock pub on the Catton Grove Estate. Avis Brown's family often visited it in the 1950s: 'We did not rent our first television until around 1958, and even then there wasn't much to watch until Anglia TV was launched the following year. Consequently, at night time, especially at weekends, the pubs were always full. The women used to go as well, you see. At the Woodcock they had a sunken garden and in the nice weather, all us kids used to play there while mum was having a drink in the pub with my sister and brother. This meant she had a bit of a life, otherwise all she did was work.'

The importance of the estate pubs to their communities was highlighted by an article in the *Eastern Evening News* about the Canary public house, which opened on the Heartsease Estate in 1961: 'On this town-size estate there is no cinema, no proper dance hall and very few opportunities for entertainment apart from the "telly". Any activities which offer an opportunity for a get-together are gratefully seized. At the Canary, the fair-sized music room is bursting with activity nearly every night of the week....In addition the public house runs a thriving social club of more than 150 members.'

Memories

Babycham was launched nationally in 1953*. It was designed to appeal to women who were beginning to play a more dominant role in post-war society. Existing tipples, including gin, cream sherry, port and stout had limited appeal, but the light, sweet sparkling drink became popular with women of all ages. A strong marketing campaign sold it as being glamorous and aspirational: whilst its deer motto became an iconic image.*

Would this happen today?

Paul Warr often went to the pub with his grandfather 'On many Saturday nights you'd find me parked outside a pub with a packet of crisps and a Vimto. I'd have only been six – can you imagine doing that today? If I wanted anything, I used to stick my head around the door, and I can still remember the cloud of smoke that hit me: it made my eyes smart. I'm very grateful for that experience, because I've never smoked a cigarette my entire life.'

Pub Entertainment

Throughout the 1940s and 1950s most pubs put on music of some kind. Subsquently, a selection of venues, together with their performers, have become part of the City's folklore.

One of most iconic entertainers was Antoinette Hannent. Antoinette, better known as Black Anna, because of the colour she habitually wore, was the daughter of one of the Italian families who migrated to Norwich in the late 19th century. In 1935 her husband took over the lease of the Jolly Butchers (Ber Street) and it was here that Anna reigned supreme until her death in 1976. Anna was an outstanding performer who became known as Norwich's Sophie Tucker. Her style of singing was particularly popular with US airmen. She was renowned for singing songs with a double entendre such as *A Lovely Water Melon.* Fans can still recall her singing *I Ain't Got Nobody* whilst standing next to a skeleton, hanging in the Jolly Butchers' lounge.

Antoinette Hannent with American servicemen, c.1950

Another popular venue was the Red Lion on St George's, the nearest pub to the Norwich School of Art, now the Norwich University of the Arts. It was a hive of activity and had a thriving youth culture. Jimmy and Beattie Beales (licensees from 1956 to 1966), fostered the contemporary music scene, and during their tenure the Red Lion is reputed to have been one of the first regular skiffle venues in Norwich. In 1958 the Alley Katz Skiffle Group, with lead vocalists Pete 'Jock' Bullen and Brian Lambert, were the pub's resident band.

Other pubs had more low-key entertainment, but most would have put on music of some kind. Kingsley Harris explains: 'Many had a piano in the corner, and literally some guy would come in and knock out a tune. Also, a lot of pubs would have what they called their resident band, who were generally regulars who played for fun. For example, the Park House, on Catton Grove Road, had the Park House Trio made up of who was available on the night. If they couldn't make the numbers up it wasn't a problem, they'd just play as the Park House Duo.'

Alley Katz Skiffle Group, 1955

Music and Dancing

During WWII one of the most popular forms of music was big band swing, as performed by the legendary Glenn Miller. The decades that followed saw the evolution of many different musical styles, including skiffle, jazz and rock 'n' roll. These developments owed much to brilliant performers and songwriters, but can also be credited to changes in society. In particular, the growth of youth culture in the 1950s: for the first time youngsters were dominating the music scene.

Although on a smaller scale, the progression of music in Norwich was very much in step with the rest of the country.

George Birch and his Band, Samson & Hercules, 1951

Do You know ?

Whether Glenn Miller ever performed in Norwich?

East Anglian music expert Kingsley Harris is unsure: 'It is rumoured that on 18 August 1944 Glenn Miller visited the Samson & Hercules having played the bandstand in Chapelfield Gardens that afternoon. Glenn had been promoted to the rank of major the day before, and it is said that he and the band stayed up most of the night celebrating. However, sadly we don't know if they played either here or in the Gardens...but it's a good story.'

Would this happen today?

In 1954 the 'Eastern Evening News' reported: '1000 children of between five and fourteen years waltzed and foxtrotted like veterans of the ballroom at the first children's dance held at the Samson & Hercules Ballroom by the Norwich Federation of Industrial Clubs. The aim was to make it "just like a grown up dance"....There were no games and no entertaining apart from the dancing....Old-fashioned dancing and the Palais Glide were the most popular.'

The Big Band Era and the Norwich Dance Halls

Big Bands were popular in the City during WWII, and continued their dominance through to the mid-1950s. The sound was a great favourite with the American airmen stationed in Norfolk, and so all Norwich's major ballrooms, including the Samson & Hercules (Tombland), the Lido (Aylsham Road) and the Gala (St Stephen's Road), engaged a mix of local and national bands, who played formal dance numbers. However, by the end of the decade tastes were changing.

Rodney Barker recalls visiting the Samson & Hercules in the late 1950s: 'It's where I met my wife, Linda, and also where my mum met my father. You went in between "Samson" and "Hercules", the two statues outside. You'd then pass through the vestibule, where they had the cloakrooms and things like that, before entering a big hall with a huge dance floor and a bandstand at the top.' By then, although they still had live music, bands were smaller and were generally made up of a guitarist, drummer and singer. Nevertheless, many dances were still formal. Rodney explains: 'It was more old-time dancing. We did ballroom or, in my case, tried to do ballroom. The floor was empty in between dances and everyone stood around the sides. The single girls sat on one edge, the lads on another. I still remember the first time I drummed up the courage to ask a girl to dance. I walked from one side of the dance floor to the other and she just said, "No thank-you." I had to walk all the

US servicemen in a victory parade, Norwich, 1945

Samson & Hercules, Tombland, 1938

way back by myself. I felt so humiliated, I never asked another girl to dance until I was 18 and saw my future wife Linda there. When the dances came to an end, normally at around 10.30pm, there used to be buses outside, waiting to go to the big estates, if you missed them you had to walk home.'

In their heyday, the ballrooms hosted a variety of events, including wedding receptions, works' dances and children's parties. But from around 1957 attendances started to fall: pastimes were changing. Youngsters no longer wanted to learn to waltz, most preferred to play the juke box, hang around cafés, listen to jazz or just bop. As they went into decline, the ballrooms did what they could to attract audiences, running such events as yo-yo and hula-hoop championships, alongside jazz clubs and jive nights. They even launched what is believed to be Norwich's first disco, as explained by Kingsley Harris: 'Geoff Watling, owner of both the Lido and Samson, promoted the first disco dance called *On the Record* at both venues in the late 1950s. Prior to that, there was a lot of what they called record hops or music nights going on, but you either had to bring along your own records or you just played the juke box. It was strange really, you paid to get in and then paid to play a record.' Change was even afoot at the Gala Ballroom, opened in 1954. The owner Eileen Page, who also taught dancing there, had always vowed she would never have rock 'n' roll performed in her ballroom, but soon realised the kids loved it. Being a businesswoman, by the late 1950s she'd adopted the strategy, if you can't beat them join them. Avis Brown was typical of the younger generation: 'I used to go out a lot; I only stayed in one night a week, and that was to wash my hair. I loved rock 'n' roll dancing. I once won a jive competition with a boyfriend at the Samson. We could do all the moves, arms over your shoulder and twirling around, it was great.'

On 31 December 1959 it was announced that Mecca, the national entertainment group, were buying both the Samson and the Lido. Locals who worried that this would be the end of an era were soon appeased. The Samson continued to hold public dances, whilst the Lido was integrated with the old Capitol cinema building and was refurbished. By October 1960 it had reopened complete with new reception rooms and two banqueting halls which seated 1000. Mecca also installed a new dance floor which addressed an interesting quirk explained by John and Glenna St Quintin: 'When we were first married [1957], we used to go to dinner dances at the Lido. On New Year's Eve there'd be hundreds of us there, and we'd all be dancing. The floor was built over an old swimming pool, and you could literally feel it going up and down.' However, one of the biggest attractions following the renovation was the installation of 450 twinkling lights in the ballroom's ceiling, giving the illusion of a romantic, star-lit night.

It sounds beautiful, but in the 1950s there was another venue that could offer (but not promise) a similar starry experience: Chapelfield Gardens. This was a favourite haunt of Silvia Buxton, who went to dances there with Colin. They enjoyed jiving, but there was a problem: 'I wore stilettos, and by the time I got home they were worn half down, because we were dancing on concrete.'

Capitol Cinema and Lido Ballroom, Alysham Road, 1954

Memories

Joan Banger recalls the impact American airmen had on the Norwich dance halls:

'In 1942 the Americans not only took over the RAF airfields, they also took over the Samson & Hercules, and so the Norwich boys were inclined to shun the place, but not so the girls. Many of the latter came to the Samson six nights a week and how they ever carried on their work in the factory or office the following day is hard to say....A Norwich boy, Gerry Hoey, a prominent figure in the London dance-band world [played at] the Samson & Hercules throughout the war years. The Americans loved Gerry Hoey and his Band, and when the strains of American Patrol were played they rocked the building, roaring their appreciation, sometimes with tears in their eyes.'

With so much emphasis on ballroom dancing, it proved quite helpful if you knew the steps, as explained by Maurice Morson: *'Most of the lads I knew went to ballroom dancing lessons; some of my mates went to the Peggy Carr School of Dancing, on Wagon and Horses Lane. I went to the Eileen Page School of Dancing, on St Stephen's Road, where the boys lined up on one side and the girls on the other. You'd hear the usual cracks, such as, "I don't fancy yours". Most of my mates went to these places for two reasons: to learn to dance and pick up the ladies. This was the era of Victor Silvester. You were instructed in things like the quickstep, waltz and the foxtrot. We ignored the tango: it was a bit too exotic for us Norwich boys.'*

Meanwhile, Rodney Barker honed his skills at the Norman School of Dancing (All Saints' Green): *'When I went there was a lady there, she wore a bouffant-type dress with lots of petticoats underneath, who tried to teach us ballroom dances. I don't think that I was a very good pupil, really. But at least I could waltz, and at a push manage a quickstep.'*

Peter and Nancy Norman at the Samson, 1960

Samson & Hercules, 1940s

Jazz and Skiffle

Jazz had been popular in Norwich in the 1920s, but after WWII it had a revival and by around 1952 it was gaining a foothold in many venues. Like the big-band sound, its growth can be credited to the American servicemen who brought their style and culture to the City, as explained by Kingsley Harris: 'Jazz was particularly picked up by youngsters. They wanted to listen to something with a bit more pace: a bit more oomph. They didn't want to be tied to bygone tastes, such as old-time dance. They were looking forward and jazz appealed to them: it had more beat.'

Jazz was performed at many venues in the City. You'd find groups starting up in the back of pubs, such as the Gibraltar Gardens, Bedford Arms or the Cat & Fiddle. More formal evenings were held at the Lido ballroom, which hosted one of the City's longest running jazz music clubs, called the Rhythm Club. John St Quintin really enjoyed going: 'It was held on a Tuesday: I went with my friends and cousins. Members could go in for 1/6d, and we all used to jive. Billy Duncan's band was one of the first to perform, later Chic Applin's band played and Max Rayner sang with them. I loved the jiving and the fact it was full of young people. The atmosphere was terrific.'

Many jazz clubs came and went, amongst their number was the Cellar Jazz Club, which met in the Orford Cellar. In February 1958 the *Eastern Evening News* announced its launch. Run by Norman Guest (booking agent at the Samson & Hercules in the 1950s and 1960s), the new club aimed to cater for all jazz tastes: traditional, modern mainstream and skiffle. It is believed that this was the first time the Cellar (located in the basement of the Orford Arms, Red Lion Street) had been used for musical entertainment, and it set the scene for the following decade, when this tiny basement became one of the City's most important music venues.

Another style of music which emerged in the late 1950s was skiffle, a kind of American folk music. Although the genres were different, and some jazz aficionados considered skiffle to be 'rough and unintelligent', there was a close link between the two. In fact, one of the earliest events put on at the Cellar Jazz Club was the 'Skiffle of the Year Contest', won by local group the Sidewinders. Similarly, another popular venue, the Grosvenor Ballroom, which opened *c.*1957 on Prince of Wales Road, held both jazz and skiffle nights.

We had hundreds of local groups playing skiffle. Kinglsley Harris explains why it was so popular: 'It attracted people who didn't necessarily want to spend hours on end practicing a classical instrument. They could just pick up anything that made a noise, such as a washboard, and join in. Folk music had always been like that, but skiffle brought it into popular culture, in that you could perform as a member of a band without being a skilled performer. You could just sit there knocking out a rhythm on your washboard and claim you were a musician. This heralded a huge change in music. Teenagers scuttled off into sheds with their friends and started skiffling with makeshift instruments, such as a double bass made from a tea chest and broom. There were no notes, and so you didn't have to read music, you didn't have to tune anything, and that's what made it popular in the youth culture. A similar principle applied to guitar playing. Although you had to learn how to play it, unlike the piano that took years to

Norwich-based skiffle groups, including the Jailbirds and the Saints, share the stage, Industrial Club, c.1957

master, if you could play three chords you could get through a whole set of skiffle.'

One of the most popular skiffle groups in the 1950s was the Saints with Tony Sheridan, who won the City's first skiffle contest, held in 1957 at the Industrial Club (Oak Street). Tony went on to have a very successful musical career, which included a recording of *My Bonnie* with the Beatles as his backing group (1961).

Memories

Albert (left) on guitar with his skiffle group at the Jolly Butchers, c.1958

Albert Cooper recalls his early music career performing jazz and skiffle: *'After leaving the air force in 1954 I returned to Norwich. Rock 'n' roll hadn't taken hold, trad jazz was the music of the time.*

'I was still in the Norwich Philharmonic Choir, we practised on King Street. One evening on my way home I passed the Jolly Butchers, on Ber Street, it was very busy and I could hear the singing. I didn't go in then, but I did a few weeks later. The lounge was a strange room. Anna had hung various items from the ceiling, including a mannequin's head. By then I'd started learning jazz, not for any particular reason, just for fun. I told Anna I'd learnt a couple of numbers, and she said I could have a go. She was standing on a beer crate, and she told me to get on a bench seat, which I did. Colin Bates her pianist at the time, who later played with Acker Bilk, accompanied me together with a scratch trad band. It went well, and after that, I performed more and more, until Anna said, why don't you come and be part of my act. I didn't get much, I think it was about 2s. 6d., but I didn't do it for the money. She called me, "my boy Albert".

'I was first introduced to skiffle music by accident. In 1956 I went to Cambridge to see an old school friend, Bernard Rudden. Bernard took me to see a chap called Stan Kelly, who later wrote "Liverpool Lullaby" for Cilla Black. He was great. His music made me feel alive. And so, I said to Bernard "Let's start a skiffle group", and that's how the Jolly Butchers' Skiffle Group was formed. There's some debate as to whether it was the City's first skiffle group, but it was definitely one of the earliest. I sang, Bernard was on guitar, a chap called Vernon played the washboard and Dave Keeley was on the tea-chest bass (we'd bought the tea chest from Lamberts' warehouse). At times we also introduced a couple of banjos. It was pretty rough music, but good fun.

'Lonny Donegan was the king of skiffle, but I suppose the musician who had the biggest influence on me was Ken Colyer. Ken was a jazz trumpeter and cornetist. He performed a mixture of blues, folk, and bluegrass, which he called skiffle. The style adopted by performers like Ken or Lonny and groups such as the Chris Barber Band was a precursor of rock 'n' roll.'

Rock 'n' Roll

Although in the late 1950s rock 'n' roll became popular in Norwich, Kingsley Harris does not believe it took hold in the same way as other styles: 'Everyone seemed to be confused by it. The people in the know recognised it as a new type of music made up of different genres, including country and jazz, all mixed together to give a lively beat. Others thought it was just a dance routine. You had a lot of people talking about rock 'n' roll. Some immediately banned it, as they associated it with rebelling kids.'

This was a period when Norwich bands who were better known for the big band sound needed to adapt their style. Amongst them was Bob Barbour. Around 1956/57 he saw the writing on the wall and restyled his band Bob Barbour and the Rockets. Unfortunately the change did not go down well with his more traditional audience. In fact the band suffered the indignity of having their inaugural gig at the Boulton & Paul Social Club cancelled because officials got cold feet about the 'rebels' it might attract. Eventually they were taken on at the Gala. Although they continued to include rock 'n' roll in their repertoire, in a bid to appease their older fans, they again rechristened themselves, this time as the Bob Barbour Orchestra.

One of the highlights of the period was when Bill Haley bought his European Tour to the Carlton (All Saints' Green) in 1957. Other rock 'n' roll artists who came to the City included a British performer billed as being 'more like Presley than Presley himself': Cliff Richard. Cliff appeared as part of the *Oh Boy Roadshow* (again at the Carlton) in 1959 with his backing group the Drifters, who were later renamed the Shadows. David Clark was in the audience, in 1996 he told the *Eastern Evening News*: 'Sitting in the 8/6d seats it was impossible to hear any of the singing above the screaming girls when Cliff changed from a pink to a white jacket while maintaining his best Elvis sneer.' Sylvia Buxton, who was also in the audience, was not too impressed: 'He was a bit spotty-faced then. I never took to him, because he wasn't a patch on Elvis...I wish he'd have come to Norwich.'

Bill Haley (left) with Franny Beecher, lead guitarist with the Comets, on tour in the UK, 1957

Sports

After the end of WWII, people wanted their everyday lives to return to 'normal', but in their leisure time they looked for a degree of escapism. This was not only provided in Norwich's cinemas and theatres but also at its sporting arenas: crowds flocked to venues across the City to see their heroes in action. Today, by far the biggest spectator sport in the City is football, back in the late 1940s the Stars, who raced motor bikes at the Firs speedway track, attracted the same size crowds as the Canaries. Although 'going to the dogs' was not as popular, greyhound racing also attracted sizeable crowds. However, one sport epitomised the era more than any of these; it may not have had the same following, but cycle speedway engendered the same fervour and pleasure, in both its sportsmen and supporters.

Cycle Speedway: The Skid Kids

The impact that cycle speedway had on young boys growing up in the aftermath of war is extraordinary. Many had lost their fathers, they had few comforts and little in the way of entertainment. In the evenings many lads met on cleared bomb sites, they could have got up to mischief, instead they made a discovery: with a few minor adaptations, the sites made brilliant cycle racing tracks. The youngsters with bikes competed against each other, those that didn't own a cycle made them from anything they could find. The movement gathered momentum, and from around 1947 the boys started to form themselves into teams. They christened themselves with names that reflected their speed and daring, such as the Eagles, Red Devils or Comets. Of course, a team needs a uniform, and so mothers and sisters were called in to make simple vests, which the boys wore with honour.

Alongside Norwich-based teams, villages set up their own squads, and soon crowds were gathering to cheer the lads on. Divisions were formed, and it was not long before teams from Norwich and Norfolk were competing nationally. Throughout the 1950s and the 1960s cycle speedway was an immensely popular sport. Some cyclists, such as Malcolm Flood, went on to make their name as professional motor-cycle speedway riders, others gave up when they went off to do national service, and their teams folded.

Norman Guest, who for many years worked as an agent in the City's music industry, was also very involved in cycle speedway, as he explained in 1998: 'I served as a Lancaster bomber pilot in WWII and when I left the RAF in the late 1940s I found cycle speedway teams established all over the place. My most local club, the Earlham Eagles, rode on a track at the top of Earlham House [nowadays a shopping centre and flats] and if a rider overshot the back straight, on leaving the bend he would career down a steep slope – where you had to concentrate to miss many trees! After a while I formed the Earlham Arrows team, and we laid a small track at the Colman Road end of North Park Avenue. The Eagles joined us there to create Earlham Cycle Speedway Club.' Soon members pitched in to build a new track, which was one of the biggest in the country, they even installed a hut, a mechanical starting gate and a banked area for spectators around three sides.

Throughout the 1950s and into the 1960s cycle speedway brought glamour, hope and excitement to many young lives – no wonder it was so popular.

Malcolm Flood (left) with arch rival Les Perritt, 1952

Dave Watson, Trevor Hedge and Cyril Atkins (l to r), c.1952

Norwich City Football Club

After the end of the war fans flocked to see the Canaries. In the 1947/8 season they finished second from bottom of Division Three South for the second year in a row and had to apply for re-election, but for the first time in the club's history home gates averaged more than 20,000. Through the 1950s, despite their humble league performances (they applied for re-election again in 1957), the Canaries notched up some memorable victories in the FA Cup competition, including a 3-1 win in January 1951 against Liverpool at Anfield and a 2-1 win against Arsenal at Highbury in January 1954.

These were the days of rosettes and rattles, of fans standing on the terraces crowding forward to see their heroes. You didn't attend a match in a replica shirt, more likely than not you'd be wearing a mac and cap, maybe with a knitted scarf. As for the players, the football idols of the 1950s were very different to today's stars. With Britain shaking off years of post-war austerity they brought a dash of excitement to many fans' lives, but they did not enjoy the millionaire lifestyle of today's professional footballers. This was the time of the maximum wage (just £20 a week in the late 1950s), which meant players did not necessarily earn any more than their fans. Terry Ryder, who played for NCFC from 1946 to 1951, was a typical footballer of his day. After leaving the game he did not even think about a celebrity-style retirement. Instead, he moved to the Heartsease, where there was nothing he enjoyed more than playing football with the boys from the estate. Having a game with Terry was a real treat for Paul Warr and his friends: 'As kids at the time, money was limited, and so we had to make our own fun. Football was the "be all and end all" in a boy's life, and so to be able to play on a field each night with a professional footballer was brilliant....I can't imagine a player being so down to earth today.'

But one thing has not changed over the years: passion and pride. In no time in City's history have these emotions been more in evidence than in 1959, when the giant-killing Canaries reached the semi-finals of the FA Cup. The Division Three side won the hearts of the City, after beating Manchester United, Cardiff City, Sheffield United and Tottenham Hotspur, and came within a hair's-breadth of a place in the final itself, until they lost 1-0 to Luton Town in the semi-final replay. In those 11 weeks, when FA Cup fever gripped the City, thousands of fans scraped together every last penny to follow the Canaries both home and away. In recognition of this support the City players travelled back with their fans on the 'Top Brass Special Train' from the Luton match. They did not hide themselves away but led the fans in chorus after chorus of *On the Ball City*.

The cup run left the team hungry for glory. The next season this became league success, when the Canaries delighted their loyal supporters by winning promotion to the second division.

Norwich City v Cardiff City at Carrow Road, 1959

Memories

Health and safety procedures at football matches were different to today. *Paul Warr recalls 'As a kid I used to go to the River End at Carrow Road. There was an unwritten rule that children could push their way down to the front so they could see. You'd sit with your feet through the metal railings. You'd be at player level, which perhaps wasn't the best view, but we had a great time. If I couldn't get a good view at the front, I'd climb up the railway sleepers at the back where the advertising hoarding was: you could get a great view up there. It wouldn't be considered safe today – but we all survived.'*

Norwich City v Cardiff City, 1959

Would this happen today?

Bobby Brennan's top tip:

An advert for Albany cigarettes, with their 'king-size filter' yet 'mature flavour' appeared in the 'Eastern Evening News' during the 1959 cup run.

Bobby Brennan, City's outside left, promoted the brand recommending it as 'an ideal cigarette for an athlete'. Ken Nethercott, City's highly acclaimed goal keeper, similarly appreciated the 'true contentment' generated by Albany's 'fine tobaccos'.

Greyhound Racing

Badges gave access to restricted viewing areas

Throughout the 1950s greyhound racing was a very popular pastime in the City.

The Boundary Park Stadium (Boundary Road) and the Norwich City Stadium (Heartsease Lane) both held regular races. The former was also used by other sports, including show jumping, and it also doubled up as a training ground for Norwich City's junior squad and third-team matches.

Many greyhound owners of the day were 'enthusiastic amateurs', amongst them was Arthur Holmes' older brother, Bob: 'He was a keen gambler and whilst I was still at school he often took me to the greyhound races. At one time he won enough to buy his own greyhound, it was called Broadland Coot, better known as Cooty. I used to take it on walks. There was an area on Mousehold, off Gilman Road, where kids rode around on their bikes, they'd worn it into a track. I often took Cooty there and he'd run around until he was exhausted: greyhounds love racing. He won Bob a lot of money, and easily paid for himself. When Bob first bought Cooty home, my mother hadn't been too pleased, but in the end she looked after him more than my brother did. When he got older, and slower, Bob announced he was going to sell him, but my mother wouldn't let him, and he became her pet.'

Glenna St Quintin's father, Jack Howe, was similarly involved in the sport : 'At times my father was very prosperous. He owned and raced greyhounds. I've known my father to have won a lot of money, and my nanny to have literally thousands underneath her mattress, and at other times he didn't have a penny. He built a private greyhound track at Costessey, but he mostly raced the dogs at Yarmouth or the Boundary Racecourse. We used to take the dogs to the track in the car. If he didn't want it to win he used to feed it before it ran; the others we didn't feed for a day or so, and so they were really keen to catch the rabbit on the wire.'

Speedway

The Firs speedway track, home of the Norwich Stars, reopened after WWII on 20 April 1946 with a challenge match against Sheffield.

The immediate post-war era was a boom time for speedway, and saw the Firs gates doubling from its pre-war days, to an average attendance of almost 20,000. The sport's popularity was at its peak. In 1947 alone, some 460,000 fans passed through the turnstiles. Demand was such that the Stadium was extended to hold 26,000. Luckily, fans did not need to choose between watching the Canaries or the Stars, as explained by journalist Derek James: 'A dream Saturday in old Norwich comprised football in the afternoon, speedway at night and fish and chips at Valoris on the way home.'

Throughout the 1950s the Norwich team attracted some of the best riders around, including the Aussies Bert Spencer and Bob Leverenz, and local lads Phil Clarke and Billy Bales (aka the Mighty Atom).

One of the highlights of the decade was the arrival of Ove Fundin, a young man from Sweden, who went on to clinch five world speedway titles. Ove (known as the 'Flying Fox' because of his red hair) came to Norwich in 1954, the following year he joined the Norwich Stars. For 10 glorious years he represented the club with pride. He was renowned for being fearless and ruthless, and was idolised by the Norwich fans. On his day no-one could touch him. In 2006, Ove was made an Honorary Freeman of Norwich. When he received the award, people stood and cheered one of the greatest speedway riders of all time, a man still regarded by many as the most talented sportsman ever to have represented the City.

BIRD CAGES
TWO-TONE ENAMELLED
From 24/9 Each
Loose's
23-25, MAGDALEN ST., NORWICH
CUSTOMERS' CAR PARK (entrance Fishergate)

Light-up—10.22 p.m.
Weather—Page 7
Wireless—Page 5

Eastern Evening News

SPEEDWAY SPECIAL

No. 21,999—Three Halfpence

Saturday, June 20, 1953

Bonds
SOLE AGENTS IN NORWICH
QUILLVEN VENETIAN BLINDS
ALL SAINTS GREEN, NORWICH

'SELL OUT' AT THE FIRS TONIGHT

Last-minute demands for Test tickets flood in

CALM BEFORE STORM

SPEEDWAY supporters from all over the country—one hardy group has even made the long journey from Wales—have been converging on Norwich today for this evening's Test match between England and Australia.

STARS' MANAGER HOLDS ENGLAND REINS TONIGHT

Autograph Hunters

An Optimist

Turn to centre pages for—
England's Prospects
Action Studies
Pen Pictures
Test History

The Firs hosts an international Test match, 1953

Norwich Stars, c.1958

Ove Fundin, c.1960

Motor Sports

In the 1950s motor sport was much less high-tech than today and hence more affordable to the enthusiastic amateur. At this time, Mike Dixon was out and about with his camera attending events across Norfolk. In this gallery are a wonderful collection of images depicting vehicles and scenes from a bygone age.

Norwich Vikings' motorcycle trial, Ringland, 1959

Motorcycle scrambling, Lyng, 1958

Stock-car racing, the Firs, Norwich, 1958

Sports-car racing, Snetterton, 1959

Motorcycle racing, Snetterton, 1959

Racing cars in the paddock, Snetterton, 1959

Different Times

Spot-welder at Barnards, 1940s

Different Times

How do you judge attitudes and actions in times gone by? Is it right to criticise and be shocked by behaviours without putting them into the context of the era?

In one sense there were many freedoms experienced in the 1950s that we envy today: it was a time when doors were often left unlocked, crime rates were low, drugs were not a problem, there were few no-go areas, and children roamed about freely and played without adult supervision. It was also a period when homosexuality was illegal, racism and sexism were acceptable and corporal punishment was the norm.

Law and Order

In the early 1950s crime rates were relatively low. Somewhat ironically, in the second half of the decade as prosperity increased so did crime: between 1955 and 1960 the number of indictable offences known to the police soared by over 60%, from 438,000 to 744,000. Why? Put simply, not only was there more to steal but it was also easier to steal: it was simpler to shoplift from a self-service supermarket than a traditional store, there were more cars on the road and valuable goods in houses.

What about the police themselves? Policing was epitomised by the television character PC Dixon of Dock Green. An avuncular figure who appeared in 434 programmes, welcoming viewers to each episode with an 'Evenin' All', a far cry from DI Jack Regan of the 1970s police drama *The Sweeney*. Was Dixon realistic? Not according to Andy Anderson, a policeman for 25 years.

Would this happen today?

A bobby's overnight duties reflected a very different Norwich economy. In the 21st century, Prince of Wales Road comes alive at 11pm, not so in the 1950s. When Andy worked the beat: 'People went home on the last buses after the pubs and cinemas turned out, and at about 11pm a great calm descended on the City. We had the place virtually to ourselves, a dog barking somewhere would make you worry and wonder who was about. Then at 4am the first railwaymen and postmen started to arrive for their early morning shift. They'd all speak to us, saying good morning in passing: fellow unfortunates.'

The work of the police was hugely different to today in terms of challenges, conditions and duties. In the 1950s the police constantly patrolled the City's streets, a very visible sign of law and order. Andy transferred from the Met to Norwich City Police in 1951: 'Norwich was divided into beats, made up of set routes around the City centre. We had beat books which contained precise instructions, including the route to be followed, the time we had to be at a set location and places which were to be given "special attention". At night we did what we called fixed-route working when you literally pressed the door of all lock-up premises. We normally patrolled singly, it was believed that working in twos encouraged gossiping! There were some exceptions to this. For example, on Saturday nights, they sent two men to Upper and Lower Goat Lanes where there were some lively pubs, including the Bluebell and the Morning Star.'

Very clearly, old-style policing was about contact with the public. The fact that the police could patrol by themselves, at a time when communication was not easy, indicates they were held in respect. Andy recalls: 'We didn't even have personal radios, instead we communicated through a system of police boxes and pillar phones, all controlled from the police station. When you were on fixed-route working you had a conference point every 40 minutes and you rang in every hour and 20 minutes. The streets all had pillar phones and if the station wanted to contact you there would be a flashing light on the top.'

But what about the 'yobs'? Maurice Morson, started his career in the City Police in 1956. He believes that offenders showed more deference to the police in the 1950s, but that this partly reflected the times: 'They were noisy, but more inhibited. There weren't the opportunities there are today: they didn't have the cars, nor the money to get a taxi home, and so they headed out of the City on the last bus. There wasn't the same access to alcohol, it wasn't readily available in general stores and pubs closed earlier. The main trouble was fighting amongst themselves and vandalism. A diluted version of what you have today.'

Last Hanging in Norwich

On 19 July 1951 Dennis Moore, who had murdered his pregnant girlfriend (Eileen Cullen), was one of two men simultaneously hung at Norwich Prison. Dennis had lived on Woodcock Road, Avis Brown's sisters knew him well: 'They both said that whatever happened in Piggy's Field, where he murdered his girlfriend, was a moment of madness, because they had never seen that boy angry or nasty. They could not believe that he'd done such a thing, but of course he lost his life for it: she lost hers and he lost his.'

Homophobia

Homosexual acts had been illegal in Britain for centuries, but so long as minors were not involved and participants acted discreetly, prosecutions were relatively rare. However, during the war there was an increase in homosexual activity, and after it ended the official mood dramatically changed. In the last full year before the war there were 320 prosecutions for 'gross' indecency, a common way to describe homosexual behaviour. By 1952 the number had risen to 1626.

The escalation was part of a government purge, supported by the press that ran articles decrying the 'secret world of pansies'. However, the mood in Britain was beginning to change. For example, there was an extensive and semi-open gay world in theatrical circles, which included such figures as Noel Coward.

Eventually, in 1954 the government set up a Departmental Committee under Sir John Wolfenden to consider homosexual offences. Despite the recommendation made in 1957 that 'homosexual behaviour between consenting adults in private' should no longer be a criminal offence it was another 10 years before homosexuality became legal in England and Wales.

As with so many 'phobias' and 'isms' public reaction was divided. In Norwich, despite the law, we already had openly gay pubs, including the Jolly Butchers on Ber Street. Albert Cooper knew the landlady, Black Anna well: 'In the 1950s the Jolly Butchers was like a nerve centre. Everyone gyrated around it because there was nothing else like it in Norwich. The clientele at the Jolly Butchers was incredible. You had a total cross-section of the community. You had lords and ladies, titled people, people from the theatre, then the old boys who lived in the dormitories upstairs. It was also known as a "gay" pub, and so it was also a centre or "camp" for the homosexual scene in Norwich. Although homosexuality was illegal, everyone turned a blind eye. The Shakespeare, on Theatre Street, was another "camp" in the 1950s. I never saw any aggression towards homosexuals at the Jolly Butchers, people were accepted for what they were.'

Racism

Before WWII about 95% of people living in Britain had been born here, whilst the remaining 5% were mostly white English and Scots whose parents had been serving the Empire overseas when they were born. During the war men from the Caribbean served with the British forces, others came to fill labour shortages in all areas from farms to factories. But after the war most went home leaving a permanent non-white population of around 30,000.

All this changed in 1948 when the British Nationality Act declared that all subjects of the King had British citizenship, which gave 800 million people living around the world the right to enter the UK. It seems extraordinary that the Act was not at all controversial. Why not? For one simple reason: it was assumed that black and Asian subjects would not want to come. This was far from the case. By 1961 the country's black and Asian population had risen to some 377,000. Many came in response to recruitment drives instigated by British employers, including the NHS and London Transport. Like today immigration divided opinion, and in some quarters gave rise to racism, most clearly illustrated by boarding houses which put up signs saying 'No dogs. No Irish. No Blacks'. Matters came to a head in the Notting Hill race riot of 1958, which in turn had been sparked by racial unrest in the St Ann's district of central Nottingham. Although no one was killed, it was an unpleasant episode since described by the political commentator Andrew Marr as 'a symbol of change rather than a bloody slaughter'.

In the News

In June 1959 a rather strange story appeared in the 'Eastern Evening News'. A picture book telling the story of the 'Three Little Pigs' printed in the USA had caused outrage because it showed the black pig to be cleverer than his white and black-and-white brethren, as he was the one who built his house out of bricks. As a result some colour-bar fanatics in the States set up a howl of protest.

Jarrolds printed the book for the British market on behalf of World Distributors Ltd. It was noted by the journalist writing the article that since the flare-up the book had been re-illustrated, and it was the black-and-white pig that built the house of brick. He concluded: 'Back to neutrality in the nursery – if not common sense in the United States.'

The Friendly Invasion

Norwich did not have a large immigrant population, but during the war and immediately afterwards it played host to American air force personnel who came into the City from bases around Norwich. Friendships were made, that endure to this day.

It was in 1942 that the United States Air Force (USAAF) launched their 'friendly invasion' of Norfolk. For the next three years at any one time there were around 50,000 USAAF personnel stationed on 18 airfields within a 30-mile radius of the City. Norwich acted like a magnet to the Americans, who made a lasting impression on locals, including Andy Anderson: 'Norwich was thronged with Americans in the 1940s. When I left off work, they seemed to be everywhere. I can still picture them sat on every bit of grass available up the Castle mound.' Similarly, Barbara Miller clearly remembers their impact: 'We always remarked that their clothes fitted so much better! Once you got to seven o'clock in the evening they descended on the City, they particularly went to places like the Samson & Hercules. On a Saturday night the "Passion Wagons", which transported the troops into the City, were all drawn up on Farmers' Avenue.' The position was reversed when dances were held on the bases. John St Quintin's cousins, Betty and Jean, were among the many young girls who went to dances at the camps, where they met their future husbands.

Although in some quarters the Americans were viewed with suspicion, especially by parents with daughters of a marriageable age, many families welcomed them with open arms. In the 1950s Glenna St Quintin's mother was a supervisor at the American Red Cross Service Club: 'The Americans came in from the camps around Norwich. They tended to home in on the Samson, although they also went to the Lido. The boys liked to be welcomed into a home, and feel they were part of the family. They always wore aftershave, and dressed smartly; their uniform was a lot better than ours. A lot of the lads came home to our house, they were nice lads.'

But what about the black airmen? It is difficult to imagine that rules of segregation applied, but in the City some venues refused entry to black Americans. In the 1950s Sylvia Buxton often saw the Americans in the cafés on King Street: 'There was one on the corner of King Street and Rose Lane, where the black Americans went. They used to separate the black and the white Americans. I think people our age weren't bothered about skin colour, but our parents were.'

The Americans brought their culture to the City. They particularly influenced our tastes in music and our dance halls. They introduced locals to such delights as peanut butter, chewing gum and coke. But most of all they were admired for their courage and sacrifice. Their time in Norwich is still commemorated at the Second Air Division Memorial Library, which has the well-chosen maxim: 'Remembering the past, inspiring the future'.

USAAF men having fun, 389 Bombardment Group 2nd Air Division, c.1943

Attitudes to Women

From the end of WWII a concerted effort was made to persuade women to leave their wartime jobs and return to the home.

In the media, women were generally portrayed as doll-like figures dressed in rustling full skirts, nipped waist, narrow bodice and made up to the nines, even whilst doing housework. The understated message of the era was that to catch and keep a man you needed curves and that the proper career was child-rearing and marriage. Even though more girls had the opportunity to extend their education, schools had to fight hard for the rights of girls. In 1951 the Head Mistress at the Blyth Grammar School for girls, criticised parents that made 'every domestic emergency an occasion for a girl's absence from school'. Four years later the Head decried parents who forced their daughters to leave before entering the sixth form using the excuse they did not need an education because 'she's only a girl' and will marry.

As highlighted in 'The World of Work' (page 98) attitudes to women in the workplace would be frowned upon today. Sexism was rife in most sectors, including offices, factories and even the police force.

When Maurice joined the City Police, there were just six WPCs in Norwich, they had very different roles to their male colleagues. Their jobs involved looking

City Police, c.1957

after children or interviewing women who had been assaulted. They never walked the beat. Maurice is the first to admit that there was an element of chauvinism, although: 'I wouldn't say it was any worse than any other workplace, it was very much in line with attitudes of the time.'

Today, if a company ran a job advert for 'single girls and young married women', as Caleys did in the *Eastern Evening News* in 1956 (see below), there would be an absolute furore. Whilst it's impossible to imagine any mainline business printing the article that appeared in the Boulton & Paul staff magazine in 1947, which described the 'challenges to men' and included the following content: 'Women in industry, sir? Darn nuisance...it's like this, you just turn your head and watch that pair of pretty legs walk up the shop and crash...a four quid job is up the spout. Then there was Peggy. She was a stunner, if ever there was one. She had everything plus. I expect she was some old johnny's private secretary before the war.... Above the racket of machinery she leans across the lathe to speak to me. I listen vaguely. You see I'm drinking in her beauty, and boy, have I got a thirst....The lathe is running, and I, like a mutt, advance the tool...and that is how the job came to be scrapped.'

However, women were not always the underdogs, and there is much evidence that they 'gave as good as they got'. In most factories jobs were regarded as either 'men's' or 'women's', as a result there tended to be segregation in the workplace. This inevitably led to behaviour that today would probably lead to disciplinary action...and the women were the worst. In the shoe trade it was said that young lads entered the ladies' machine room at their peril. At the Norvic factory (on St George's) there was a chance that they'd be bundled into one of the huge baskets used to transport sewn uppers around the factory, whilst at Christmas they'd probably lose their trousers!

Segregation even extended into the City's coffee shops. Lambert's Oriental Café, located in the basement of Lambert's confectionery and tobacconist shop in London Street, was one of the last such City establishments to be a male-only preserve. In October 1960 an article in the *Eastern Evening News* decried the change: 'Not long ago there were three coffee shops in Norwich reserved exclusively for men. Now there is only one and before long that will be opened to women...it is an institution that will be sadly missed in the City. There is certainly room for one such place.'

In the light of the above it is unsurprising that in the 1950s one of most iconic toys of all times was born: Barbie. The doll was an instant hit. In its first year of production (1959) more than 350,000 were sold. Barbie's appearance was a precise reflection of Western society's attitude to women at the time: long-legged, small waisted and voluptuous. Barbie represented all that the marketing fraternity believed that a woman should want to be in the 1950s: glamorous, famous, wealthy and popular. Which leads to another important question: compared with the celebrity culture of the 21st century, how much has actually changed?

Childcare

Two very clear messages come across about childcare in the 1950s. On the one hand, from a young age children had extensive freedoms to roam with little or no supervision, on the other, discipline was often brutal and violent.

John Chilvers recalls having loving and responsible parents, 'but they didn't think twice about letting me go into the City by myself when I was only seven.' John's experience was typical. On Saturday mornings droves of unaccompanied children descended on the City. Queues of boisterous children would form outside the cinemas clutching their sixpence entrance money waiting for the commanding figure of the commissionaire to allow them in. Then the 'sixpenny rush' for seats would erupt in a cacophony of noise and excitement. Later they'd flock to the Cattle Market or maybe the Castle Museum. Some would go and gaze at the toys in Jarrolds or, from 1956, have a ride on Curls escalator. Kids would be sent out all day to play, and expected back when it was dark: adult supervision was minimal. Those who recall the era, would never dream of allowing their grandchildren the same leeway, yet many remember it as one of the best parts of growing up.

The same cannot be said of corporal punishment. Corporal punishment, defined as 'causing deliberate pain to a child in response to the child's undesired behaviour and/or language', was allowed in English schools until 1986. In the immediate post-war era it was the norm at Christine Perfect's primary school: 'Discipline was much stronger than it is now. If you'd been naughty...one teacher, a Mr Hurn, called you to the front of the class where you had to bend over and he'd whack you on the bottom with a black plimsoll.' Such behaviour was not only accepted but treated as the norm. There are numerous examples of teachers who were given free rein to bully their pupils. Lynn Preston enjoyed attending the Colman Road School where she was one of the few to pass the 11+ exam, but she had the misfortune to upset one of her teachers: 'She was vicious. She whacked me cruelly with a rubber plimsoll on my hand for no good reason: I was messing around with the wheels on my roller skates and the noise irritated her. The problem was the power of teachers. I was very scared of that woman and lost sleep because she picked on me. Parents could not help: they were deferential to authority and concerned that if they came "up the school" it would only make things worse. If you got on the wrong side of a particularly nasty teacher life was a misery.'

Peter Watson, c.1954

Lynn Preston, c.1958

In Conclusion

Banter in the workplace, giving children extra freedoms, having policemen on the beat, are aspects of the 1950s that many would like to see restored. But flogging in schools, sexism, homophobia and racism are all rightly condemned. Thus, although we may now decry the constant need to be 'politically correct', few would argue that a change in legislation and attitudes was necessary.

Our outlook and behaviour will continue to evolve. Inevitably, in the same way we look back at the 1950s, in years to come our descendants will view our generation and its actions with a mix of admiration and disapproval. After all we are all moulded by the times in which we live.

Cows on the way to the Cattle Market, St George's Plain, Colegate, c.1958

Epilogue

We would like to finish with an important question: how many of the features that epitomised Norwich in the 1950s have endured into the 21st century?

Somewhat ironically, although we have retained most of the ancient buildings, a host of them dating from medieval times, many of the hallmarks of the immediate post-war era have vanished.

Most noticeably the manufacturing industries that we relied upon to bring wealth and prosperity to the City have all but disappeared. Factories have given way to the residential, retail, catering or finance sectors: often a combination of all four. Now, all that reminds us that St George's was once home to the great Norvic shoe factory is the Last Wine Bar (named after a shoemaker's modelling tool). Chapelfield, is no longer associated with chocolate, now it is a shopping mall. In the 21st century the only heavy metal you will hear at Riverside, comes from the huge entertainment venues.

Hordes of cyclists no longer arrive in the City on their way to work: the bike has given way to the car. This has brought tremendous changes to roads, as planners have constantly sought to cater to the needs of the motorist. We have seen the introduction of car parks, flyovers and much destruction: all in the name of progress. Interestingly, the trend is gradually being reversed, as cycle tracks, park and ride schemes and pedestrian precincts progressively appear.

On Saturday mornings children don't travel into the City to visit the Cattle Market, whilst the 'sixpenny rush' has long gone and the escalators in Debenhams (previously Curls) hold little allure. Schools have evolved in line with the national education system. Many of the institutions that flourished in the 1950s are still open, though the Blyth, C.N.S. and Hewett, along with the secondary schools, are now comprehensives. Additionally, Norwich is home to two universities, whilst City College is one of the largest further-education establishments in the country.

The City's library has moved from Charing Cross, and is now housed in the iconic Forum. It is no longer a place to whisper and tiptoe around, instead it offers a meeting place, and access to anything from books to computer games alongside a multitude of events: no wonder it is one of the most popular public libraries in the UK.

The City's major hospital is still the Norfolk and Norwich, but it has relocated out of the City. The former site has been redeveloped, for residential use.

All of the 1950s cinemas have closed. In their stead new multiplex venues have flourished. However, the Theatre Royal has regained its status as a leading venue for live performances, and the Maddermarket continues to delight audiences. The night-time economy has changed beyond recognition. No more will youngsters dance the evening away at the Samson & Hercules or the Lido, rushing to catch the last bus home at 10.30pm – that's the time they now arrive at one of the City's many night clubs. The Canaries still entertain and frustrate crowds in equal measure at Carrow Road, but we no longer go to the dogs or enjoy the spectacle of motorcycle speedway in the City.

Grocery shopping is mostly done at supermarkets. In the face of this increased competition, stallholders on Norwich Market have successfully diversified. Although still home to many splendid and popular food stalls, it is not accurate to describe it as a 'provisions market'.

Bonds is now John Lewis and Curls is Debenhams. Jarrolds has not only survived, but flourished and expanded. It is now recognised both locally and nationally as the City's flagship independent store, despite the development of two huge, modern shopping centres, Castle Mall and Chapelfield.

For better or for worse, the City has undoubtedly changed. Has it improved? In some respects, undoubtedly yes, in others, definitely not. Do you like it more?.... That's for you to say.

Additional Information

Bibliography

Anderson, A. P. and Storey, N. R. 'Norwich, Eighty Years of the Norwich Society', Sutton Publishing, 2004.

Archant Publications Including the *Eastern Daily Press* and the *Eastern Evening News*, various dates.

Axon, Jo 'Sidecars', Shire Publications, 2007.

Baker, Patricia 'Fashions of a Decade', Facts on File, 1991.

Barfield, T. J. 'Scott built a Dynamo', Laurence, Scott & Electromotors, *c.*1962.

Barr, Neville and Newham 'The Story of the Norwich Players & the Creation of the Maddermarket Theatre', Leiston Press, 2011.

Blackwell, Michael and Carole 'Norwich Theatre Royal: The First 250 Years', Connaught Books, 2007.

Bowman, Martin W. 'Images of War: Norwich Blitz', Pen & Sword Military, 2012.

Briers, Frank *et al* 'Norwich and its Region', Norwich Local Exec. Committee of the British Association, 1961.

Brooks, Pamela 'Norwich Street by Street', Breedon Books Publishing, 2006.

Brown, Mike 'Life in the 1950s', Pitkin Publishing, 2014.

Catton Grove Community Centre 'Catton Grove Memories, 1935 – 1965', self published, 2015.

Clayton, Eric 'The First 100 Years of Telephones Viewed From Norwich', British Telecom, 1980.

Cope, A.B. 'The Book of the Norwich Festival', Norwich Festival Society Ltd, 1951.

Cossey, Peter 'Continuous Performances: Memories of Norwich Cinemas, 1946 - 1961', self-published, 2015.

Durbin, Gail 'The Past Displayed', Norfolk Museums Service, 1984.

Feeney, Paul 'A 1950s Childhood', The History Press, 2009.

Green, Barbara and Young, Rachel M. R. 'Norwich: The Growth of a City', Norfolk Museums Service, 1981.

Gurney-Read, Joyce 'Trades & Industries of Norwich', Crowes of Norwich, 1988.

Gurney-Read, Joyce Miscellaneous collection of information retained in the Local Studies Section, Norfolk & Norwich Millennium Library, various dates.

Gurney-Read, Joyce 'Some of Norwich's Family Stores – A Study', self-published, 1985.

Harman, Janet 'An Introduction to Council Housing In Norwich', Thesis (M.A.), U.E.A., 1972.

Harmer, F. W. 'The Story of a Norwich Industry', self-published, *c.*1947.

Harris, Kingsley 'Albert Cooper, A Chronicle of Norwich's King of the Blues', Hannah Publications, 2003.

Holmes, F. and M. 'The Old Courts and Yards of Norwich', Norwich Heritage Projects, 2015.

Holmes, F. and M. 'The Story of the Norwich Boot and Shoe Trade', Norwich Heritage Projects, 2013.

Holmes, F. and M. 'Norwich Pubs and Breweries, Past and Present', Norwich Heritage Projects, 2011.

Hunter, Nick 'Popular Culture: 1940 –1959', Raintree, 2014.

Jacobs, Norman and Kemp, Mike 'Norwich Speedway', Tempus Publishing Ltd, 2004.

Jacobs, Norman 'Speedway in East Anglia', Tempus Publishing Ltd, 2000.

James, Rowland Pierce and Rowley 'City of Norwich Plan', The City of Norwich Corporation, 1945

Johnson, Paul '20th-Century Britain: Economic, Social and Cultural Change', Longman, 1994.

Kelly's 'Directory of the City of Norwich', various dates.

Kybird, Bas 'Thirty Years with Norwich Police', self-published, 2009.

Leighton, Sophie 'The 1950s Home', Shire Publications, 2014.

Lewis, Peter 'The Fifties', William Heinemann Ltd, 1978.

Malpas, P. and Murie, A 'Housing Policy and Practice', fifth edition, Macmillan Press, 1999.

Marr, Andrew 'A History of Modern Britain', Macmillan, 2008.
McLean, J. J. 'A Fine City, Fit for Heroes', unpublished, 2011.
Meeres, Frank 'A History of Norwich', Phillimore, 1998.
Meeres, Frank 'The Story of Norwich', Phillimore & Co. Ltd, 2011.
Mile Cross Community Festival C'mtee 'Mile Cross Memories: Moments from the Past', self-published, 1993.
Mile Cross History Research Group 'Milestones to Mile Cross', Mile Cross History Research Group, 1995.
Morson, Maurice 'Norwich Murders', Wharncliffe Books, 2006.
Morson, Maurice 'A Force Remembered', Breedon Books Publishing Company, 2000.
Mottram, R. H. 'If Stones Could Speak', Richard Clay and Company Ltd, 1953.
Moynahan, Brian 'Road to Recovery, 1950s', The Reader's Digest Association Ltd, 2007.
Nobbs, George 'Norwich: City of Centuries', George Nobbs Publishing, 1978.
Norwich City Council Planning Services 'Conservation Area Appraisal: Mile Cross', HMSO, 2009.
Norwich City Football Club '100 Great Football Memories', Jarrold Publishing, 2002.
Norwich Heritage Projects 'A Market For Our Times', Norwich Heritage Projects, 2010.
Norwich Labour Party Housing Policy Group 'Norwich Housing Report', self-published, *c.*1977.
Norwich Town Planning Committee 'Norwich Planning Handbook', self-published, 1968, 1972, 1982.
Ogley, Davison & Currie 'The Norfolk and Suffolk Weather Book', Froglets Publications Ltd, 1993.
Pollard, Sidney 'The Development of the British Economy 1914 - 1967', Edward Arnold Ltd, 1969.
Pressley, Alison 'The 50s & 60s: The Best of Times', Index Books Ltd, 2009.
Pritchard, Anthony 'British Family Cars of the 1950s and 1960s', Shire Publications, 2010.
Rawcliffe, Carole and Wilson, Richard 'Norwich since 1550', Hambledon and London, 2004.
Reed, Paula 'Fifty Fashion Looks That Changed the 1950s', Octopus Publishing Group, 2012.
Sedgwick, Michael 'Classic Cars of the 1950s and 1960s', Tiger Books International, 1997.
Temple, Clifford 'Clifford Temple Remembers Norwich', Panda Books Publishing, 1983.
True North 'Memories of Norwich', True North Books Ltd, 1999.
Walker, Susannah '1950s Modern British Style and Design', Shire Publications, 2012.
Walshe, Bevan, Sealy & Phillipson 'A Knight on the Box', Anglia Television Ltd, 1999.
Williams, Nick 'St James Mill, Norwich', Jarrolds & Sons Ltd and Norwich HEART, 2012.
Williams, Nick 'City of Industries', Norwich HEART, 2013.
Yorke, Trevor 'The 1940s & 1950s House Explained', Countryside Books, 2010.

Websites

www.archives.norfolk.gov.uk	Information about the extensive archives relating to the history of Norfolk held at the Norfolk Record Office.
www.georgeplunkett.co.uk	An outstanding collection of 20th-century photographs of Norwich.
news.bbc.co.uk/onthisday	A summary of major UK headlines, covering the period 1950 to 2005.
www.musicfromtheeastzone.co.uk	A wonderful website, managed by Kingsley Harris, containing extensive information on the Norfolk and Suffolk music scene.
www.picture.norfolk.gov.uk	A superb website operated by the Norfolk County Council Library and Information Service which contains over 17,000 images of people, places and events from across the country.

Index

Acknowledgements

We are very grateful to all who have generously shared information with us. Without their help this book could not have been written.

Special thanks must be given to Penny Clarke for her advice and help in editing the book.

Philip Armes greatly assisted by sharing his memories and giving us access to his photographic collection. We are again obliged to Jonathan Plunkett for allowing us to print so many of George Plunkett's historic photographs.

The staff at both the Norfolk County Council Library and Information Service and the Norfolk Record Office have given much guidance and also permission to use and reproduce their material. Particular thanks to Clare Everitt, who looks after Picture Norfolk, for her help in locating photographs.

We are indebted to all who shared their memories with us and who allowed us to reproduce personal images.

Newspaper reports give a wonderful insight into events as they happened. We extend our appreciation to Archant, in particular Rosemary Dixon, for allowing us to access their archive and for allowing us to reproduce photographs. We are also indebted to Derek James and Kingsley Harris for sharing their knowledge of the period with us.

We have made much use of printed works; all publications and relevant websites are listed in the bibliography. Further information on photographic resources can be found on page ii.

Finally we apologise if we have inadvertently failed to acknowledge any of our sources. Anyone who has not been contacted is invited to write to the publisher so that full recognition can be given in subsequent editions.

Philip Armes 1923 - 2017

It was with great sadness that we learnt of the death of our friend Philip. Over the years Philip has provided us with images from his large and well-ordered collection of local photographs. When we started this book he was one of the first people we spoke to and, as normal, he went to great trouble to seek out interesting pictures. He also delighted in explaining the background behind each photo. He was a wonderfully generous and kind man whose help we greatly appreciated.

Philip worked for Norwich City Council as a photographer doing both still and cine work. Perhaps his best known film is of a journey around Norwich in a police car. Made in 1950 it was made to help the City Engineers plan their road-widening schemes. Now in the East Anglian Film Archive, it is a delightful reminder of a City recognisable, but vastly changed.

Much of Philip's work was to photograph the City for planning purposes. As such, his images are not posed or intended to make any artistic statement. Instead they carry an authenticity of exactly what Norwich was like at the time.

His collection remains an important historical record of an era when Norwich was undergoing both renovation and major redevelopment. Philip recorded those changes and preserved that record. Like the Plunkett collection it is an invaluable part of Norwich's heritage. Thank you Philip.

Norwich Heritage Projects

Norwich Heritage Projects is a voluntary organisation which is self funding. We are a small group of volunteers who aim to promote Norwich's rich past. Additional information, including audio and visual recordings can be found on our various websites:

www.norwich-heritage.co.uk

www.norwichshoes.co.uk

www.norwich-yards.co.uk

www.norfolkstainedglass.org

www.norwich-pubs-breweries.co.uk

www.norwich-market.org.uk